Name

Worksheet **1** Side **1**

a a

a a a a a a a

a a a a a a a

Worksheet **1** Side **2**

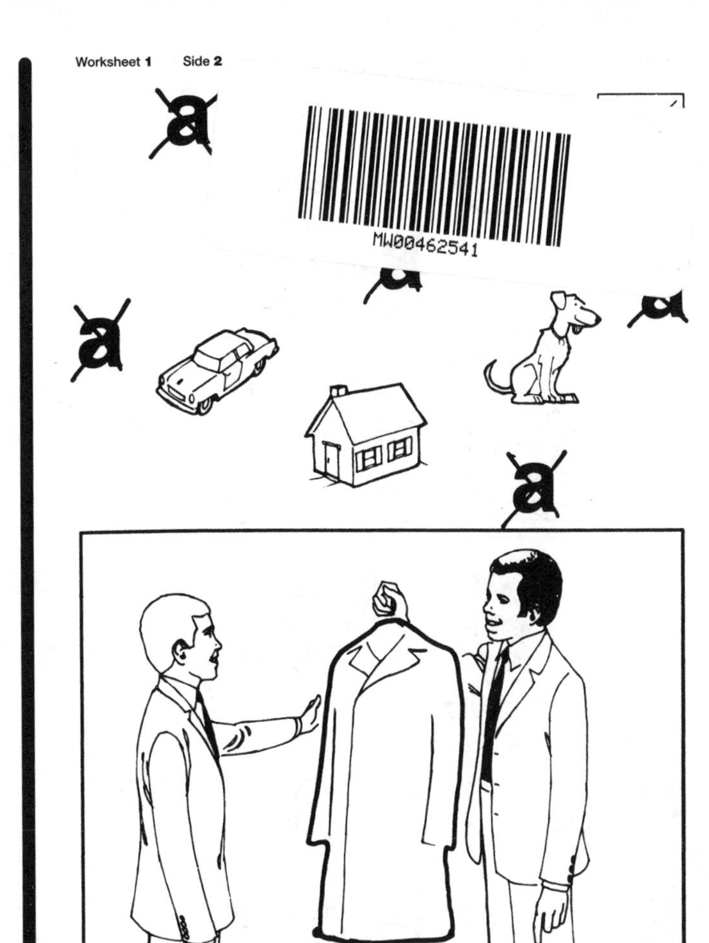

Name

Worksheet **2** Side **1**

a a a a a a a

a a a a a a a

Worksheet **2** Side **2**

Name ______________________ Worksheet 3 Side 1

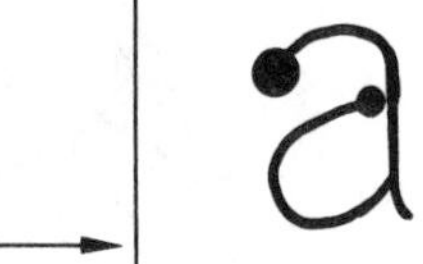

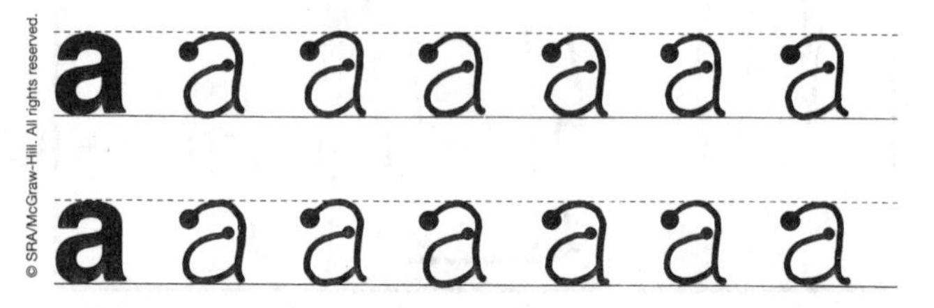

Worksheet 3 Side 2

Name ______________________ Worksheet 4 Side 1

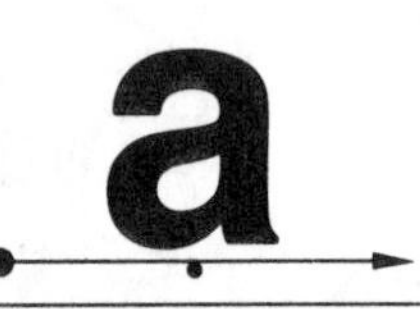

Worksheet 4 Side 2

Name ____________________ Worksheet **5** Side **1**

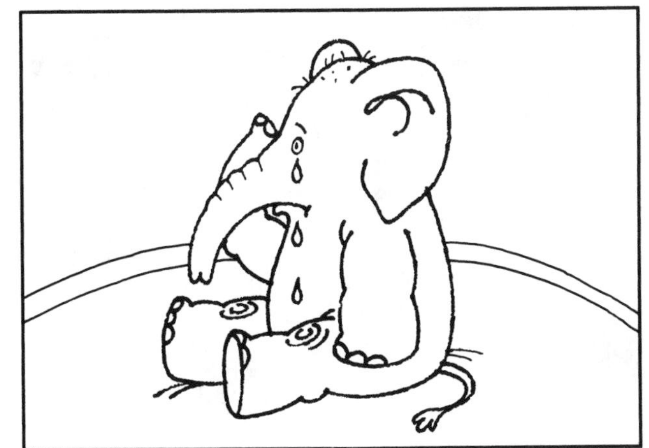

a a

a a a a a a a

a a a a a a a

Worksheet **5** Side **2**

Name ____________________ Worksheet **6** Side **1**

a a

a a a a a a a

a a a a a a a

Worksheet **6** Side **2**

Worksheet 7 Side 1

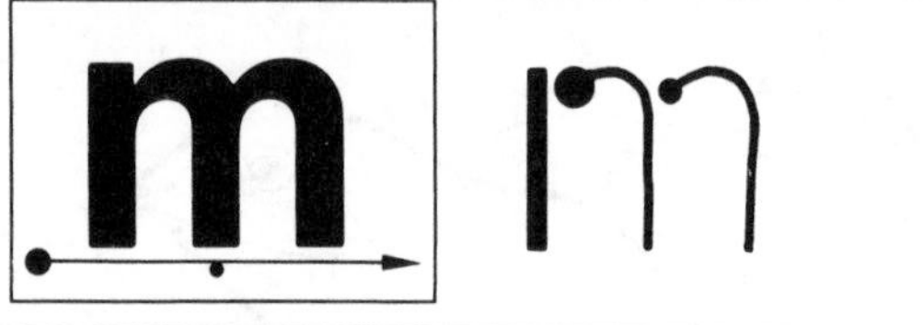

m m m m m m

m m m m m m

Worksheet 7 Side 2

Name

Worksheet 8 Side 1

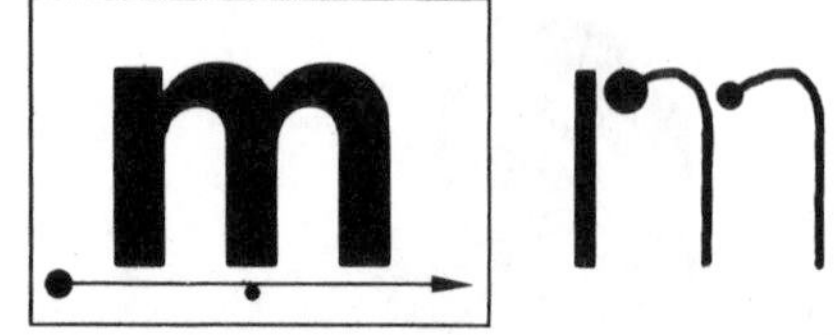

m m m m m m

m m m m m m

Worksheet 8 Side 2

Name 

Worksheet 9 Side 1

m

m m m m m m m

m m m m m m m

Worksheet 9 Side 2

Name

Worksheet 10 Side 1

a a a a a a a

a a a a a a a

Worksheet 10 Side 2

Name 

Worksheet 11 Side 1

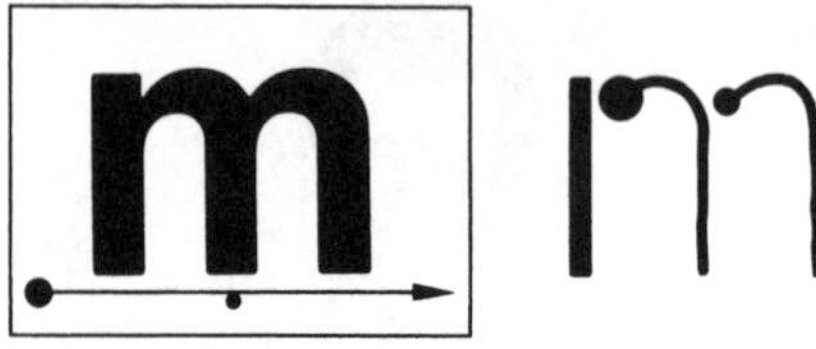

m m

m m

Worksheet 11 Side 2

Name

Worksheet 12 Side 1

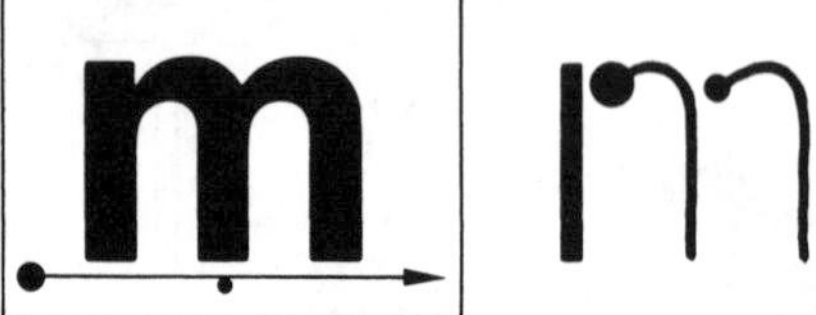

m m

m m

Worksheet 12 Side 2

a

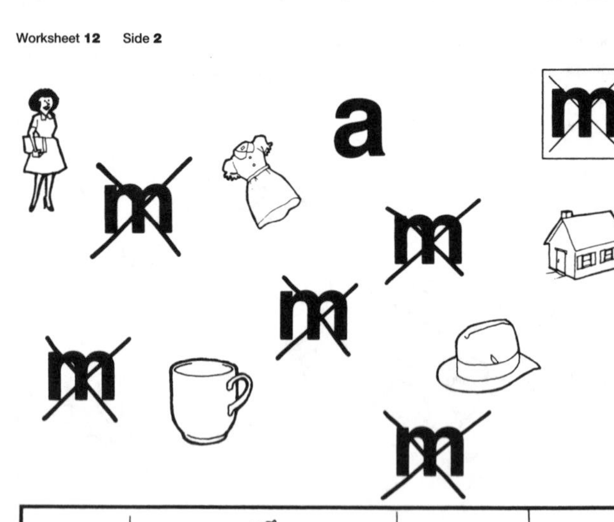

Name ______

Worksheet 13 Side 1

a

a a a a a a a

a a a a a a a

Worksheet 13 Side 2

Name ______

Worksheet 14 Side 1

m

a

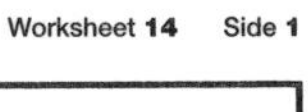

a

a a a a a a a

a a a a a a a

Worksheet 14 Side 2

Name________________ Worksheet **15** Side **1**

a
m

m

m

Worksheet **15** Side **2**

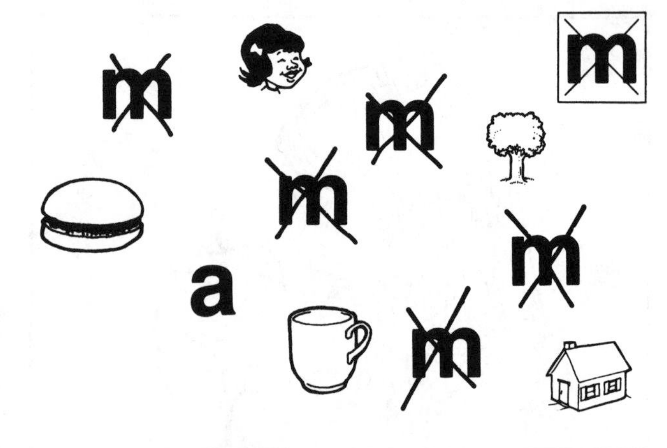

Name________________ Worksheet **16** Side **1**

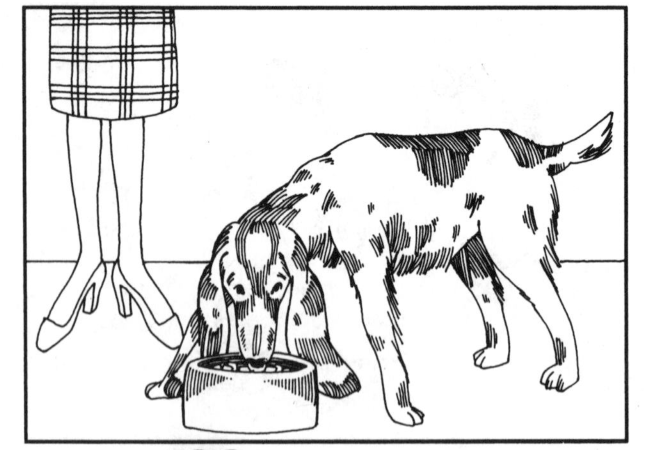

m
a

a

a

Worksheet **16** Side **2**

Name ______________________ Worksheet **17** Side **1**

a

s

S

s S S S S S S

s S S S S S S

Worksheet **17** Side **2**

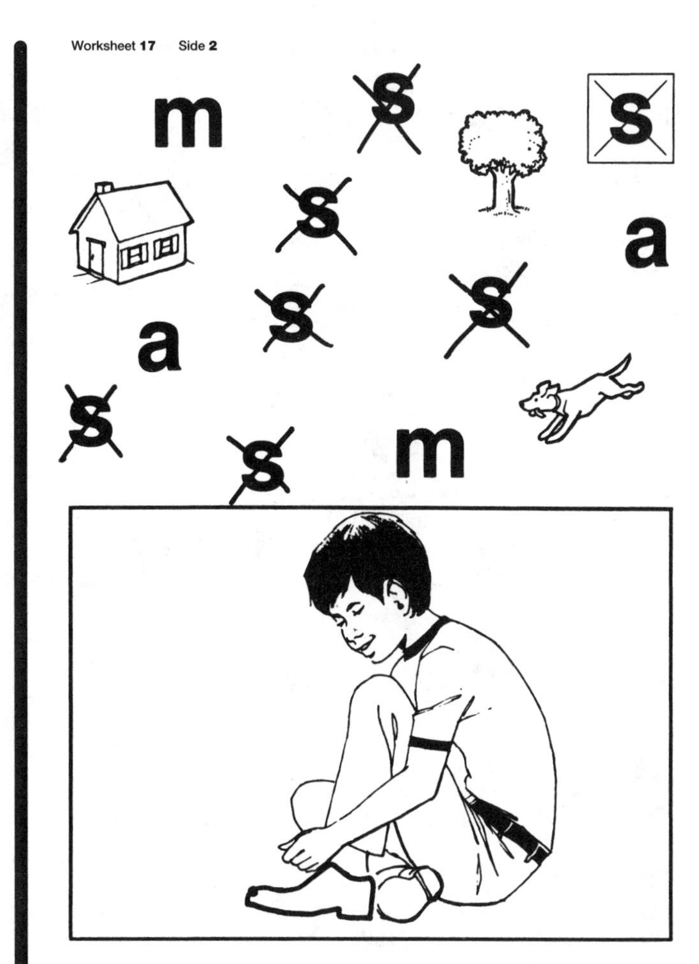

Name ______________________ Worksheet **18** Side **1**

m

s

S

s S S S S S S

s S S S S S S

Worksheet **18** Side **2**

Name

Worksheet 19 Side 1

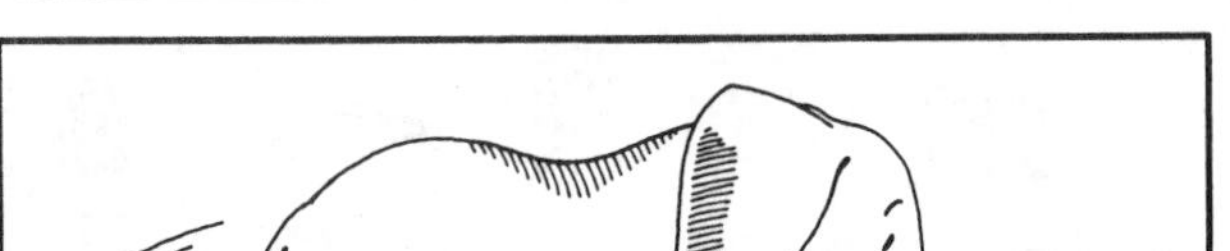

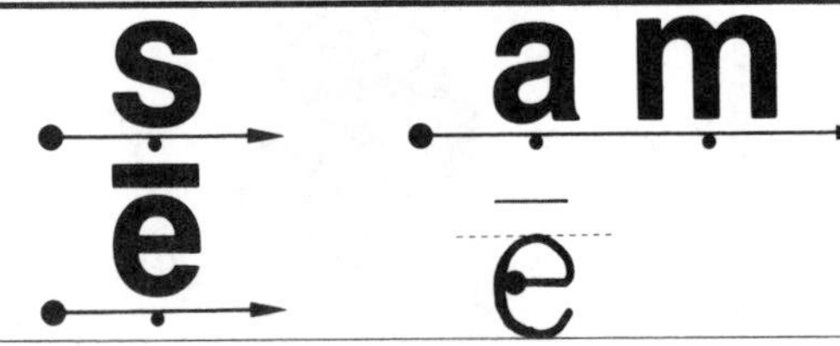

s am

ē e

ē e e e e e e

ē e e e e e e

Worksheet 19 Side 2

a a a m s a s a m a a

Name

Worksheet 20 Side 1

ē ma

s s

s s s s s s s

s s s s s s s

Worksheet 20 Side 2

s ē ē ē a ē a ē ē s ē

Name________________________ Worksheet 21 Side 1

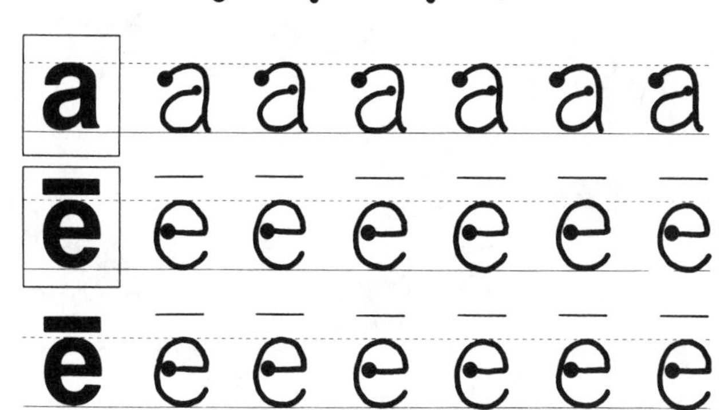

mē

a a a a a a a

ē e e e e e e

ē e e e e e e

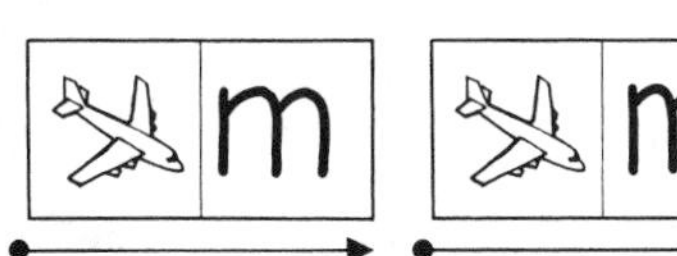

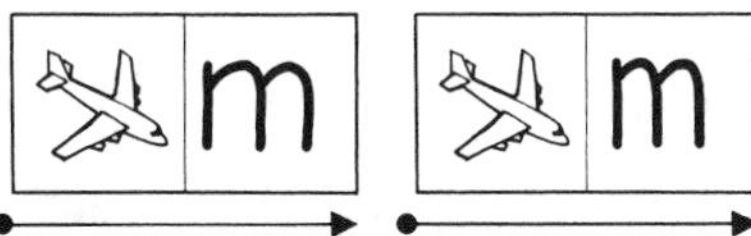

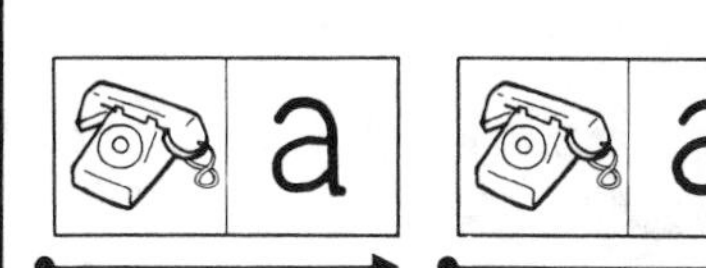

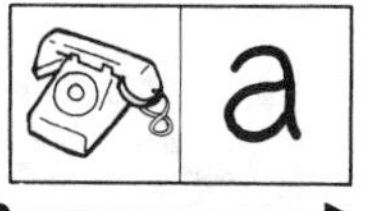

Worksheet 21 Side 2

Name________________________ Worksheet 22 Side 1

sa

ē e e e e e e

s s s s s s s

s s s s s s s

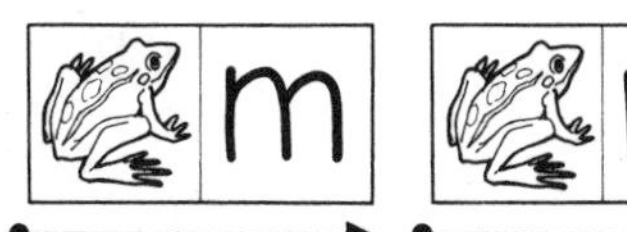

Worksheet 22 Side 2

ē s a ē ē ē m ē ē a ē s m ē

Name

Worksheet **23** Side **1**

ē m

ē e e e e e e

m m m m m m

m m m m m m

 ē

 ē

 ē

 a

 a

 a

Worksheet **23** Side **2**

m a s m m m m ē m m s m ē a m

Name

Worksheet **24** Side **1**

s ē

a a a a a a a

r r r r r r r

r r r r r r r

 m

 m

 m

 s

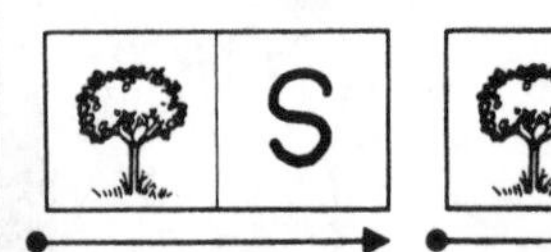 s

 s

Worksheet **24** Side **2**

r r r r s m r a r m ē r r r m

Name ____________________ Worksheet 25 Side 1

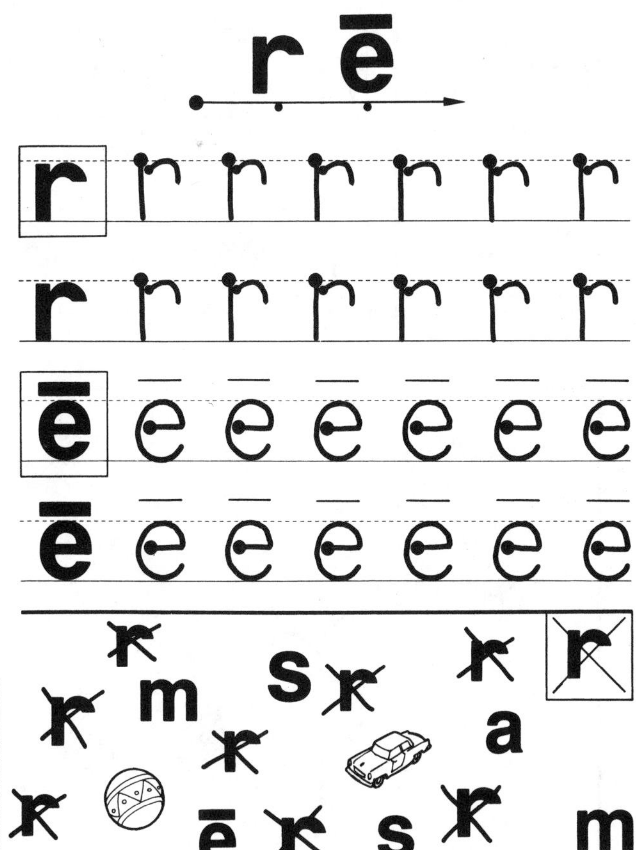

Worksheet 25 Side 2

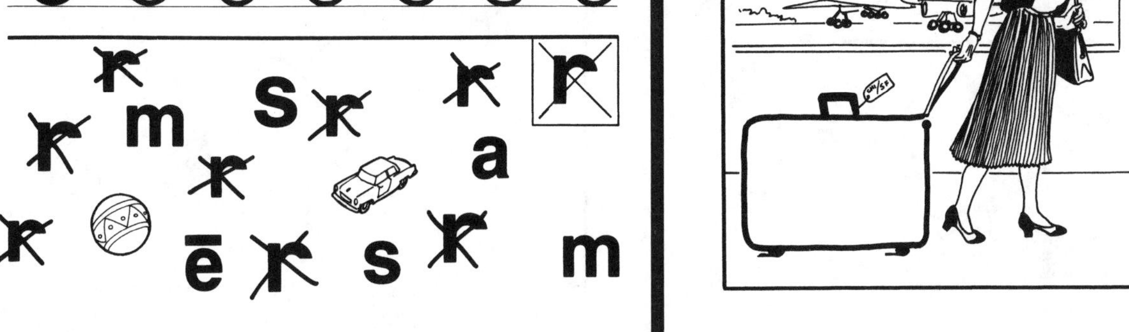

Name ____________________ Worksheet 26 Side 1

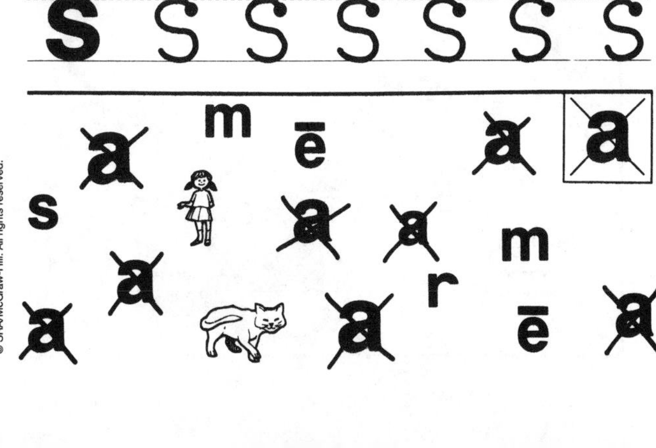

Worksheet 26 Side 2

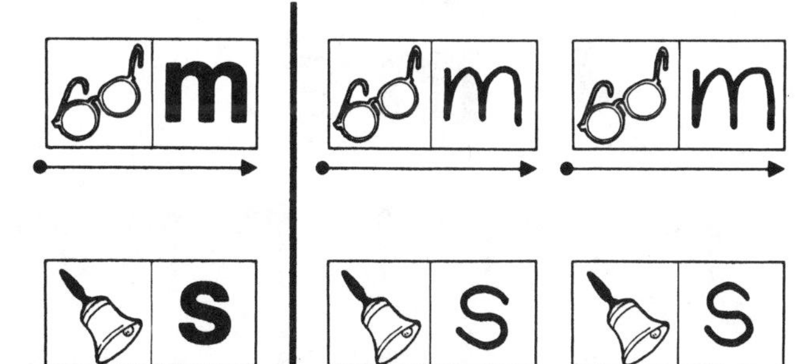

Name ______________________ Worksheet 27 Side 1

r a

ē e e e e e e

ē e e e e e e

a a a a a a a

a a a a a a a

m s m m m ē m s a r r m m m m

Worksheet 27 Side 2

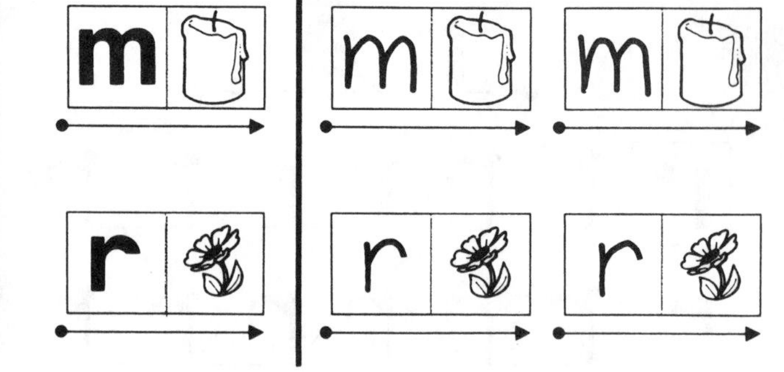

Name ______________________ Worksheet 28 Side 1

m ē

r r r r r r r

r r r r r r r

d d d d d d d

d d d d d d d

s m d d d ē d d d d a a d r d

Worksheet 28 Side 2

s s s

ē ē ē

Name 

Worksheet **29** Side **1**

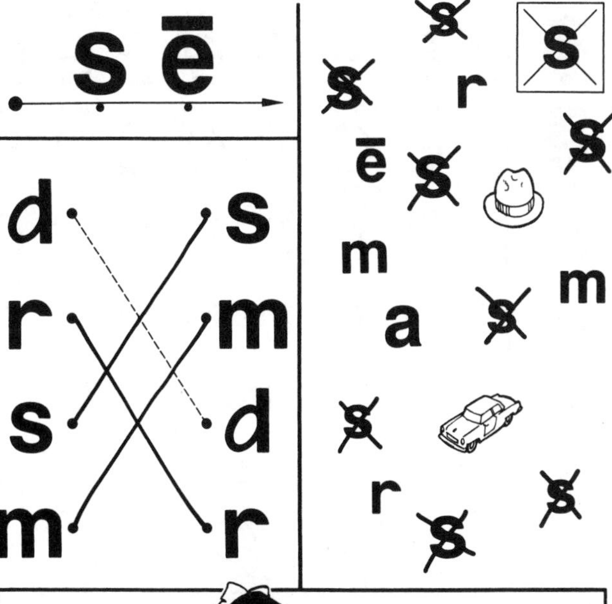

Worksheet **29** Side **2**

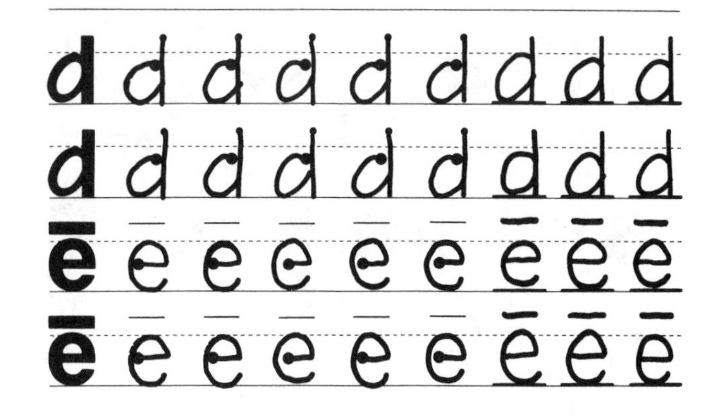

Name

Worksheet **30** Side **1**

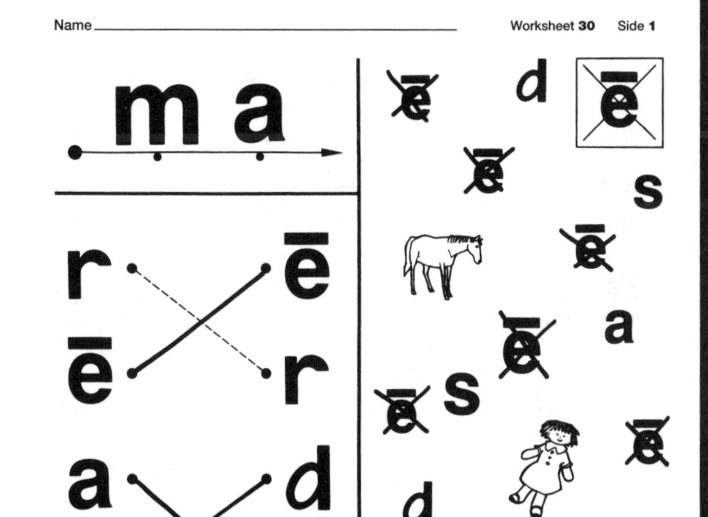

Worksheet **30** Side **2**

m m m m m m m
m m m m m m m
s s s s s s s s s
s s s s s s s s s

s s s s
a a a a
m m m m
r r r r

© SRA/McGraw-Hill. All rights reserved.

Name
Worksheet 31 Side 1

r a
s
a
d
m
m
a
s
d

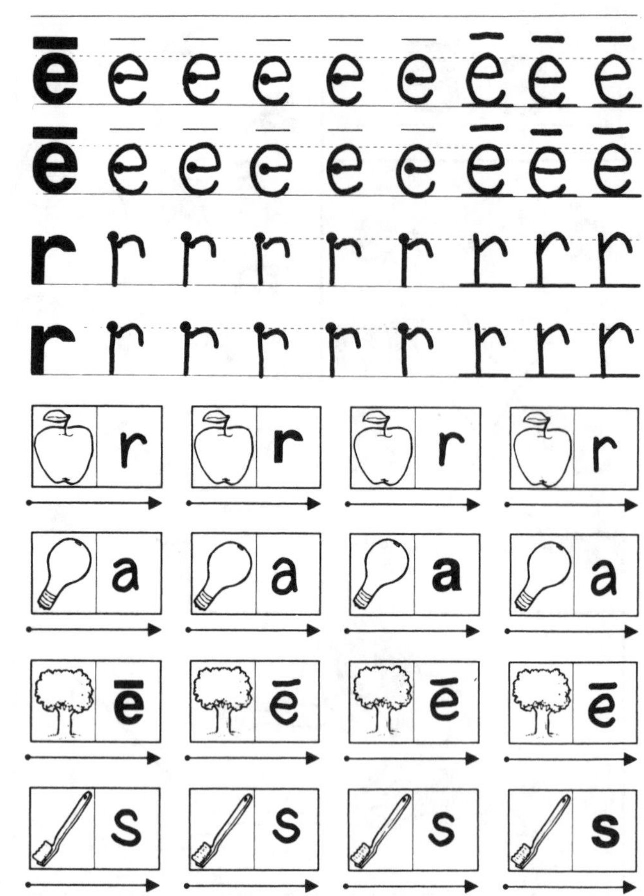
Worksheet 31 Side 2

16

Name
Worksheet 32 Side 1
m ē
s
r
f
a
m
ē
r
a
s
f
ē
m

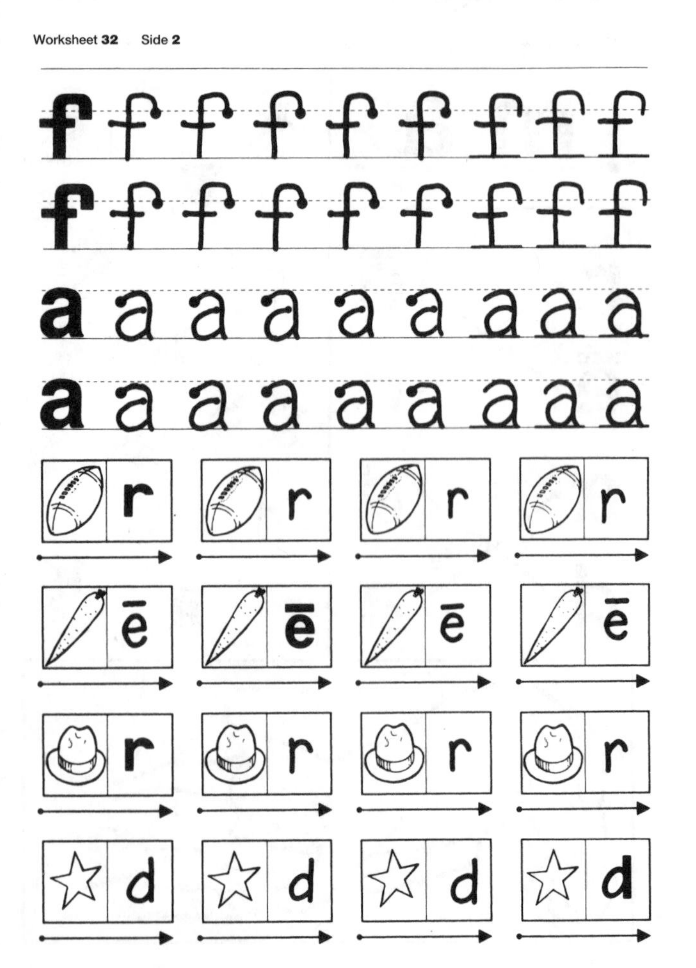
Worksheet 32 Side 2

Name ____________________ Worksheet 33 Side 1

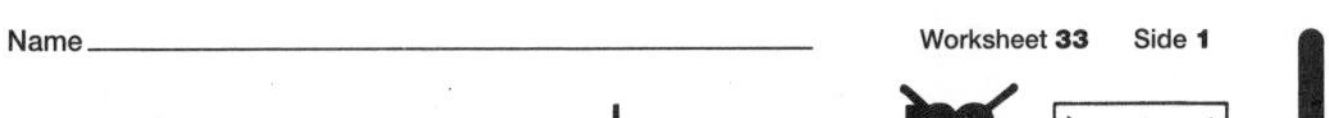

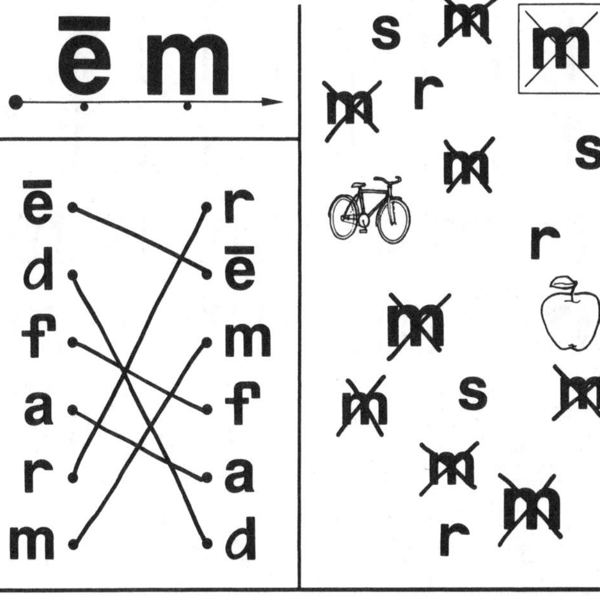

Worksheet 33 Side 2

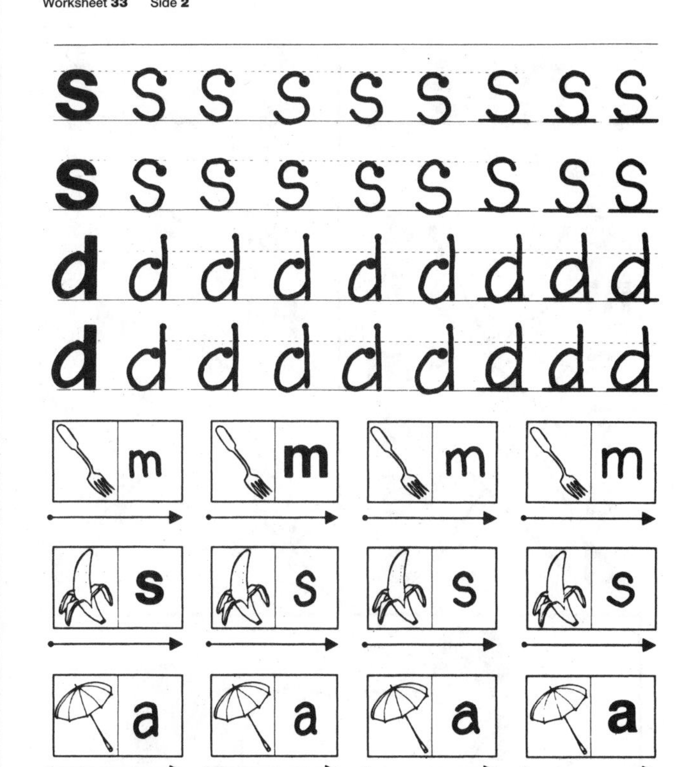

Name ____________________ Worksheet 34 Side 1

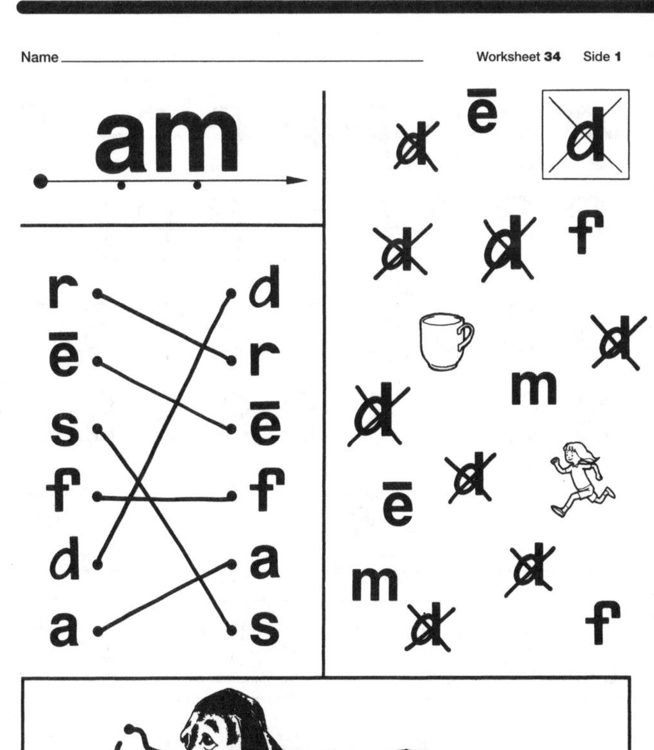

Worksheet 34 Side 2

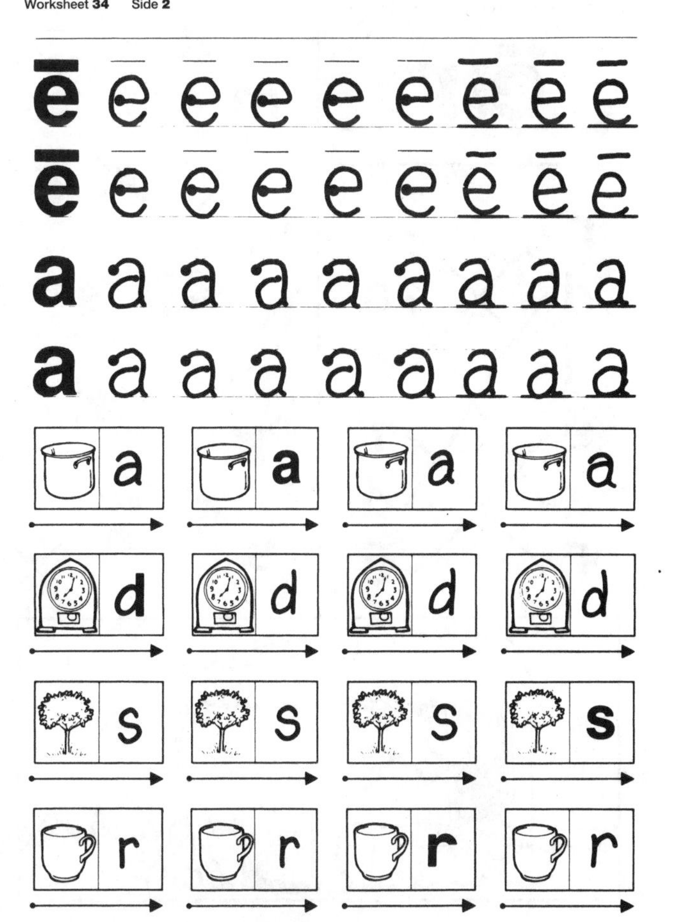

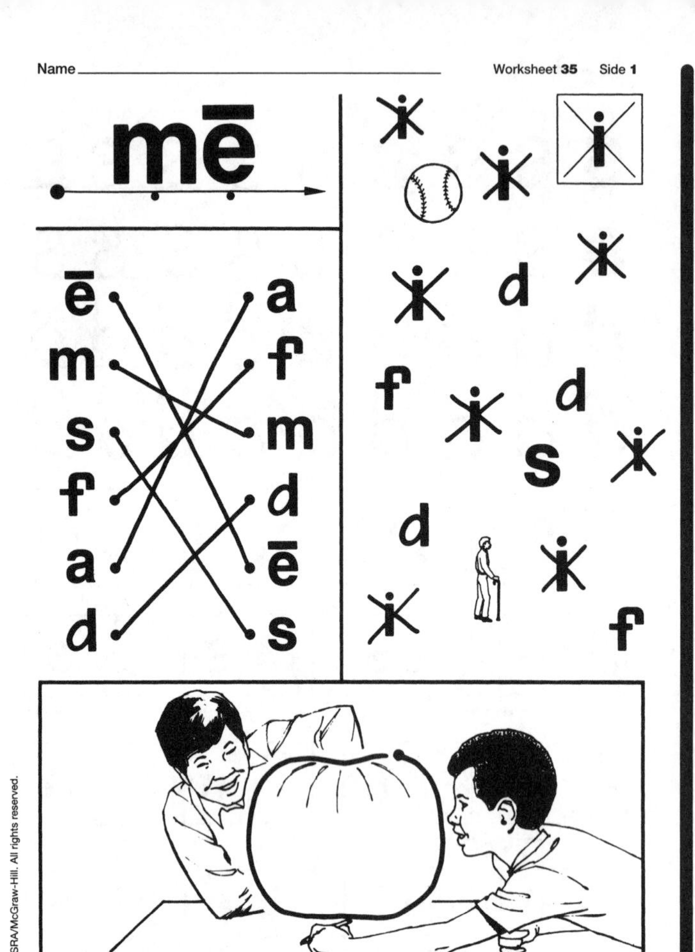
Name
Worksheet 35 Side 1
mē
ē m s f a d
a f m d ē s
f d s d f
© SRA/McGraw-Hill. All rights reserved.

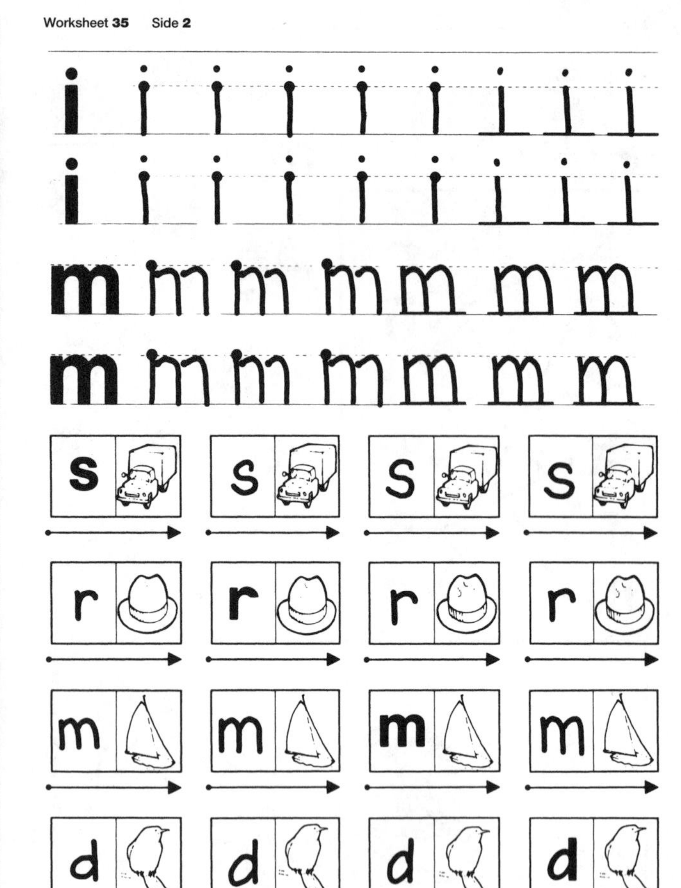
Worksheet 35 Side 2
i
i
m
m
s s s s
r r r r
m m m m
d d d d

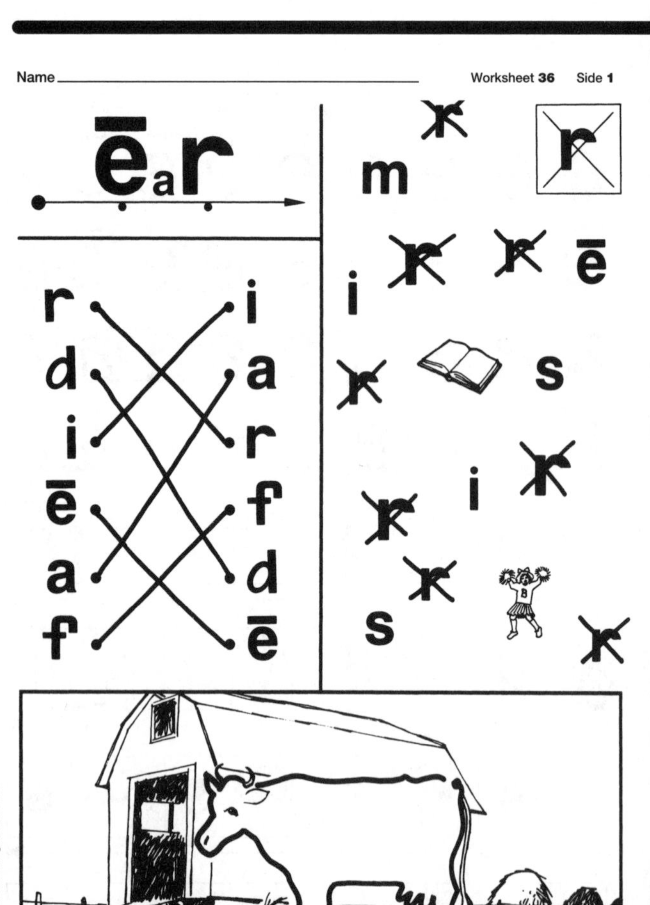
Name
Worksheet 36 Side 1
ēar
r d i ē a f
i a r f d ē
m ē i s s
© SRA/McGraw-Hill. All rights reserved.

Worksheet 36 Side 2
f
f
s
s
ē ē ē ē
r r r r
f f f f
m m m m

Name ____________________ Worksheet **37** Side **1**

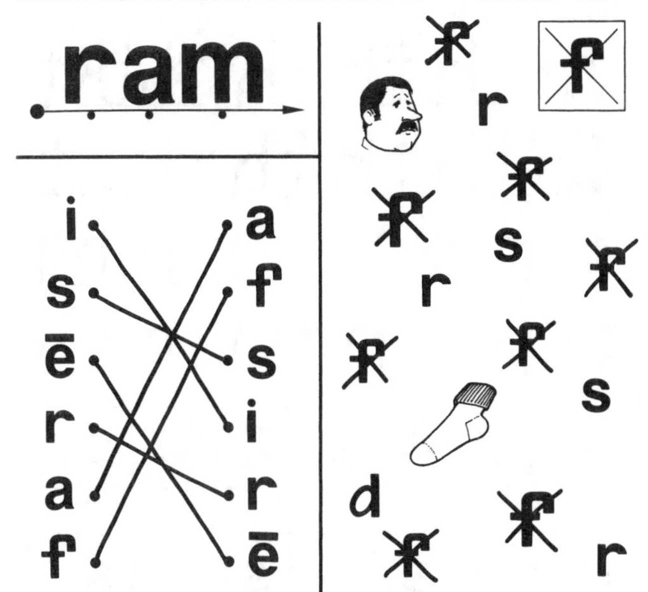

Worksheet **37** Side **2**

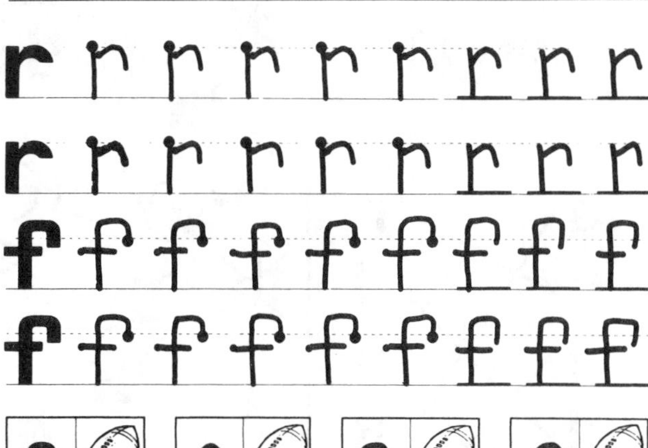

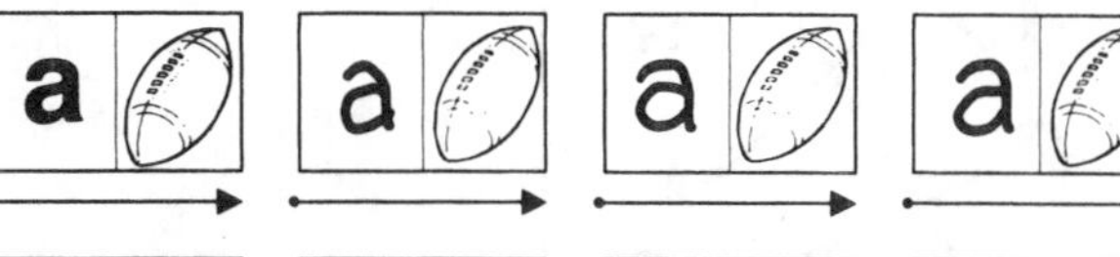

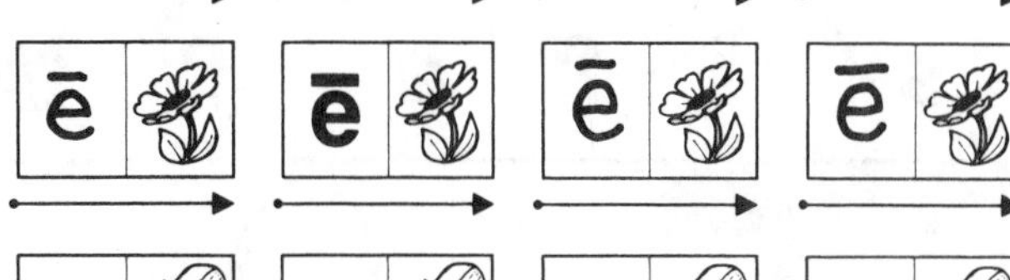

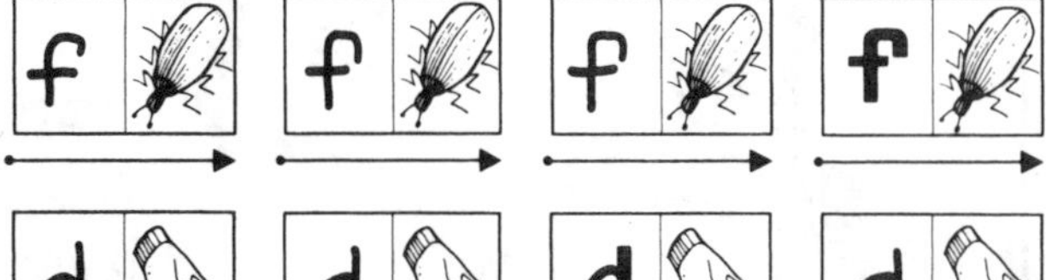

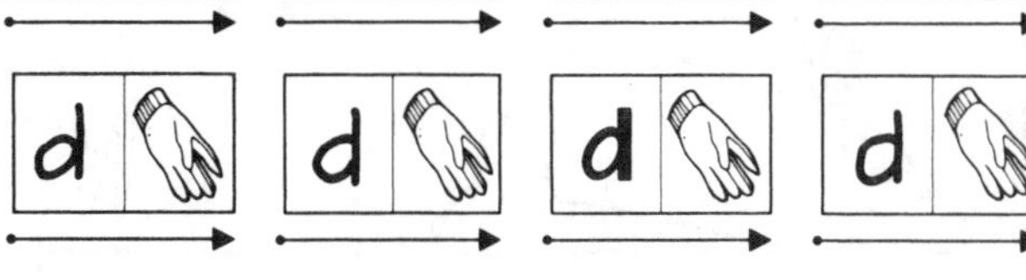

Name ____________________ Worksheet **38** Side **1**

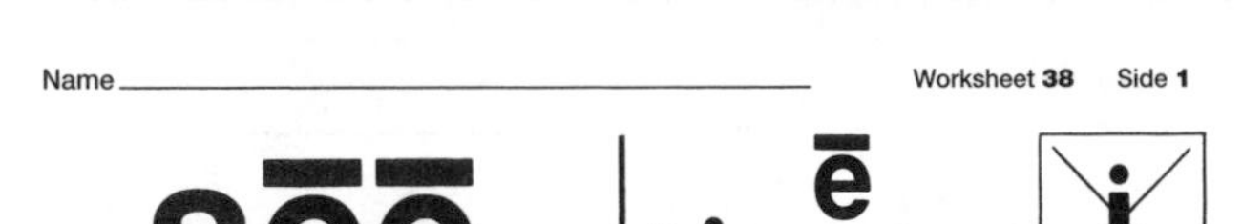

Worksheet **38** Side **2**

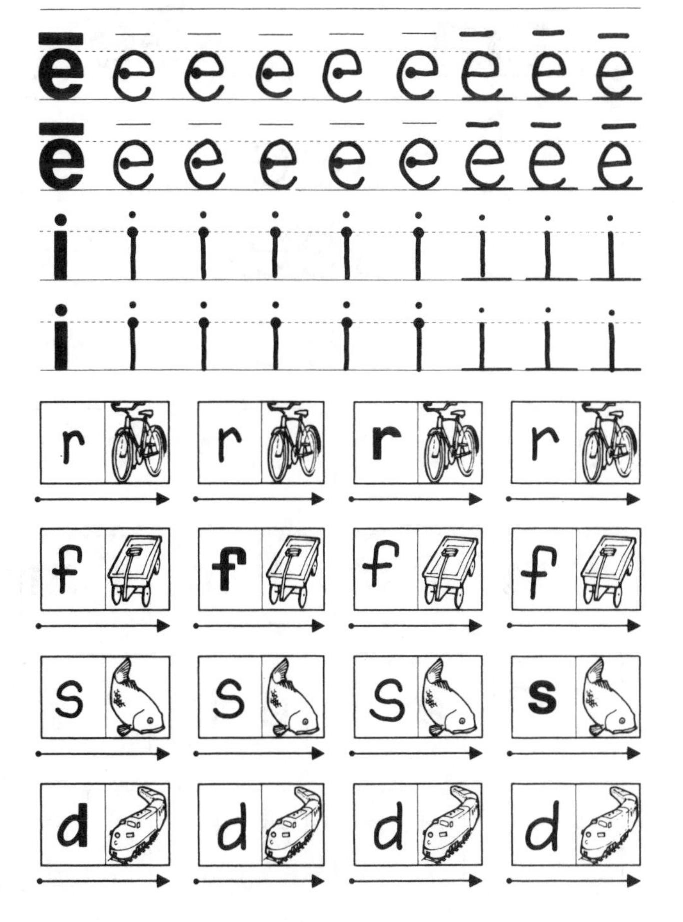

Name
Worksheet 39 Side 1
am
a r i d f s
r d s a i f
th f r s
© SRA/McGraw-Hill. All rights reserved.

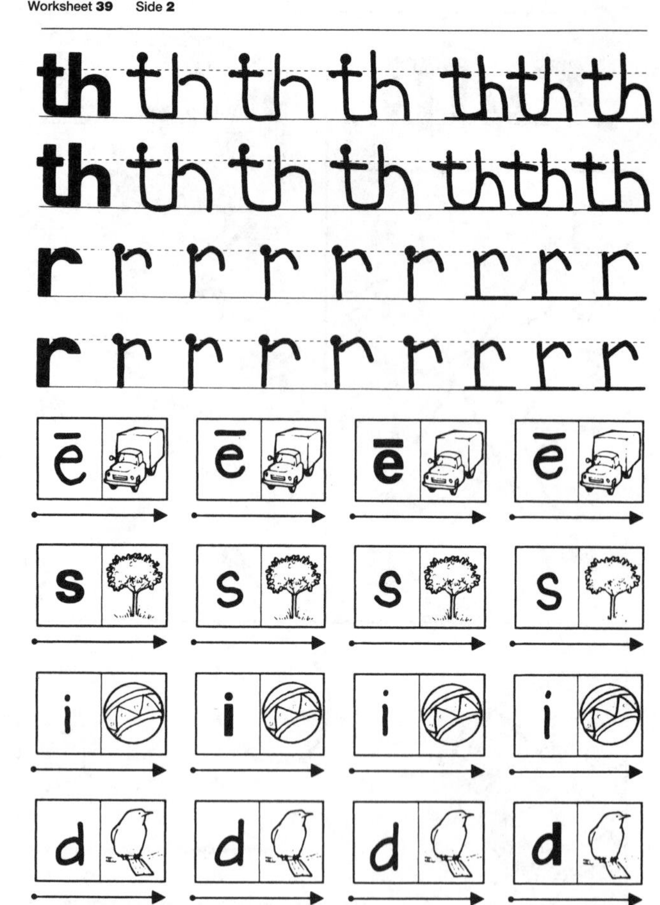
Worksheet 39 Side 2
th th th th th th th
r r r r r r r r r
ē s i d

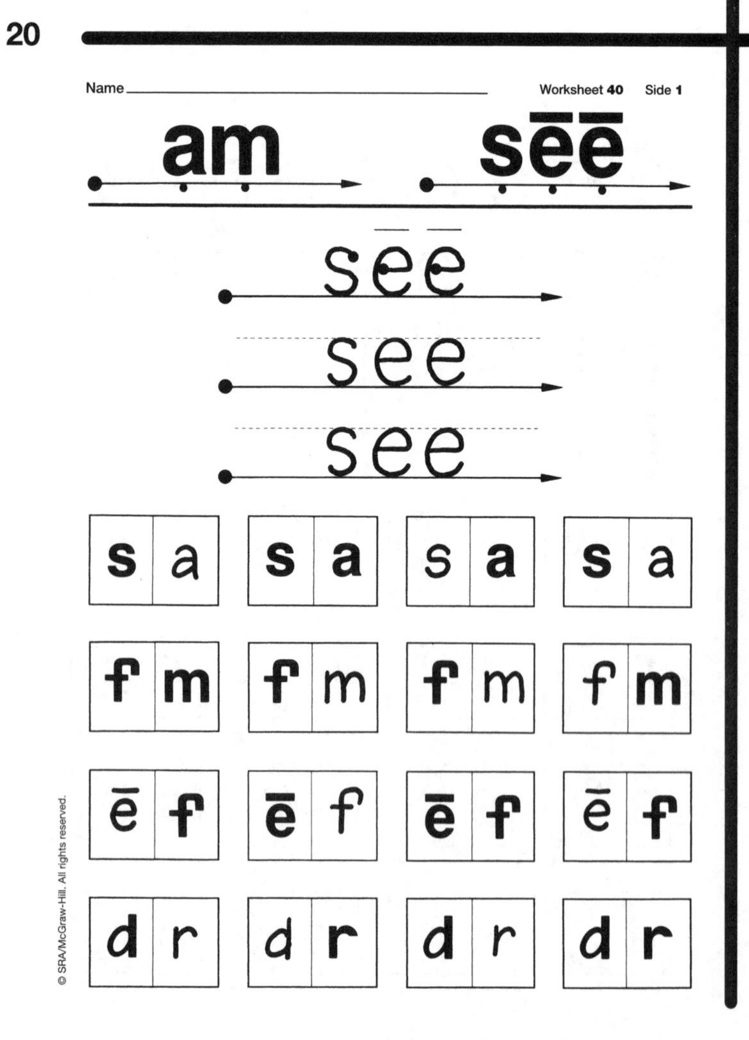
Name
Worksheet 40 Side 1
am
sēē
see
see
see
s a
f m
ē f
d r
© SRA/McGraw-Hill. All rights reserved.

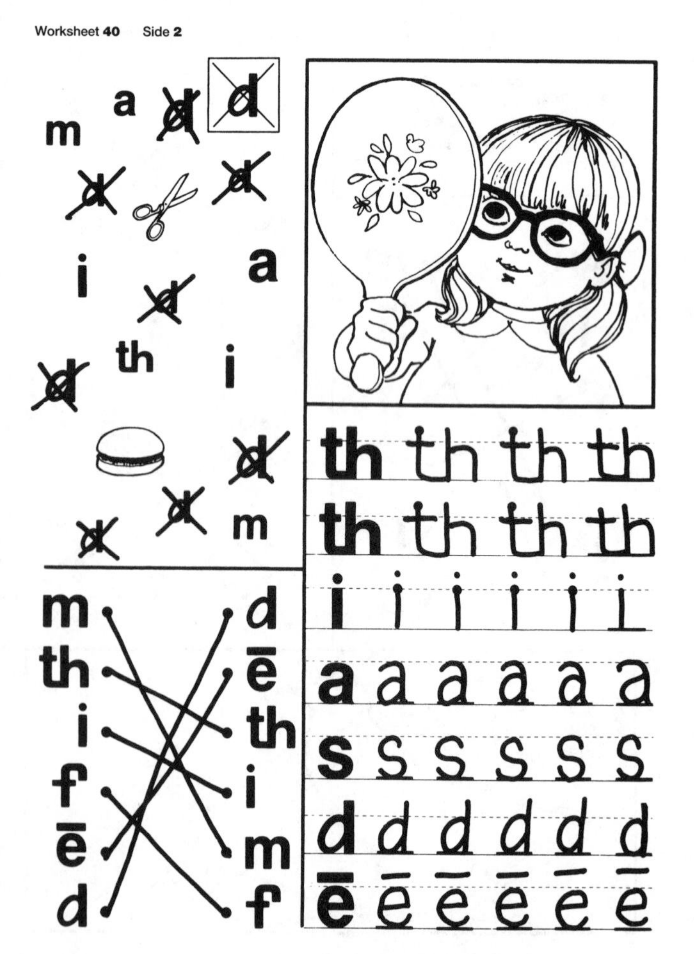
Worksheet 40 Side 2
m a d
i a
th i
m
m th i f ē d
d ē th i m f
th th th th
i i i i i i
a a a a a a
s s s s s s
d d d d d d
ē ē ē ē ē ē

Name ______________________ Worksheet **41** Side **1**

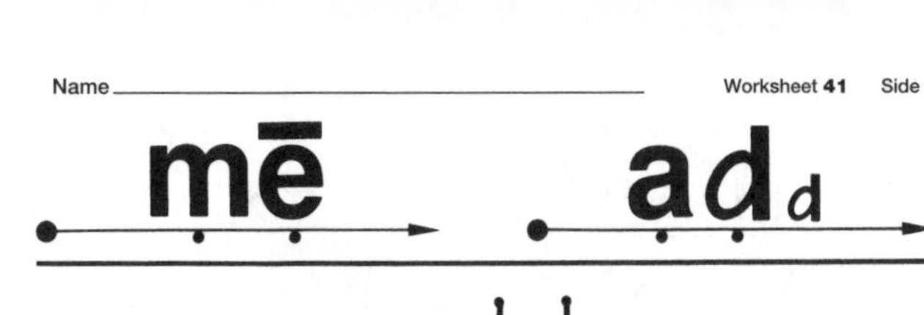

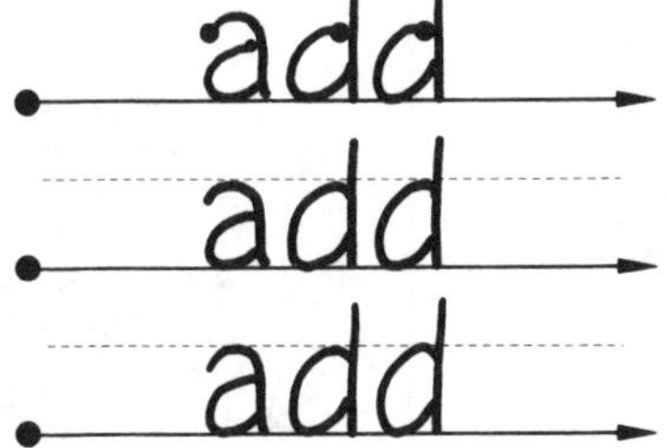

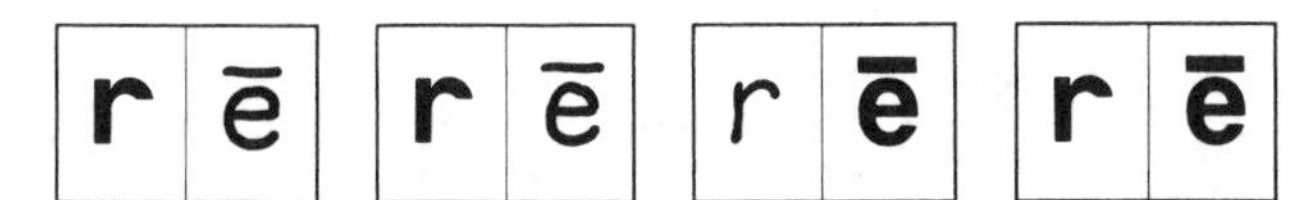

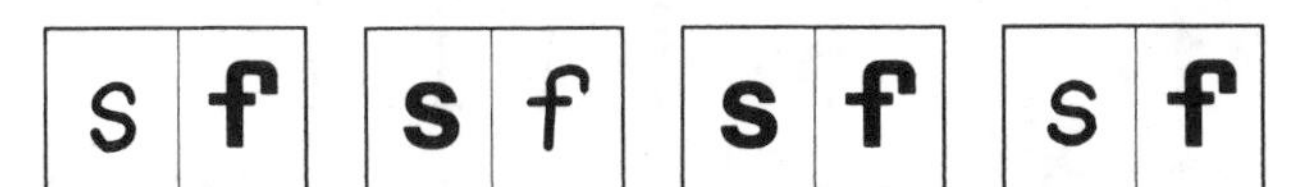

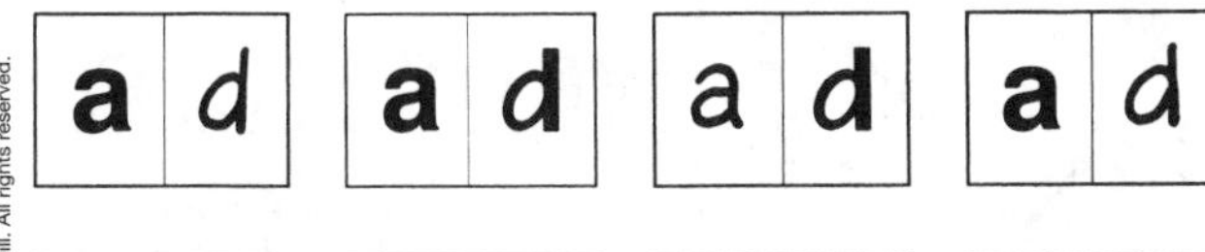

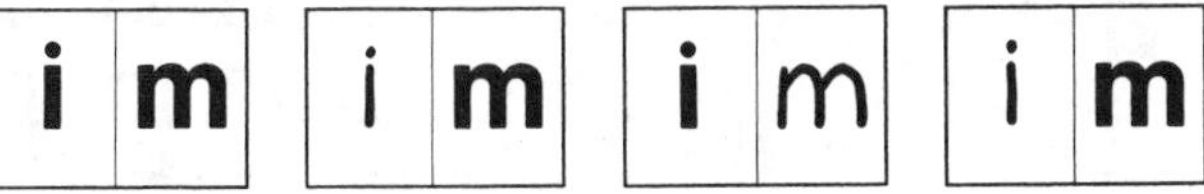

Worksheet **41** Side **2**

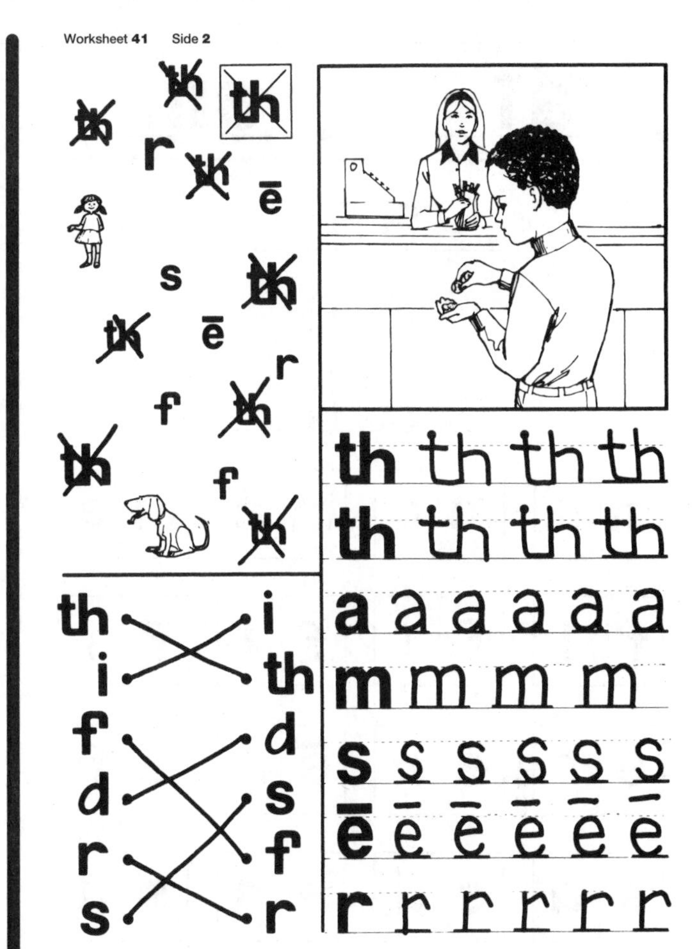

Name ______________________ Worksheet **42** Side **1**

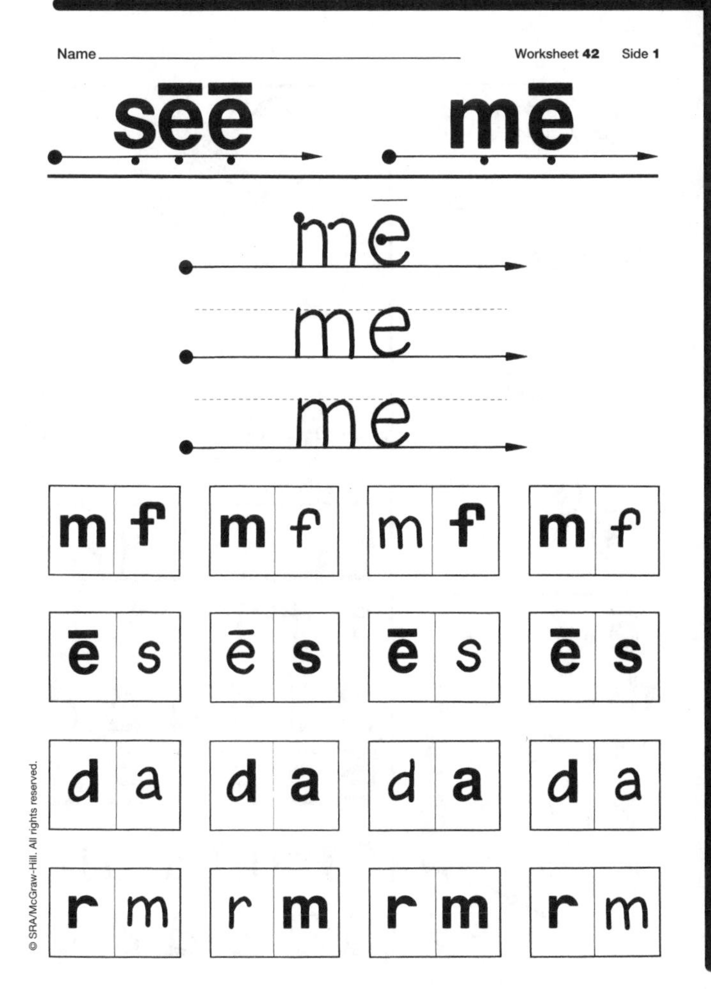

Worksheet **42** Side **2**

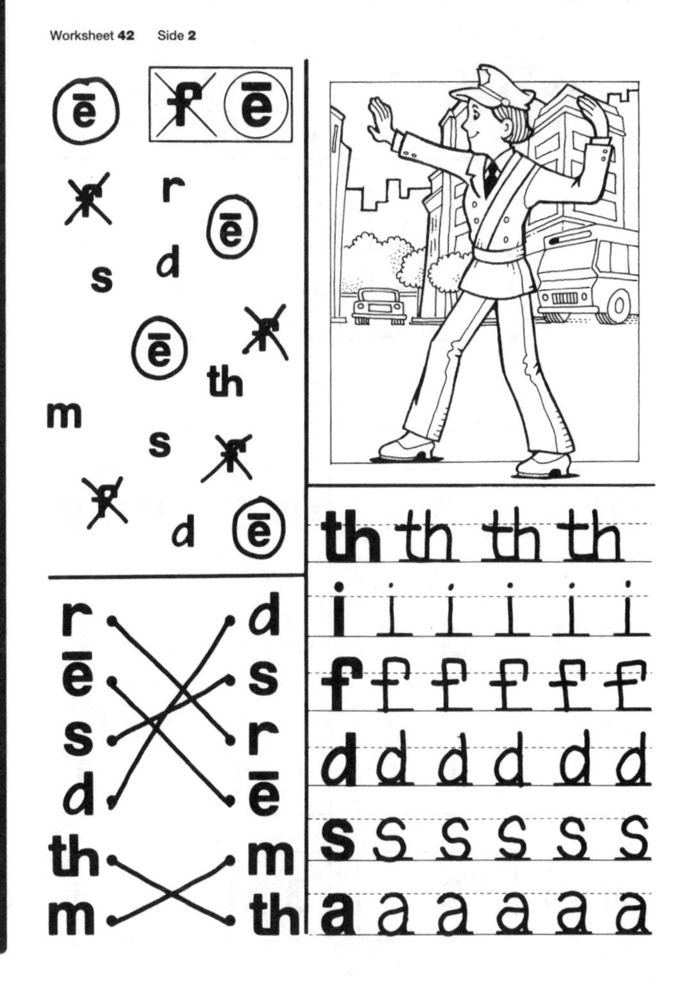

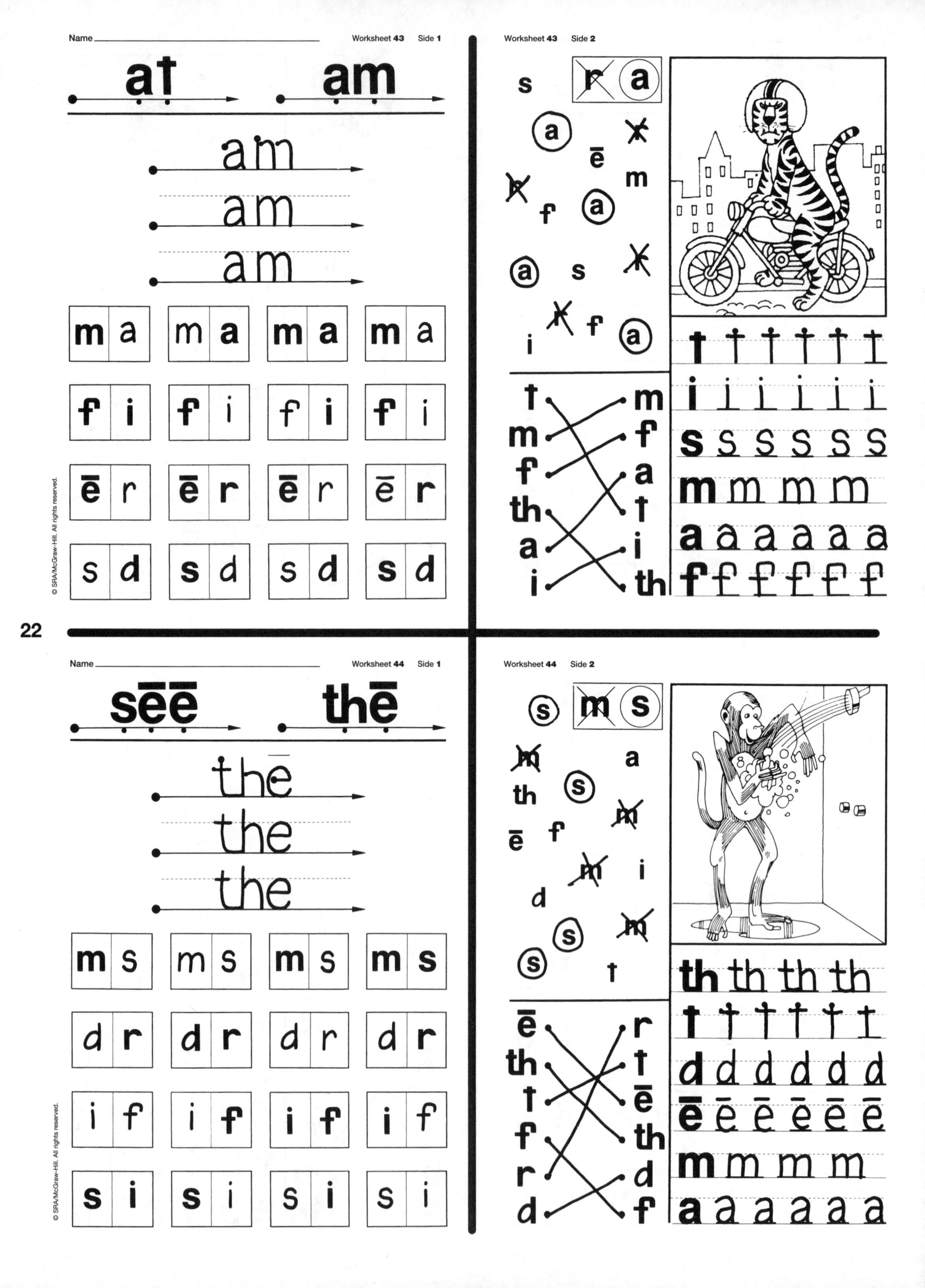

Name
Worksheet 43 Side 1
at am
am
am
am
m a m a m a m a
f i f i f i f i
ē r ē r ē r ē r
s d s d s d s d
Worksheet 43 Side 2
s r a
a
ē
m
f
a
a s
f
i a
t m
m f
f a
th t
a i
i th
t t t t t t
i i i i i i
s s s s s s
m m m m
a a a a a a
f f f f f f
22
Name
Worksheet 44 Side 1
sēē thē
the
the
the
m s m s m s m s
d r d r d r d r
i f i f i f i f
s i s i s i s i
Worksheet 44 Side 2
s m s
m a
th s
m
ē f
m i
d
s
m
s
t
ē r
th t
t ē
f th
r d
d f
th th th th
t t t t t t
d d d d d d
ē ē ē ē ē ē
m m m m
a a a a a a
© SRA/McGraw-Hill. All rights reserved.
© SRA/McGraw-Hill. All rights reserved.

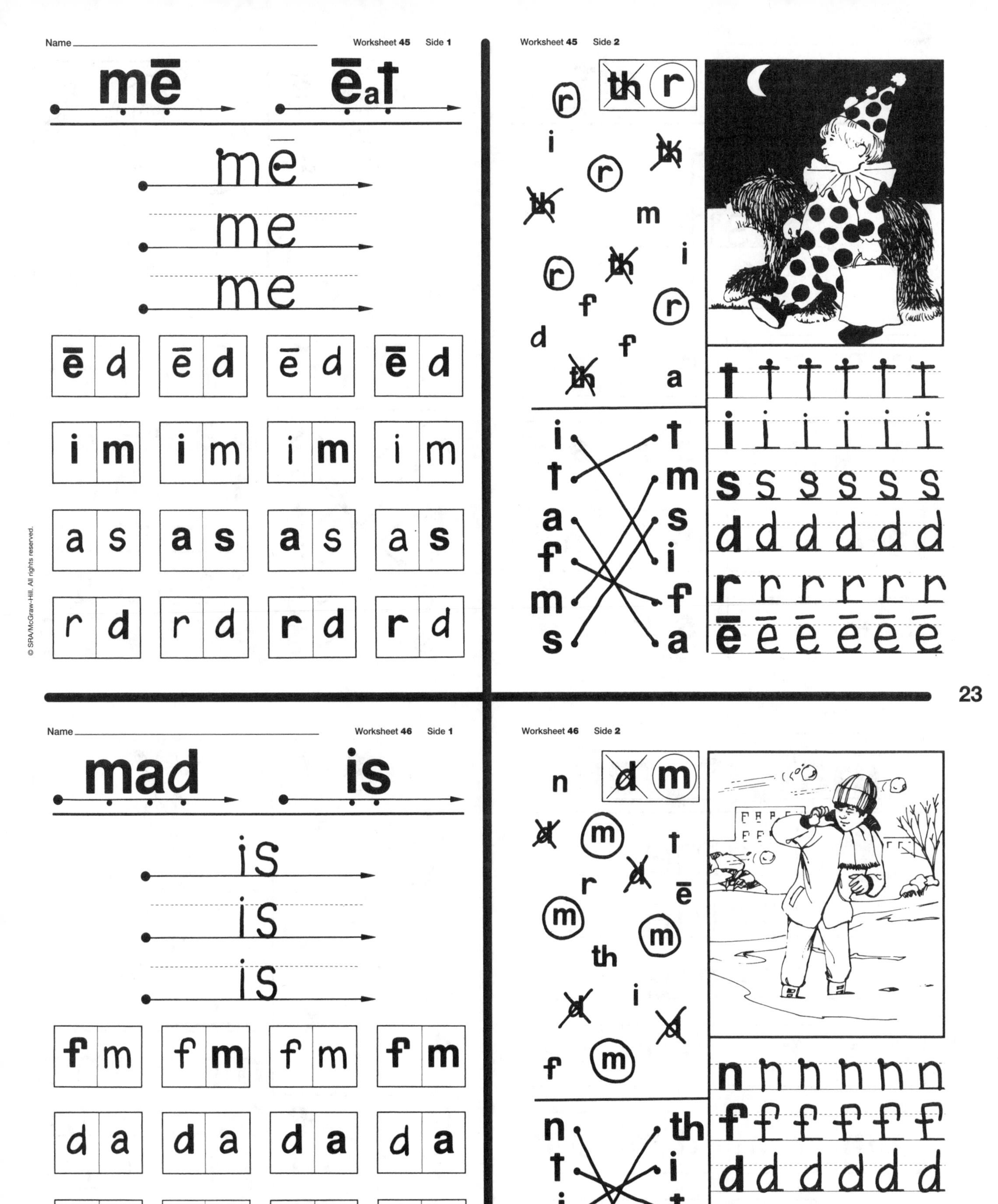
Name
Worksheet 45 Side 1
mē ēat
me
me
me
Worksheet 45 Side 2
th r
Name
Worksheet 46 Side 1
mad is
is
is
is
Worksheet 46 Side 2
d m

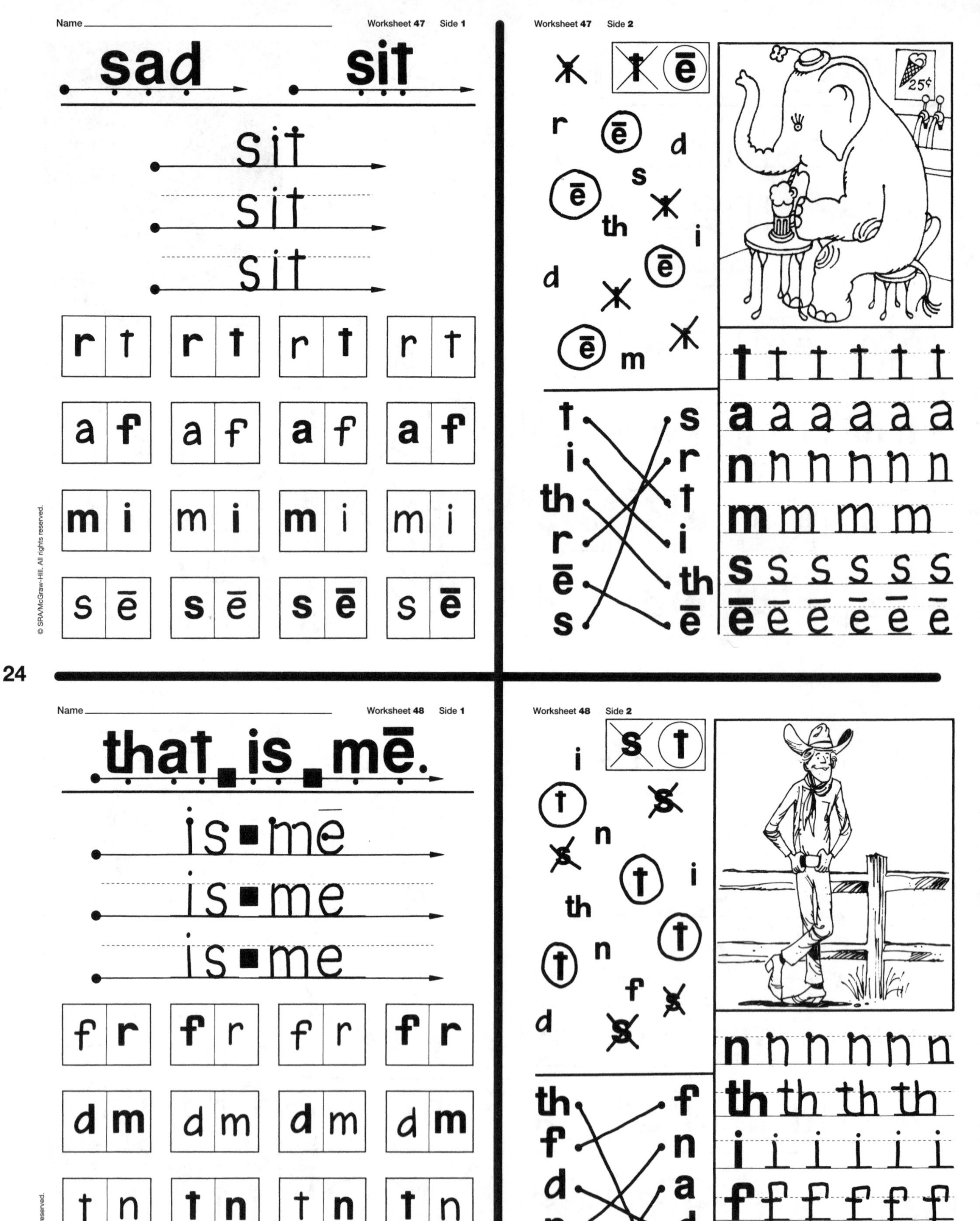
Name
Worksheet 47 Side 1
sad sit
sit
sit
sit
© SRA/McGraw-Hill. All rights reserved.
Worksheet 47 Side 2
25¢
Name
Worksheet 48 Side 1
that is mē.
is mē
is me
is me
© SRA/McGraw-Hill. All rights reserved.
Worksheet 48 Side 2

Name ______________________ Worksheet **49** Side **1**

sēē▪mē▪ēat.

see▪me

see▪me

see▪me

n ē	n ē	n ē	n ē
r n	r n	r n	r n
i f	i f	i f	i f
d t	d t	d t	d t

Worksheet **49** Side **2**

f a

f t i a s f th a f a t n f a i

n → m
r → th
i → r
th → f
f → i
m → n

n n n n n n
t t t t t t
s s s s s s
m m m m
d d d d d d
r r r r r r

Name ______________________ Worksheet **50** Side **1**

it▪is▪fat.

it▪is▪fat.

it▪is▪fat.

it▪is▪fat.

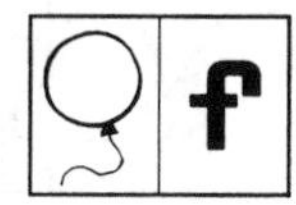 a | f

 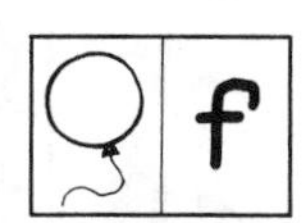 

a | f | f | a

f | a | a | f

f | a | f | a

Worksheet **50** Side **2**

i n

n th i t c n i n d th f n i i c

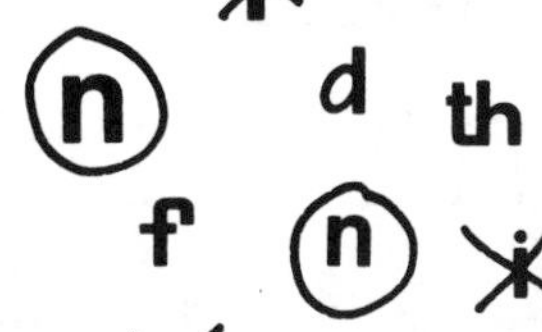

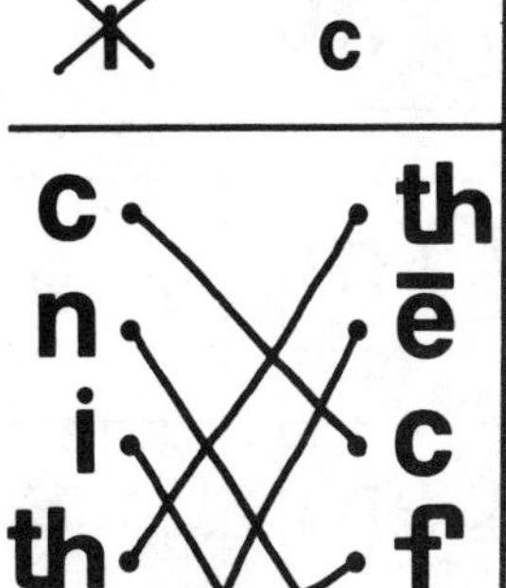

c → th
n → ē
i → c
th → f
f → n
ē → i

c c c c c c
t t t t t t
f f f f f f
n n n n n n
m m m m
i i i i i i

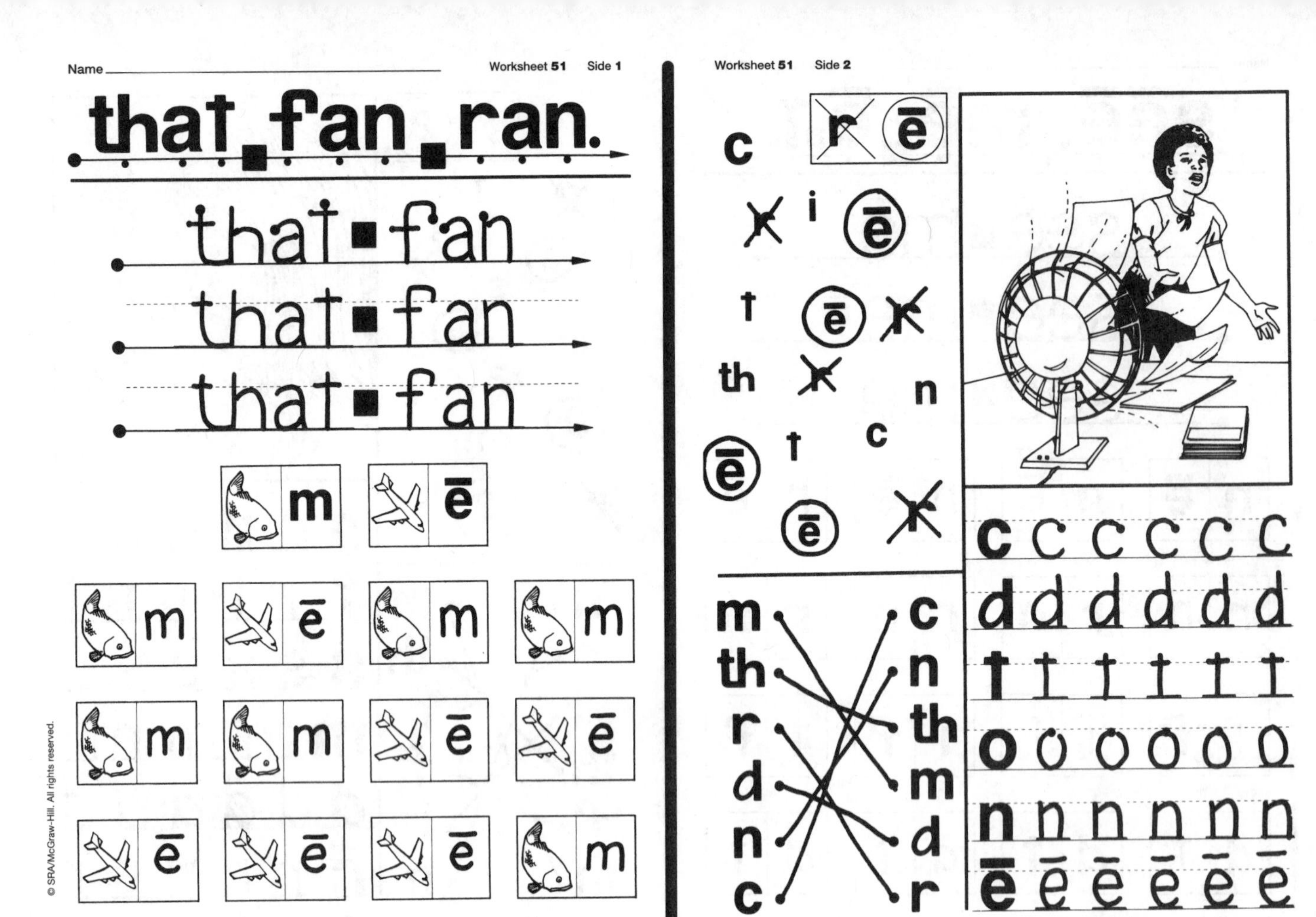
Name
Worksheet 51 Side 1
that fan ran.
that fan
that fan
that fan
m ē
© SRA/McGraw-Hill. All rights reserved.
Worksheet 51 Side 2
r ē
c c c c c c
d d d d d d
t t t t t t
o o o o o o
n n n n n n
ē ē ē ē ē ē

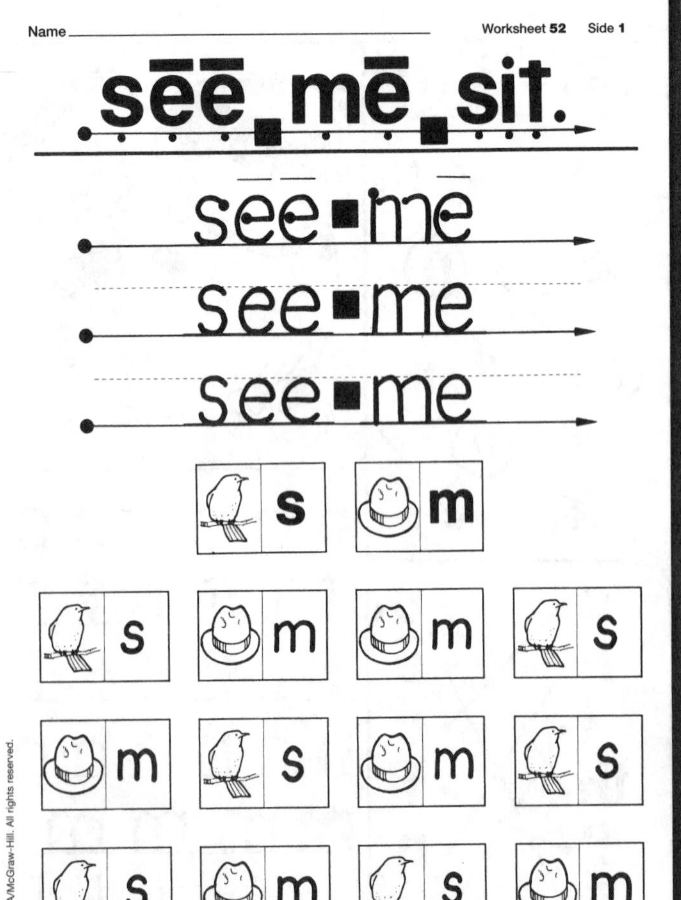
Name
Worksheet 52 Side 1
sēē mē sit.
see me
see me
see me
s m
© SRA/McGraw-Hill. All rights reserved.

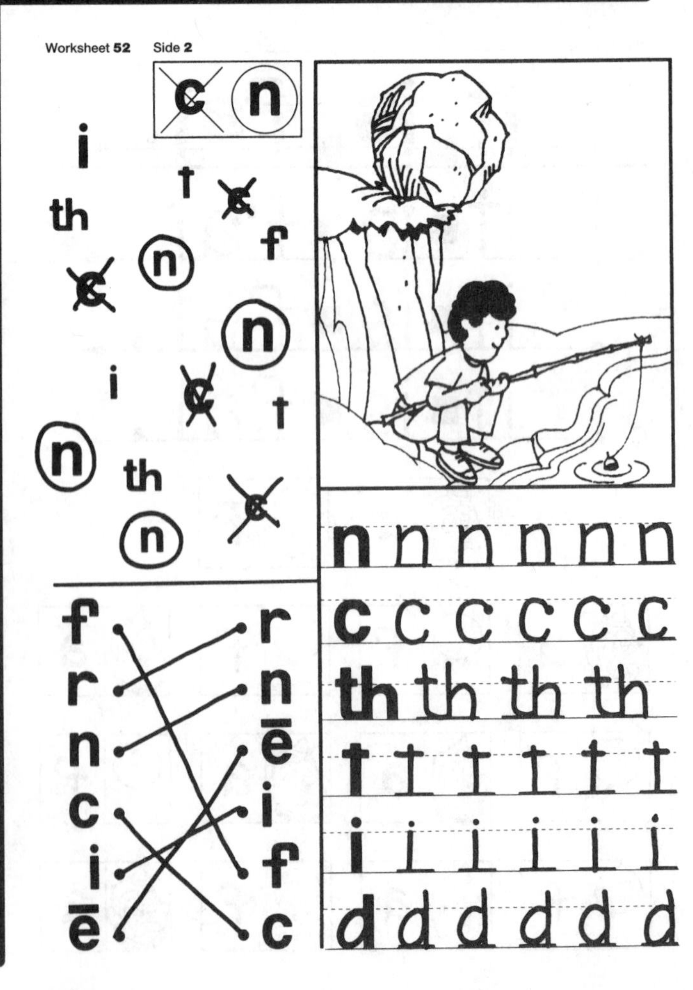
Worksheet 52 Side 2
c n
n n n n n n
c c c c c c
th th th th
t t t t t t
i i i i i i
d d d d d d

Name ______________________ Worksheet **53** Side **1**

thē sad man

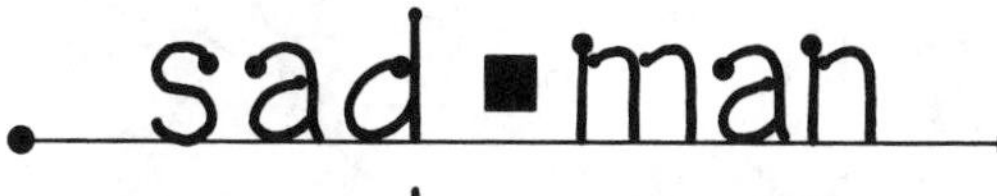

sad man

sad man

sad man

 a	 ē

 ē	 a	 a	 ē
 a	 ē	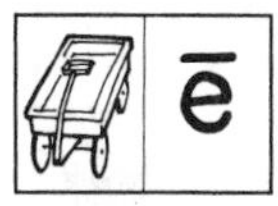 ē	 a
 a	 a	 ē	 ē

Worksheet **53** Side **2**

n f c

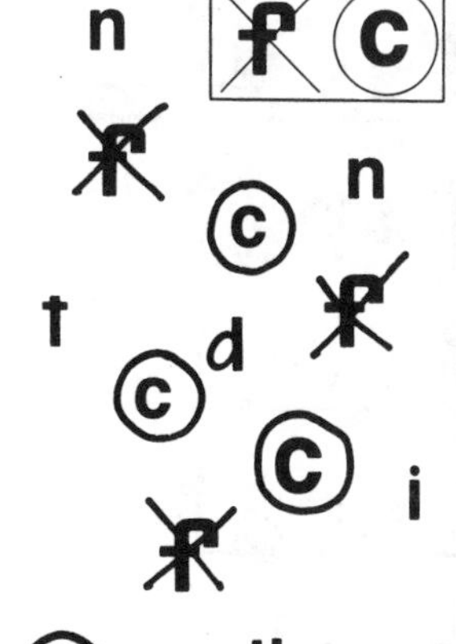

f c n c t d f c c i f c th ē f

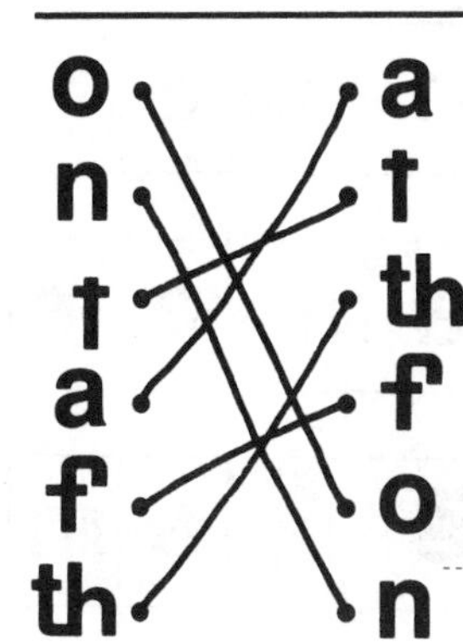

o	a
n	t
t	th
a	f
f	o
th	n

n n n n n n

o o o o o o

m m m m m

t t t t t t

ē ē ē ē ē ē

r r r r r r

Name ______________________ Worksheet **54** Side **1**

mad at mē

at me

at me

at me

 f	 d

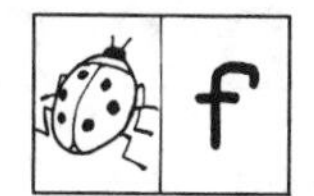 f	 d	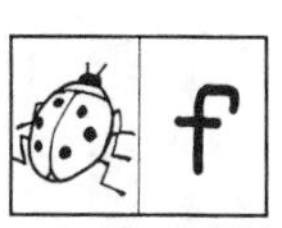 f	 d
 d	 d	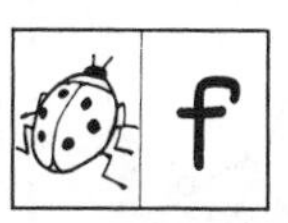 f	 f
 f	 f	 d	 d

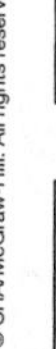

Worksheet **54** Side **2**

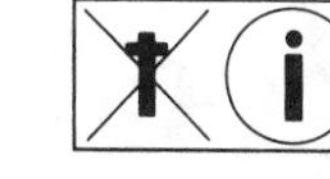

c t i

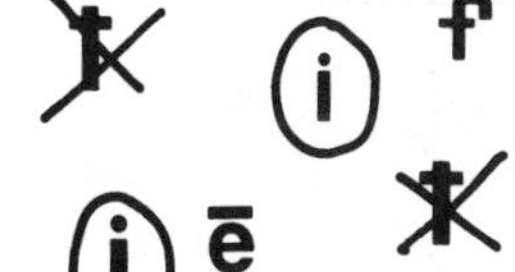

t i f i ē t n t i i c th t n

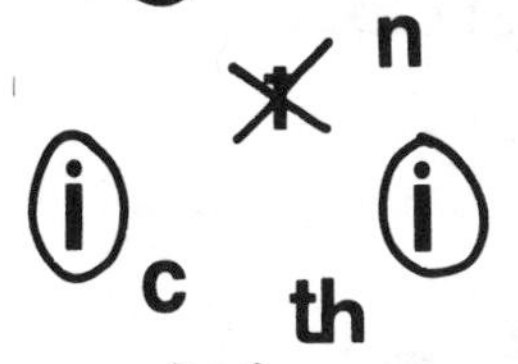

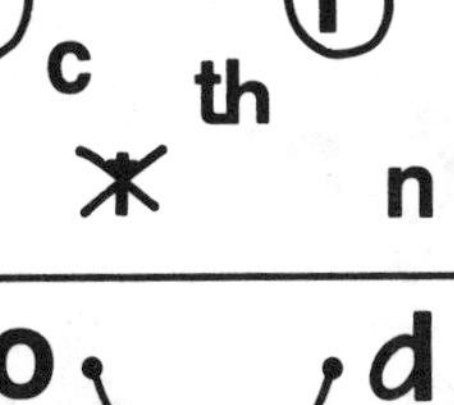

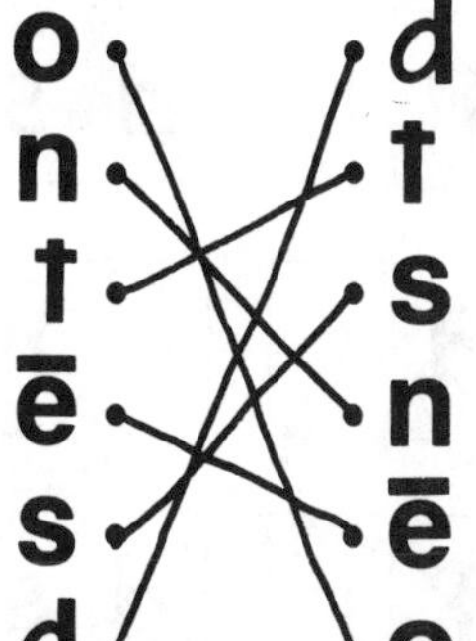

o	d
n	t
t	s
ē	n
s	ē
d	o

c c c c c c

o o o o o o

n n n n n n

t t t t t t

s s s s s s

a a a a a a

Name ____________________ Worksheet **55** Side **1**

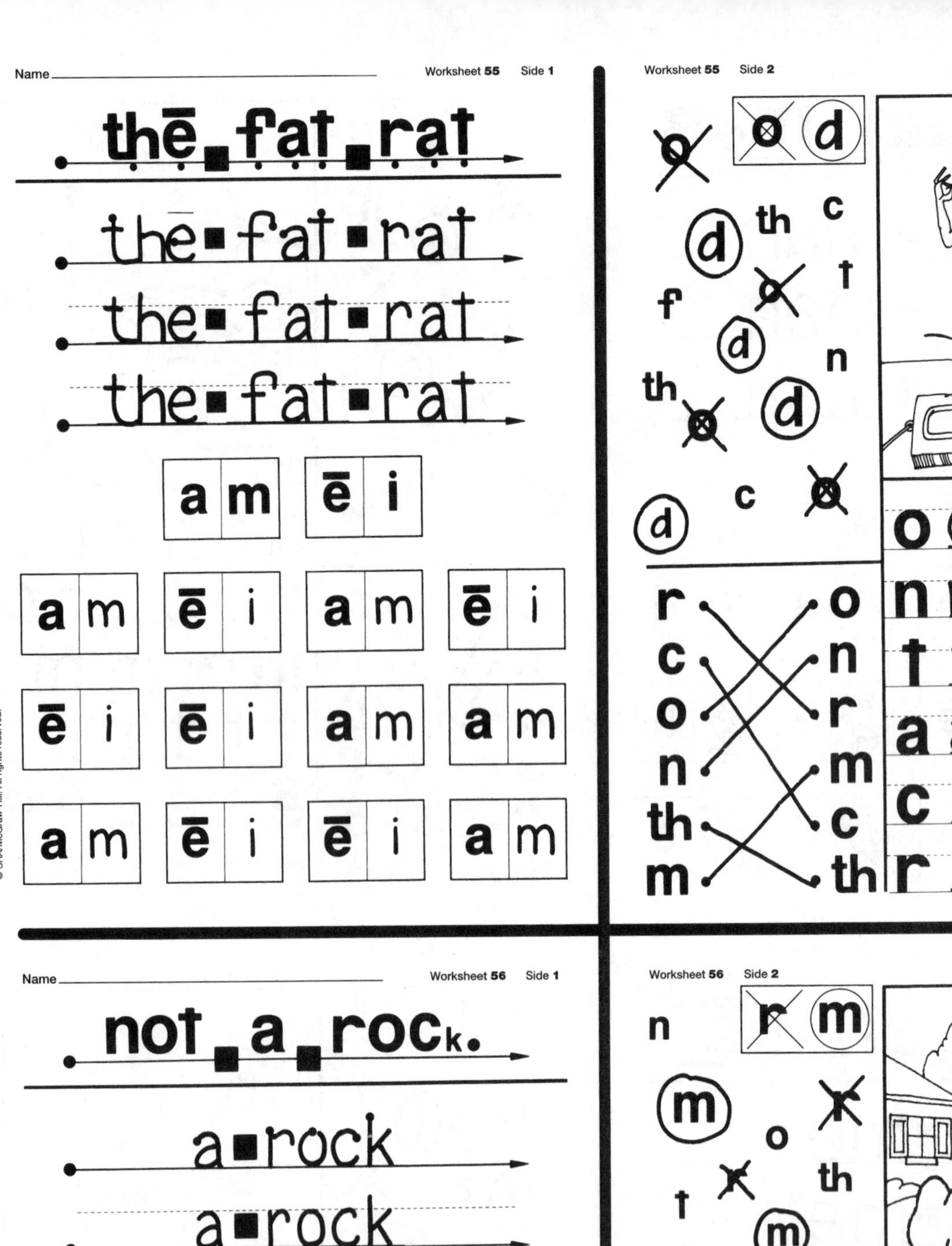

thē fat rat

the fat rat

the fat rat

the fat rat

a	m

ē	i

am	ēi	am	ēi
ēi	ēi	am	am
am	ēi	ēi	am

Worksheet **55** Side **2**

o d

d th c f t d n th d c d

r	o
c	n
o	r
n	m
th	c
m	th

o o o o o o

n n n n n n

t t t t t t

a a a a a a

c c c c c c

r r r r r r

Name ____________________ Worksheet **56** Side **1**

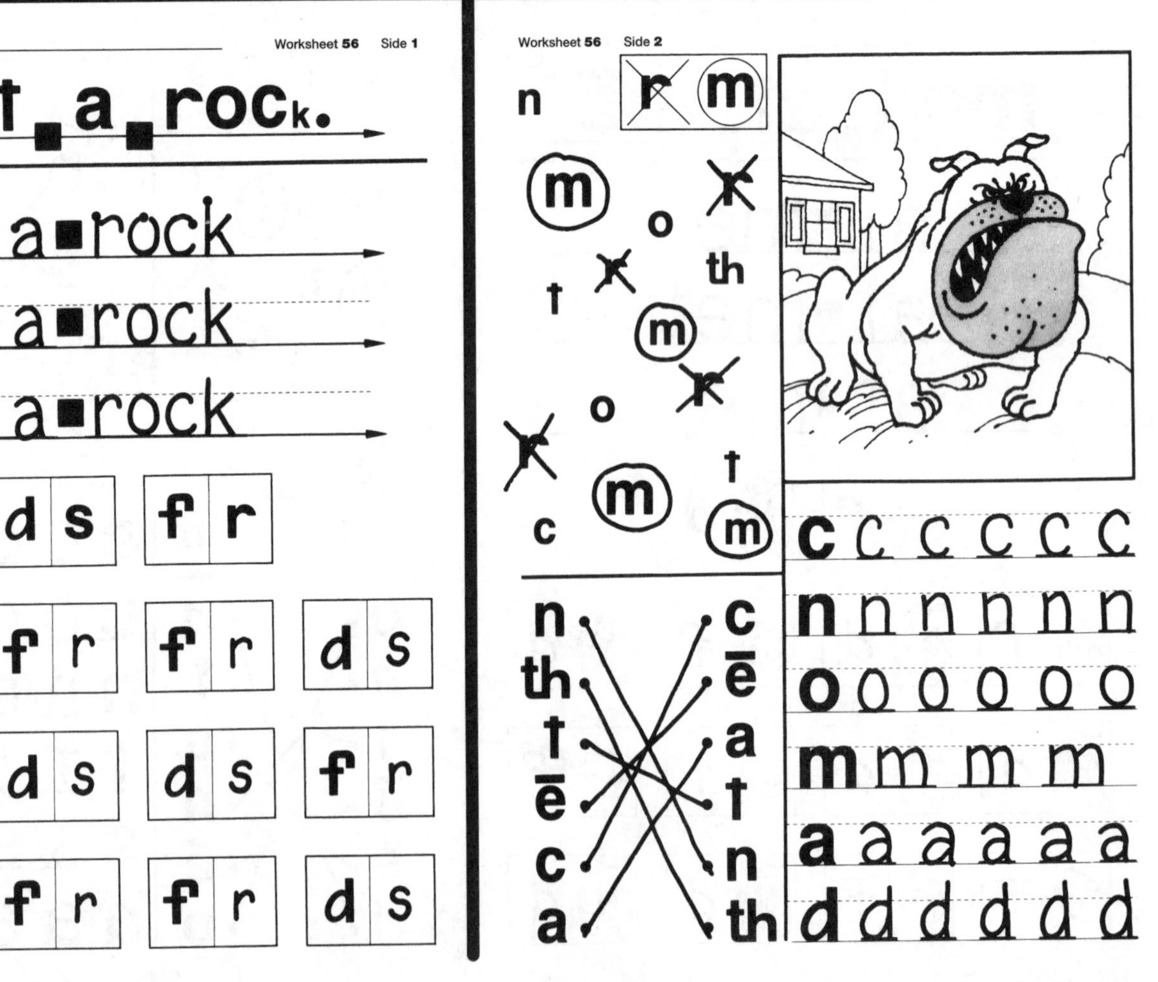

not a rock.

a rock

a rock

a rock

d	s

f	r

ds	fr	fr	ds
fr	ds	ds	fr
ds	fr	fr	ds

Worksheet **56** Side **2**

r m

n m o r t th m r o r t c m m

n	c
th	ē
t	a
ē	t
c	n
a	th

c c c c c c

n n n n n n

o o o o o o

m m m m

a a a a a a

d d d d d d

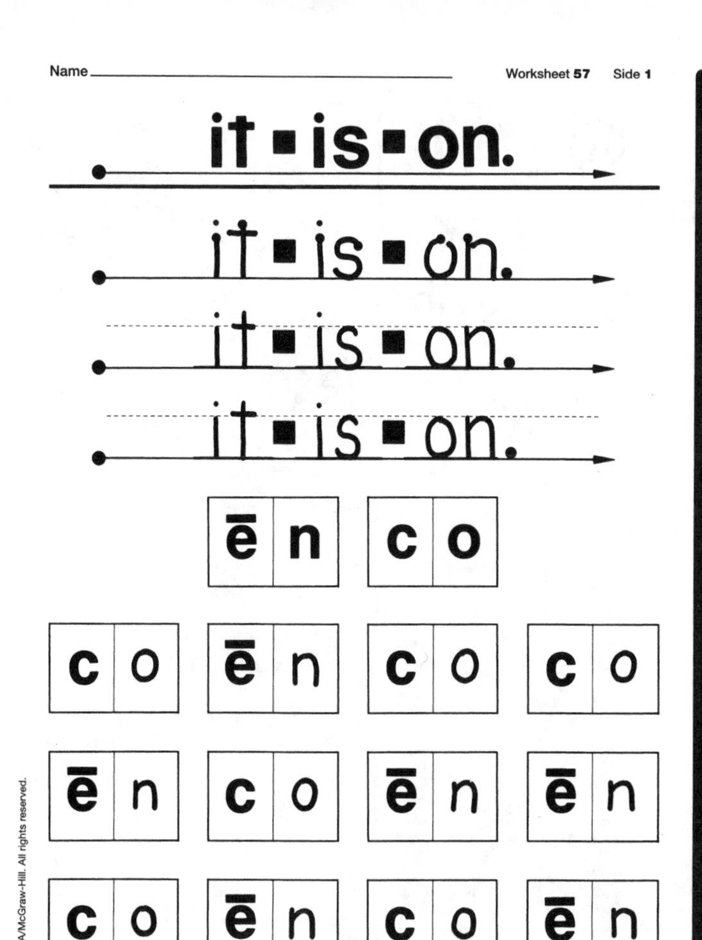
Name

Worksheet **57** Side **1**

it is on.

it is on.

it is on.

it is on.

ē	n		c	o

c o	ē n	c o	c o
ē n	c o	ē n	ē n
c o	ē n	c o	ē n

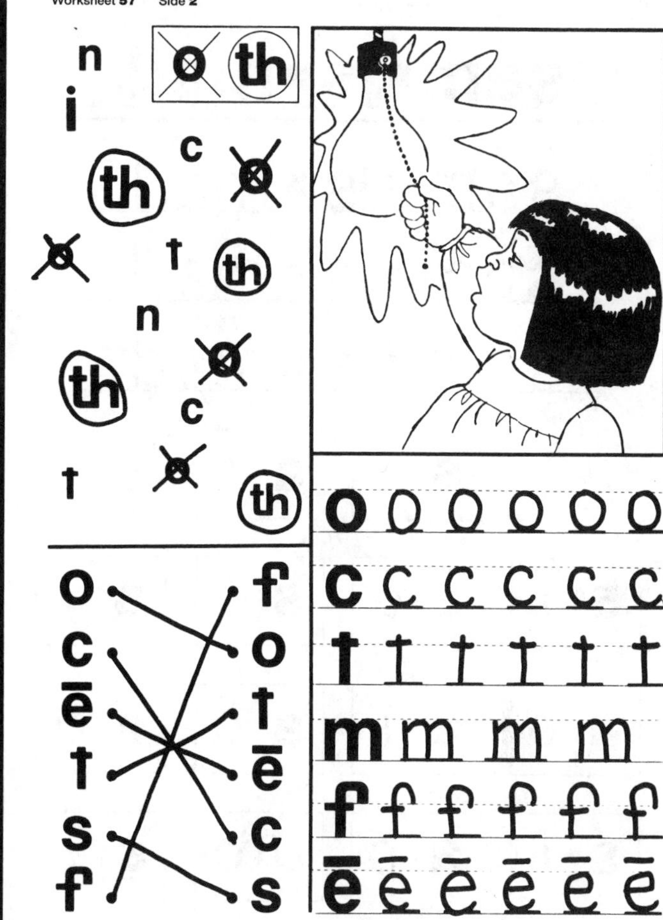
Worksheet **57** Side **2**

o th

n i c th o o t th n th o c o t th

o	f
c	o
ē	t
t	ē
s	c
f	s

o o o o o o
c c c c c c
t t t t t t
m m m m
f f f f f f
ē ē ē ē ē ē

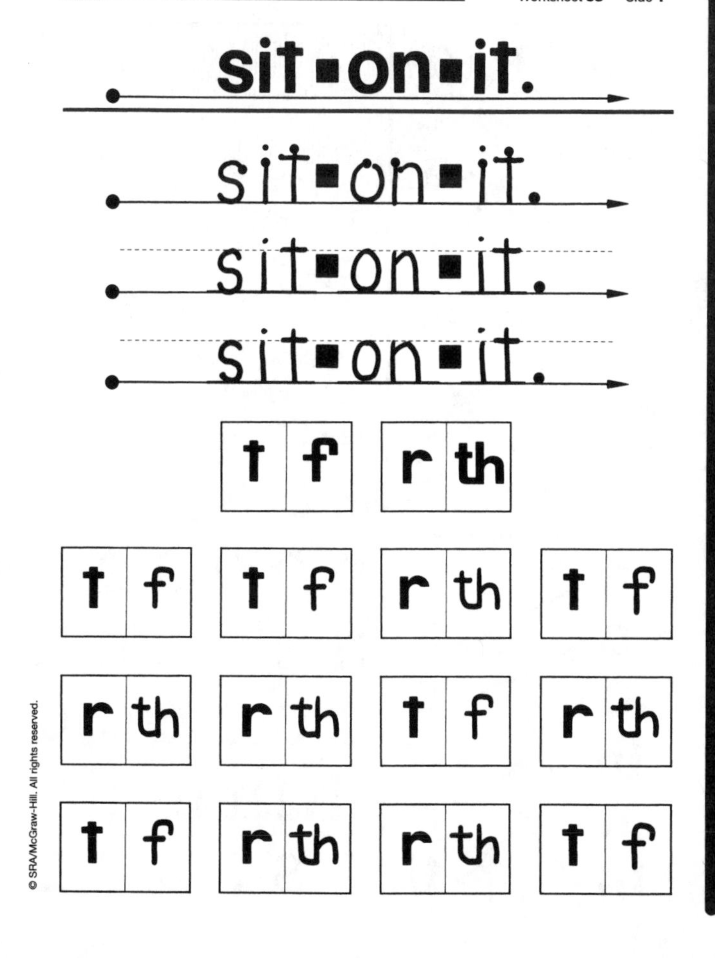
Name

Worksheet **58** Side **1**

sit on it.

sit on it.

sit on it.

sit on it.

t	f		r	th

t f	t f	r th	t f
r th	r th	t f	r th
t f	r th	r th	t f

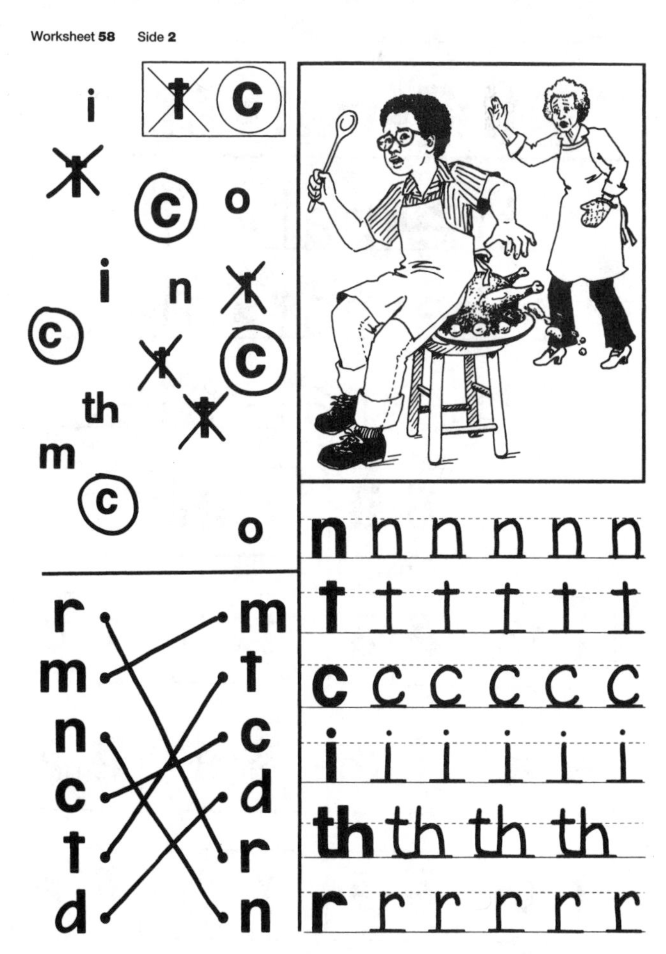
Worksheet **58** Side **2**

t c

i t c o i n t c c t th t m c o

r	m
m	t
n	c
c	d
t	r
d	n

n n n n n n
t t t t t t
c c c c c c
i i i i i i
th th th th
r r r r r r

Name

Worksheet 59 Side 1

sam is mad.

sam is mad.

sam is mad.

sam is mad.

s	i

a	o

s i	a o	s i	s i
a o	s i	a o	a o
s i	a o	a o	s i

Worksheet 59 Side 2

n ā r th n t n r th c r t n i

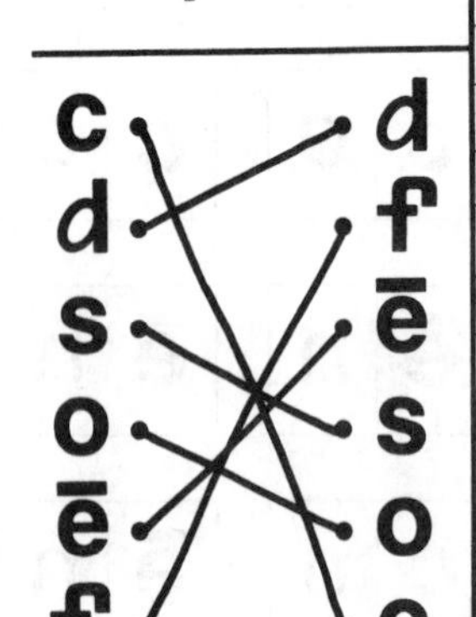

c	d
d	f
s	ē
o	s
ē	o
f	c

a a a a a a

m m m m

o o o o o o

t t t t t t

s s s s s s

ē ē ē ē ē ē

Name

Worksheet 60 Side 1

thē rat āte.

thē rat āte.

the rat ate.

the rat ate.

ē	ā

t	th

t th	ē ā	t th	t th
ē ā	t th	ē ā	ē ā
t th	ē ā	t th	ē ā

Worksheet 60 Side 2

c n a

a o n ā a c a n t a ā n a n o

ā	n
c	ā
o	c
th	m
n	o
m	th

a a a a a a

o o o o o o

n n n n n n

c c c c c c

th th th th

s s s s s s

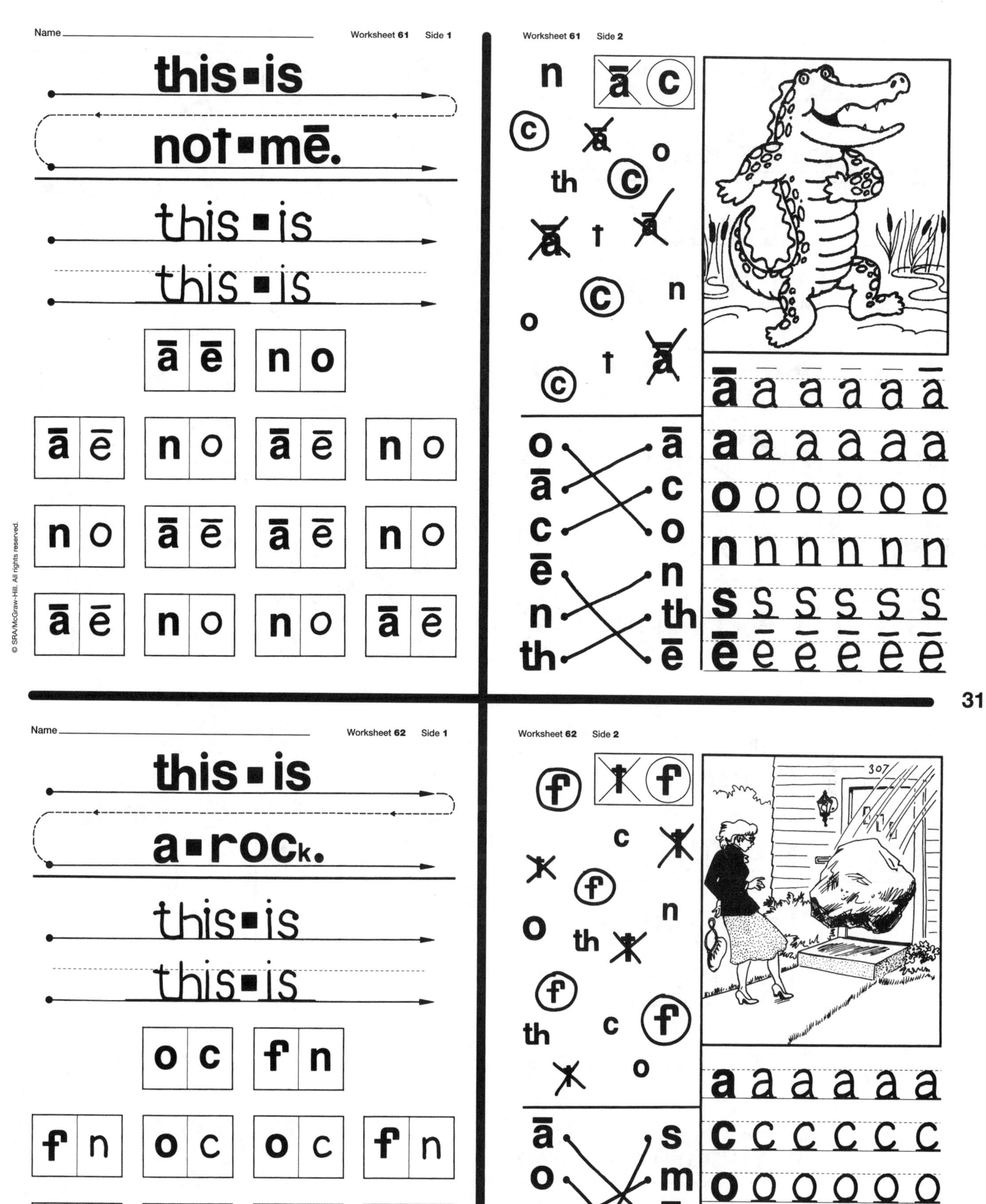

Name
Worksheet 61 Side 1
this is
not mē.
this is
this is
ā ē no
Worksheet 61 Side 2
Name
Worksheet 62 Side 1
this is
a roc k.
this is
this is
oc fn
Worksheet 62 Side 2

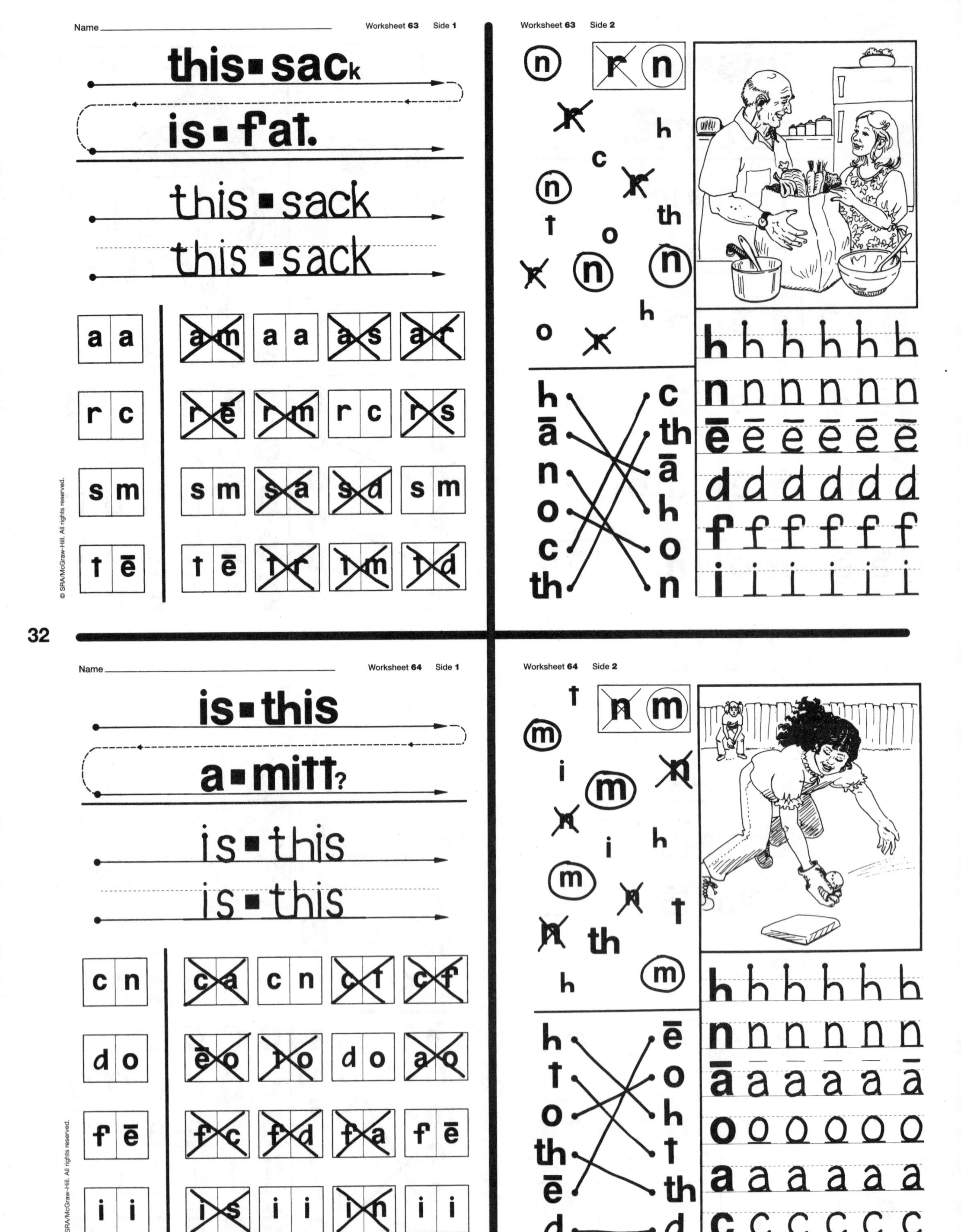

Name
Worksheet 63 Side 1
this sack
is fat.
this sack
this sack
a a
r c
s m
t ē
Worksheet 63 Side 2
h
ā
n
o
c
th
c
th
ā
h
o
n
32
Name
Worksheet 64 Side 1
is this
a mitt?
is this
is this
c n
d o
f ē
i i
Worksheet 64 Side 2
h
t
o
th
ē
d
ē
o
h
t
th
d

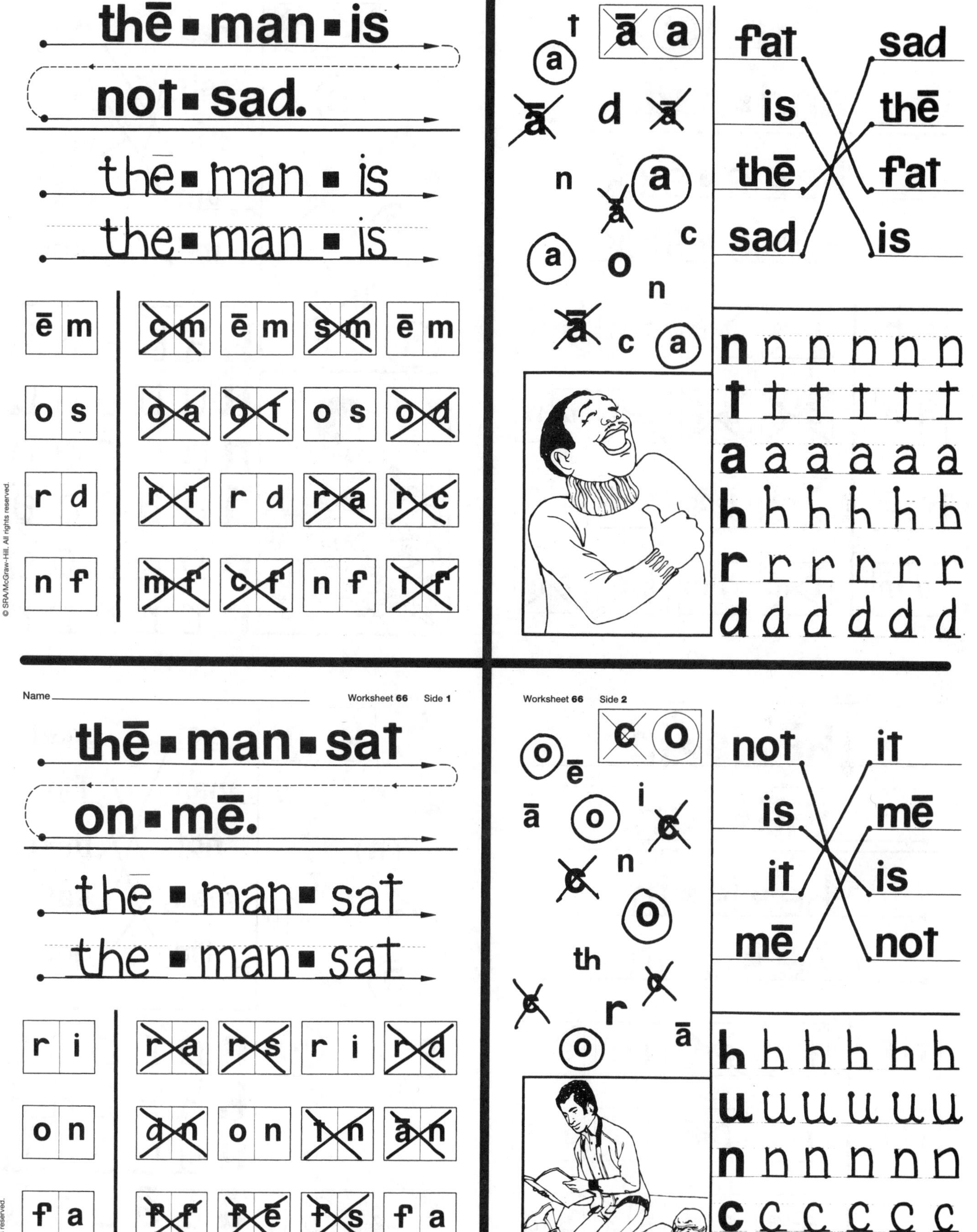

Name
Worksheet 65 Side 1
thē man is not sad.
the man is
the man is
ēm
os
rd
nf
Worksheet 65 Side 2
fat
is
thē
sad
sad
thē
fat
is
n t a h r d
Name
Worksheet 66 Side 1
thē man sat on mē.
the man sat
the man sat
ri
on
fa
ēē
Worksheet 66 Side 2
not
is
it
mē
it
mē
is
not
h u n c s i

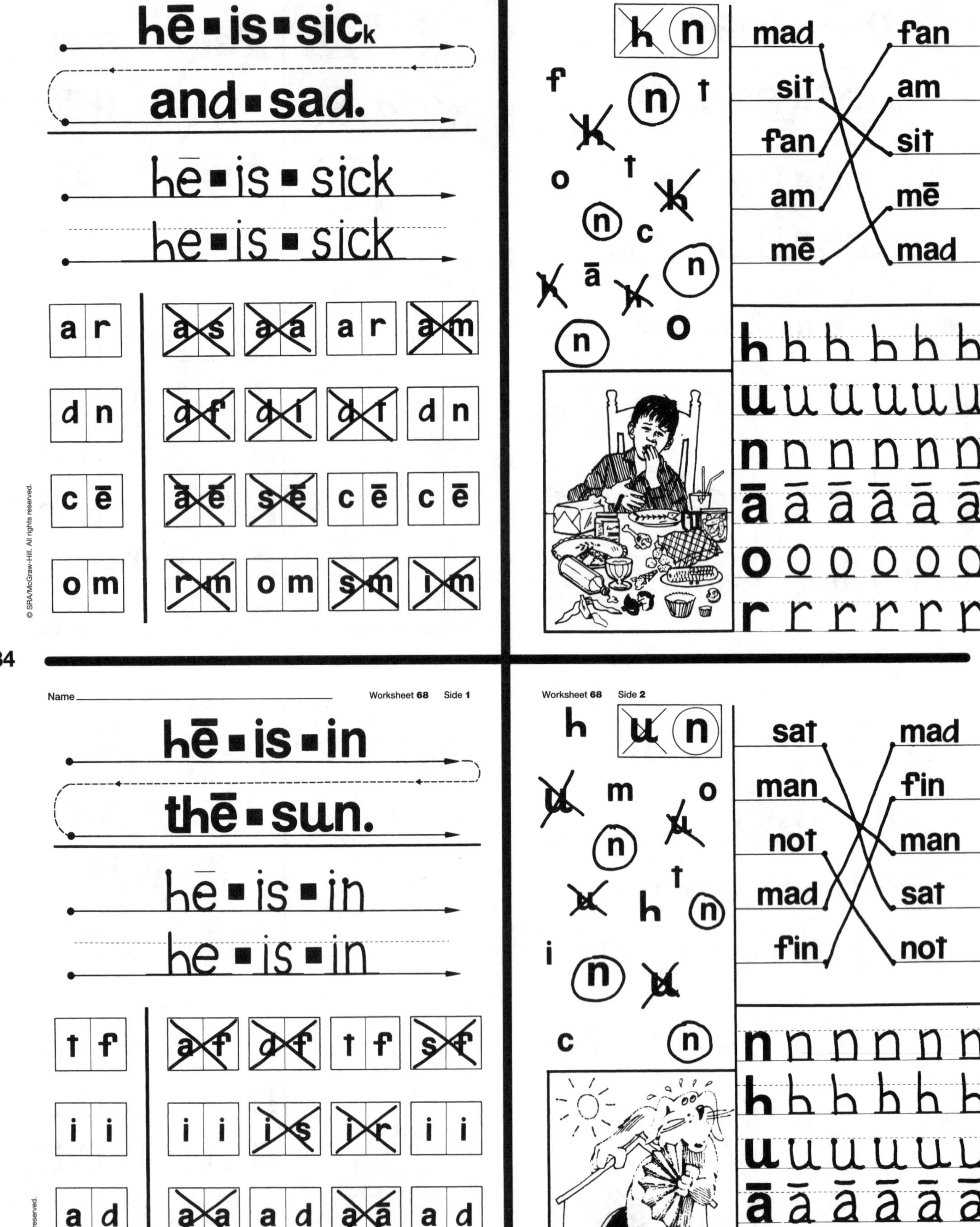

Name ______ Worksheet 67 Side 1

hē is sick and sad.

hē is sick

he is sick

a r	a s	a a	a r	a m
d n	d f	d i	d f	d n
c ē	ā ē	s ē	c ē	c ē
o m	r m	o m	s m	i m

Worksheet 67 Side 2

h n

f n t h o t h n c n ā h h o n

mad	fan
sit	am
fan	sit
am	mē
mē	mad

h h h h h h

u u u u u u

n n n n n n

ā ā ā ā ā ā

o o o o o o

r r r r r r

Name ______ Worksheet 68 Side 1

hē is in thē sun.

hē is in

he is in

t f	a f	d f	t f	s f
i i	i i	i s	i r	i i
a d	a a	a d	a ā	a d
h n	ē n	s n	f n	h n

Worksheet 68 Side 2

h u n

u m o n u t u h n i n u c n

sat	mad
man	fin
not	man
mad	sat
fin	not

n n n n n n

h h h h h h

u u u u u u

ā ā ā ā ā ā

m m m m

s s s s s s

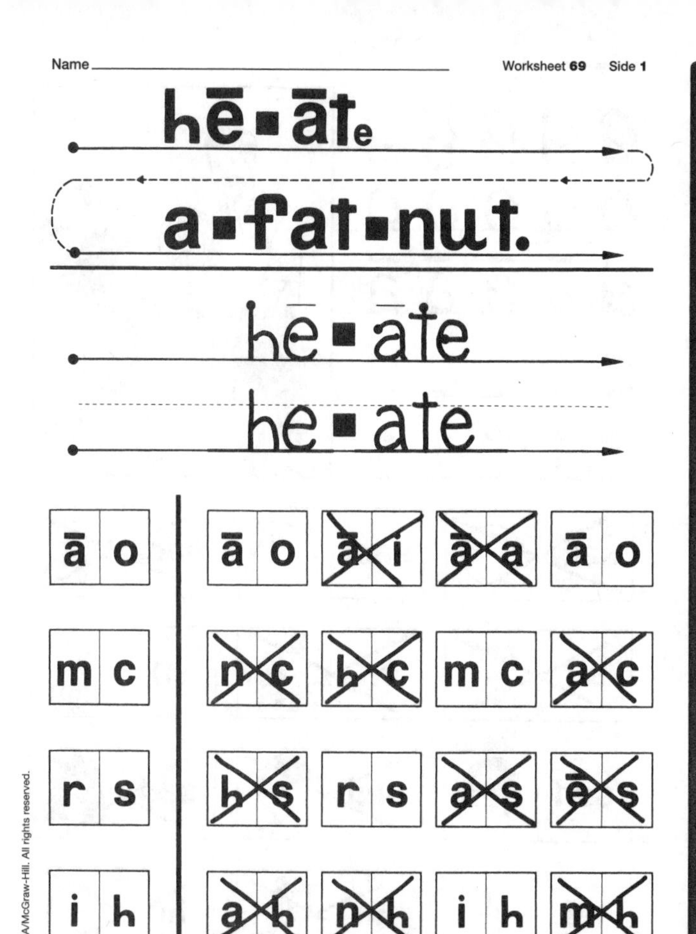
Name
Worksheet 69 Side 1
hē ■ āte
a ■ fat ■ nut.
ā o
m c
r s
i h
© SRA/McGraw-Hill. All rights reserved.

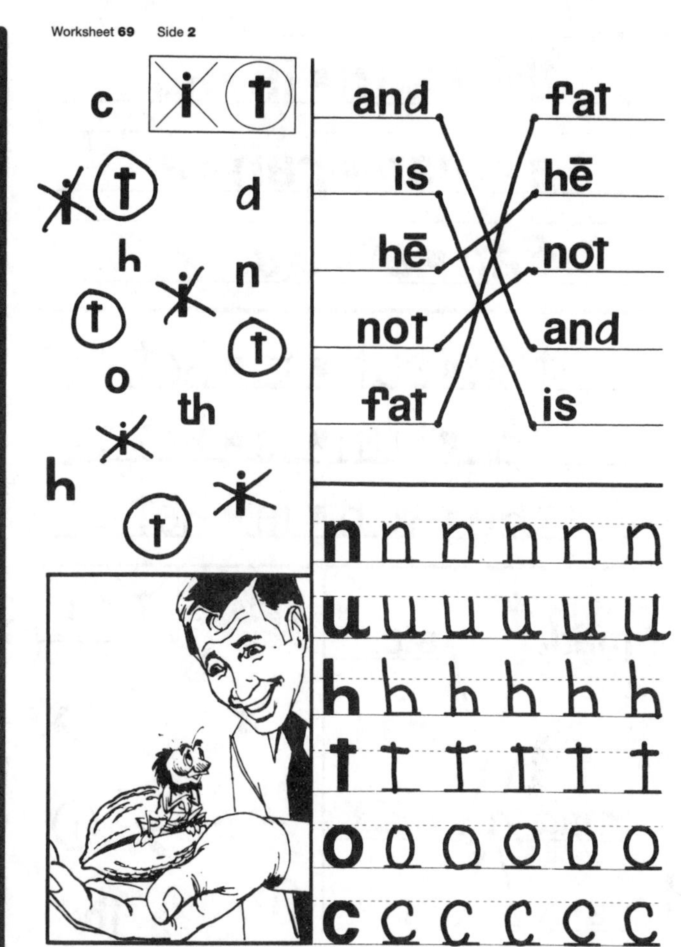
Worksheet 69 Side 2
and
is
hē
not
fat
fat
hē
not
and
is

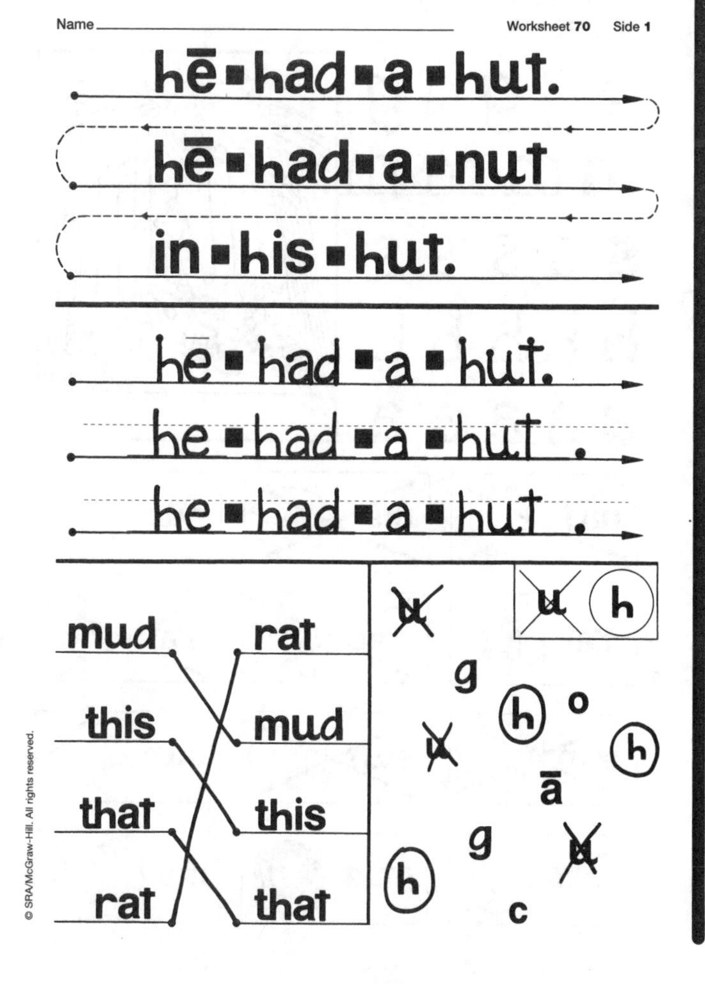
Name
Worksheet 70 Side 1
hē ■ had ■ a ■ hut.
hē ■ had ■ a ■ nut
in ■ his ■ hut.
mud
this
that
rat
rat
mud
this
that
© SRA/McGraw-Hill. All rights reserved.

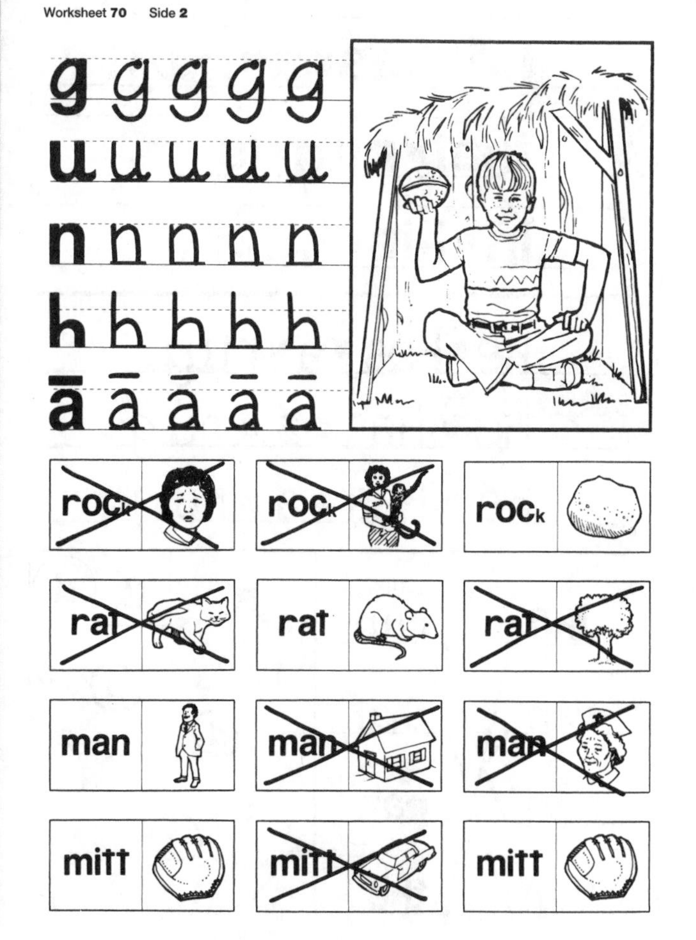
Worksheet 70 Side 2
rock
rock
rock
rat
rat
rat
man
man
man
mitt
mitt
mitt

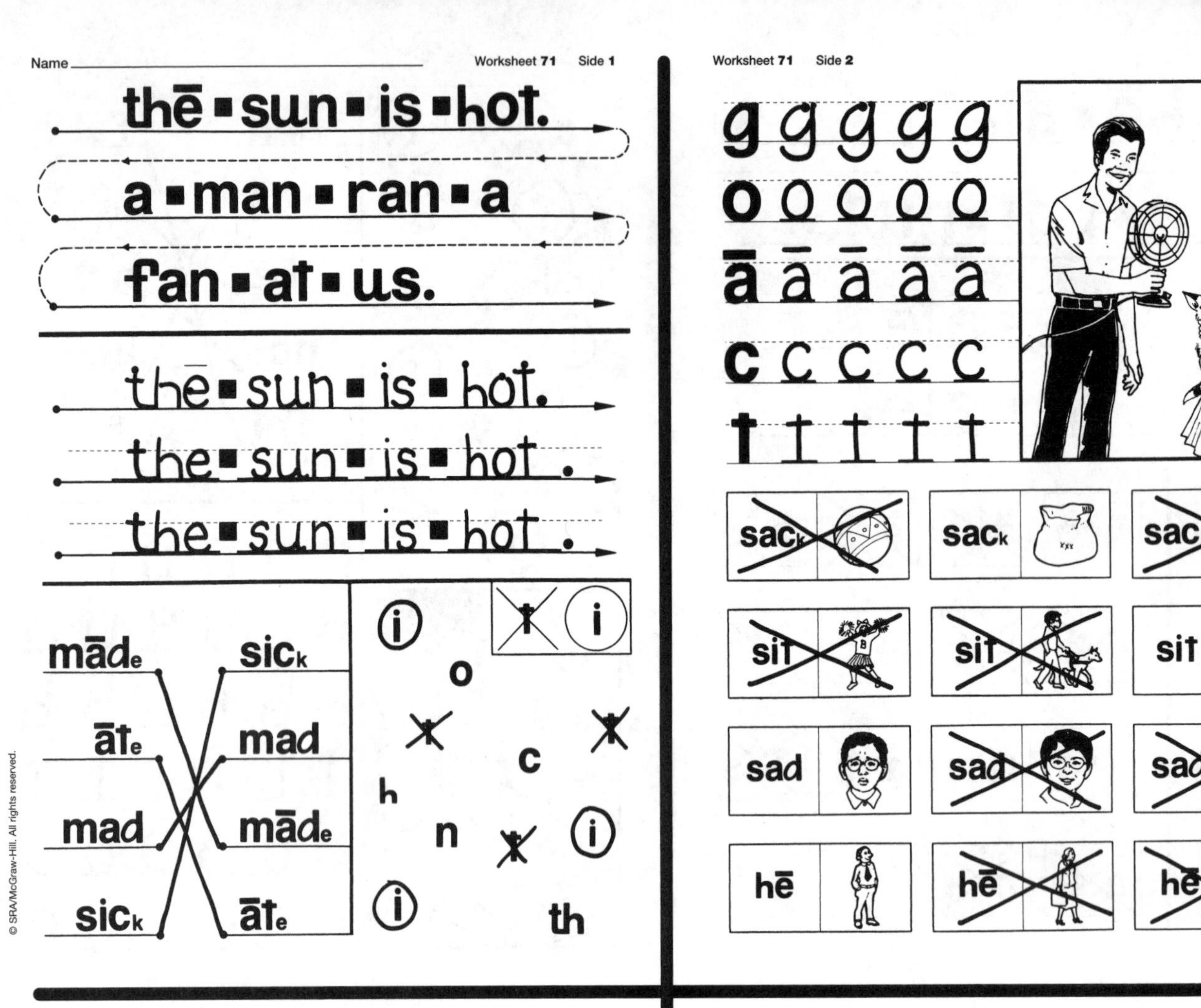

Name ____________________ Worksheet 71 Side 1

thē ■ sun ■ is ■ hot.
a ■ man ■ ran ■ a
fan ■ at ■ us.

thē ■ sun ■ is ■ hot.
the ■ sun ■ is ■ hot.
the ■ sun ■ is ■ hot.

mādₑ — sicₖ
ātₑ — mad
mad — mādₑ
sicₖ — ātₑ

i o c h n th

Worksheet 71 Side 2

g g g g g
o o o o o
ā ā ā ā ā
c c c c c
t t t t t

sacₖ sacₖ sacₖ
sit sit sit
sad sad sad
hē hē hē

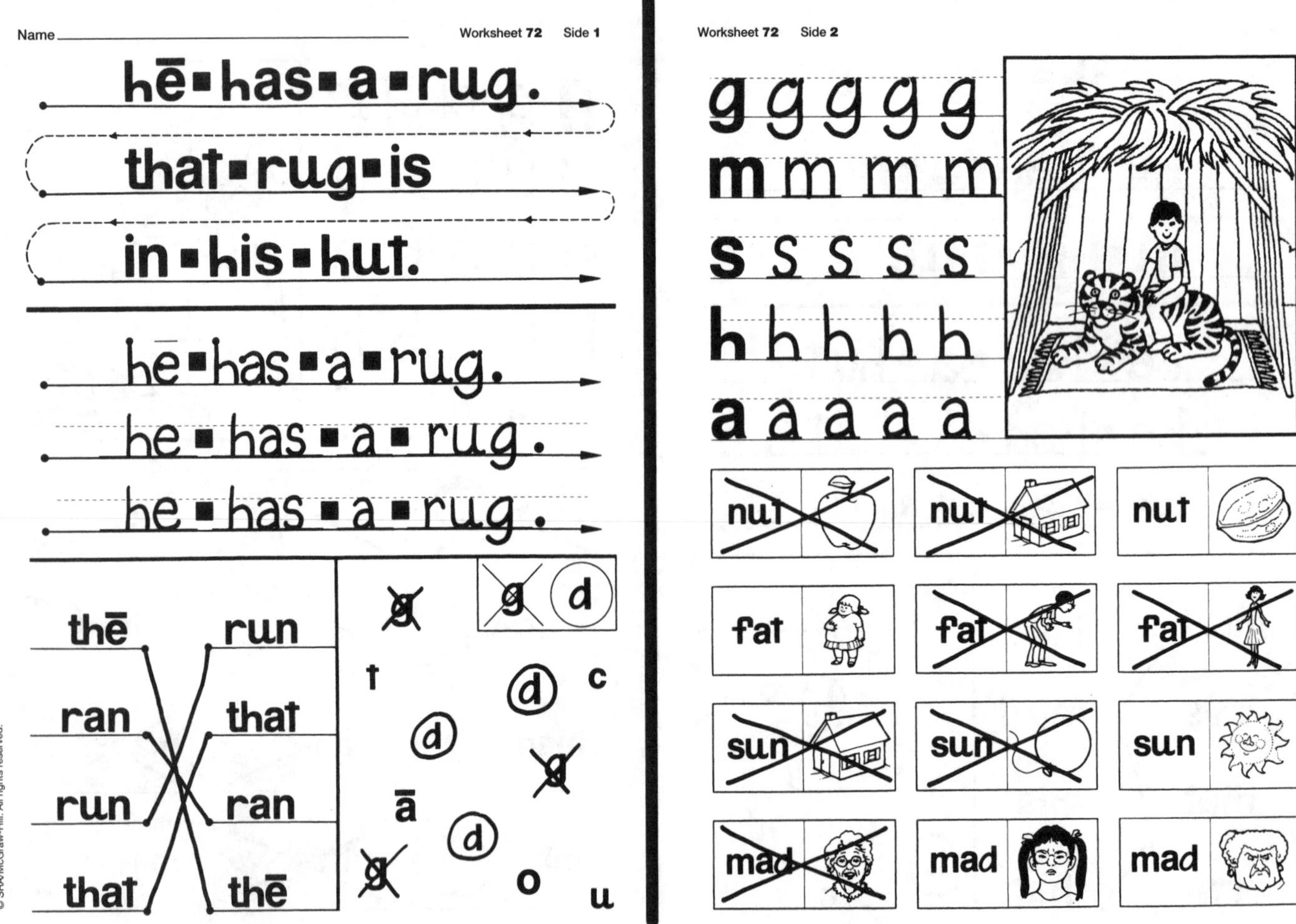

Name ____________________ Worksheet 72 Side 1

hē ■ has ■ a ■ rug.
that ■ rug ■ is
in ■ his ■ hut.

hē ■ has ■ a ■ rug.
he ■ has ■ a ■ rug.
he ■ has ■ a ■ rug.

thē — run
ran — that
run — ran
that — thē

g d t c d d ā o u

Worksheet 72 Side 2

g g g g g
m m m m
s s s s s
h h h h h
a a a a a

nut nut nut
fat fat fat
sun sun sun
mad mad mad

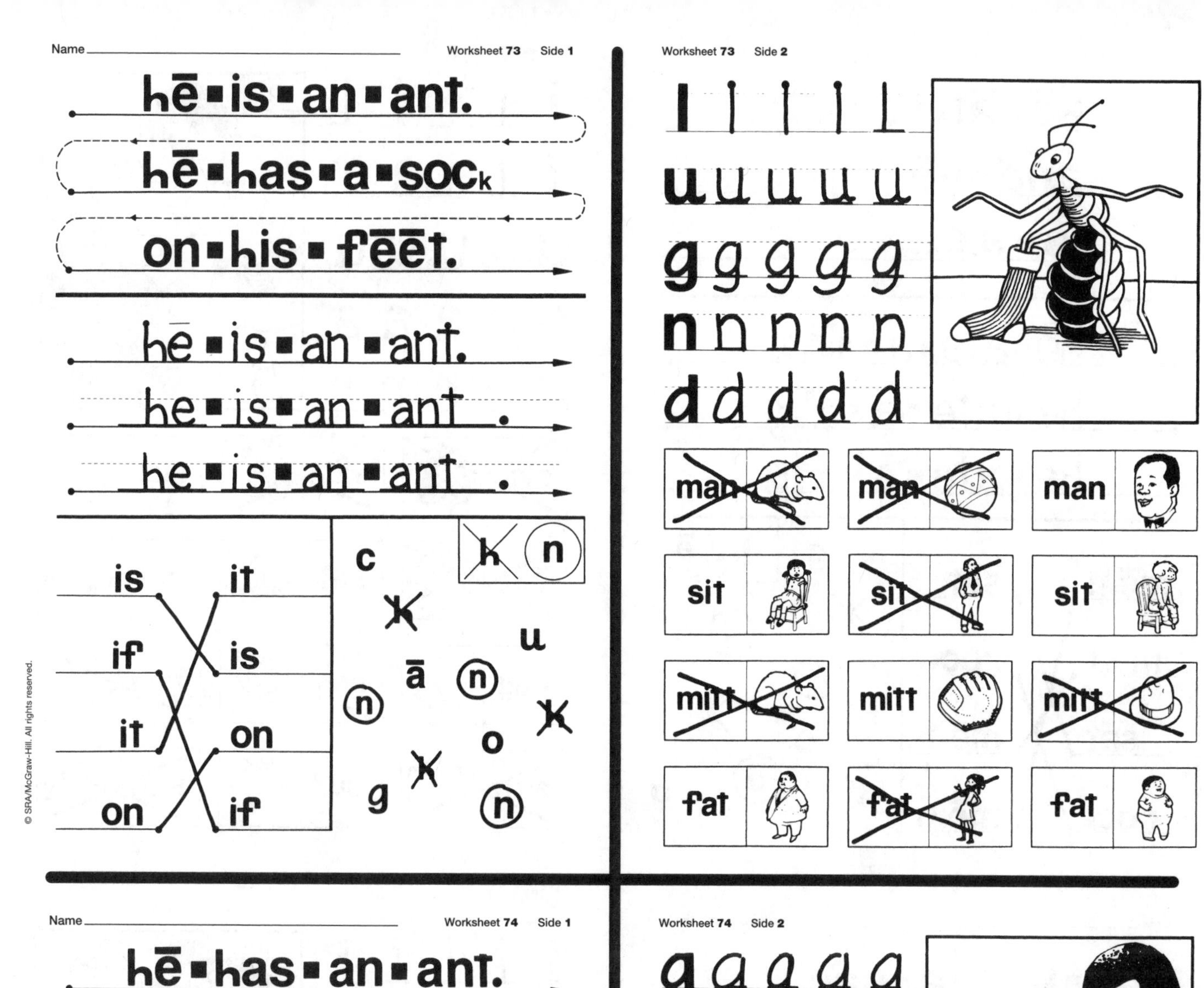

Name ________________

Worksheet 73 Side 1

hē is an ant.
hē has a sock
on his fēēt.

hē is an ant.
he is an ant.
he is an ant.

is — it
if — is
it — on
on — if

h n

c k u ā n n k o k g n

Worksheet 73 Side 2

l l l l l
u u u u u
g g g g g
n n n n n
d d d d d

man man man
sit sit sit
mitt mitt mitt
fat fat fat

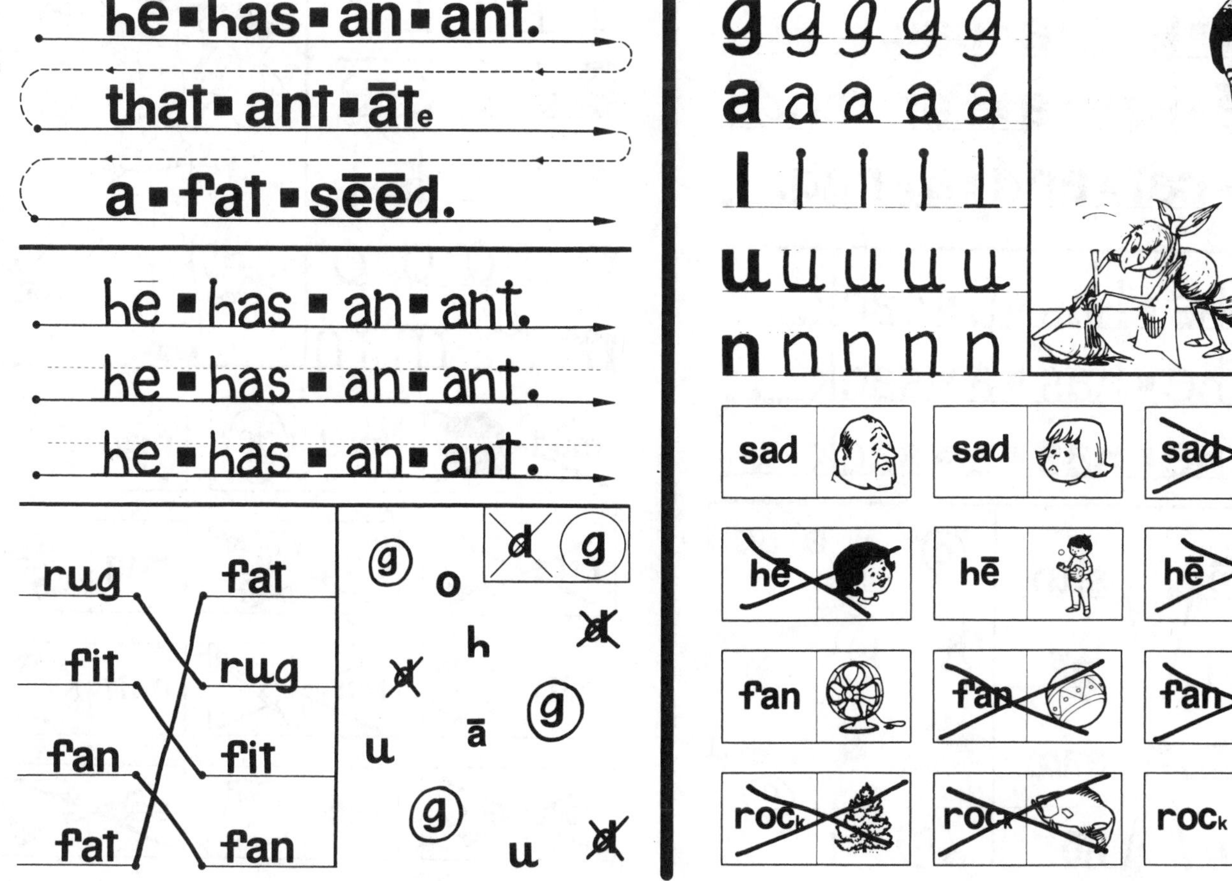

Name ________________

Worksheet 74 Side 1

hē has an ant.
that ant āte
a fat sēēd.

hē has an ant.
he has an ant.
he has an ant.

rug — fat
fit — rug
fan — fit
fat — fan

d g

g o d h d g ā u g u d

Worksheet 74 Side 2

g g g g g
a a a a a
l l l l l
u u u u u
n n n n n

sad sad sad
hē hē hē
fan fan fan
rock rock rock

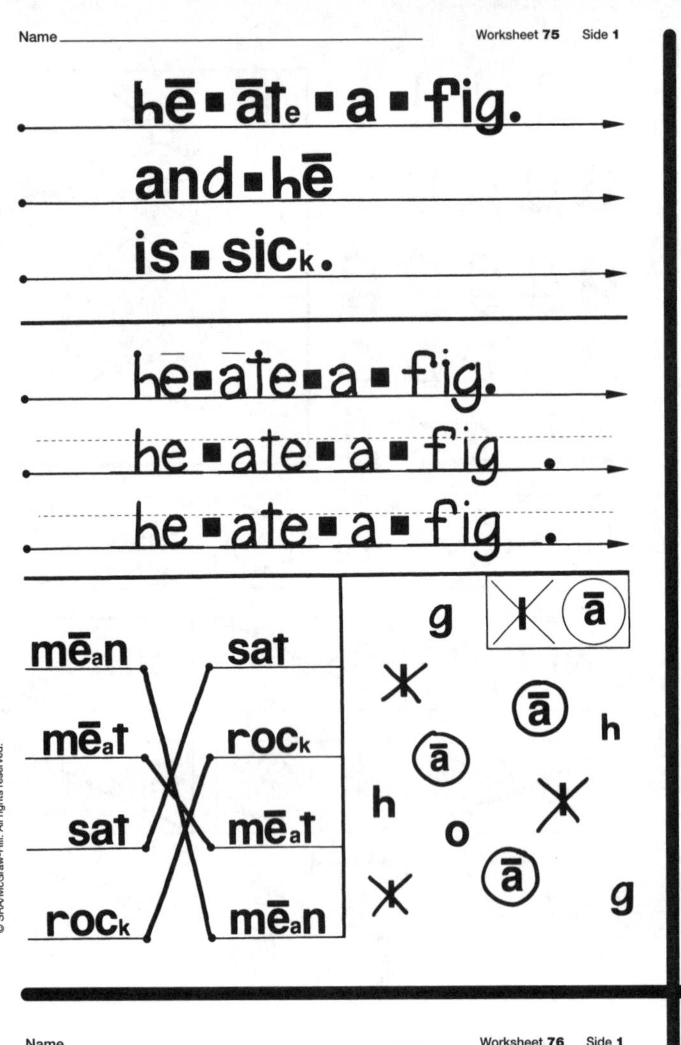
Name
Worksheet 75 Side 1
hē ▪ āte ▪ a ▪ fig.
and ▪ hē
is ▪ sick.
hē ▪ āte ▪ a ▪ fig.
he ▪ ate ▪ a ▪ fig .
he ▪ ate ▪ a ▪ fig .
mēan
sat
mēat
rock
sat
mēat
rock
mēan
g
ā
h
ā
ā
h
o
ā
g
© SRA/McGraw-Hill. All rights reserved.

Worksheet 75 Side 2
I I I I I
i i i i i
u u u u u
a a a a a
r r r r r
sick
sick
sick
rat
rat
rat
rag
rag
rag
sun
sun
sun

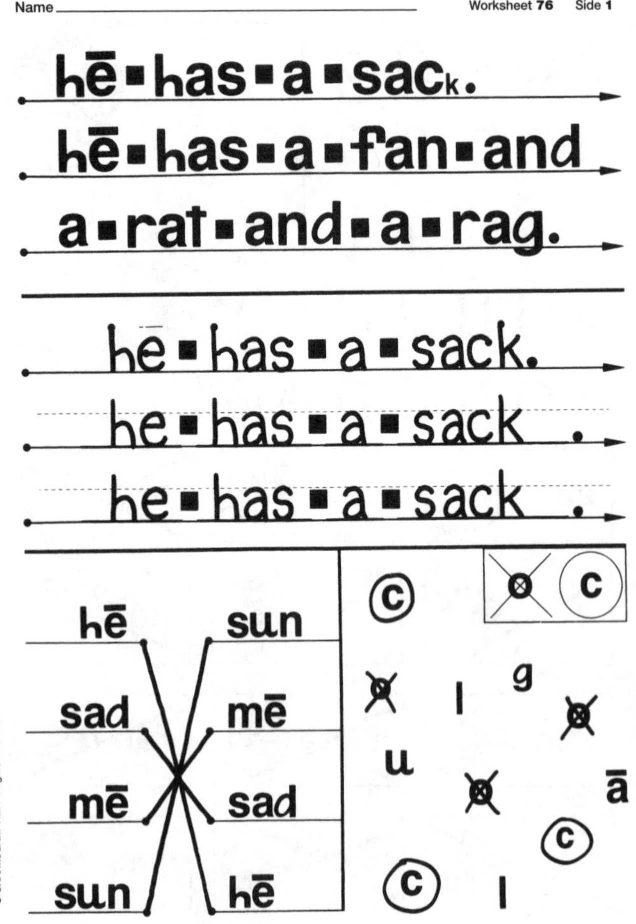
Name
Worksheet 76 Side 1
hē ▪ has ▪ a ▪ sack.
hē ▪ has ▪ a ▪ fan ▪ and
a ▪ rat ▪ and ▪ a ▪ rag.
hē ▪ has ▪ a ▪ sack.
he ▪ has ▪ a ▪ sack .
he ▪ has ▪ a ▪ sack .
hē
sun
sad
mē
mē
sad
sun
hē
c
c
g
I
u
ā
c
c
I
© SRA/McGraw-Hill. All rights reserved.

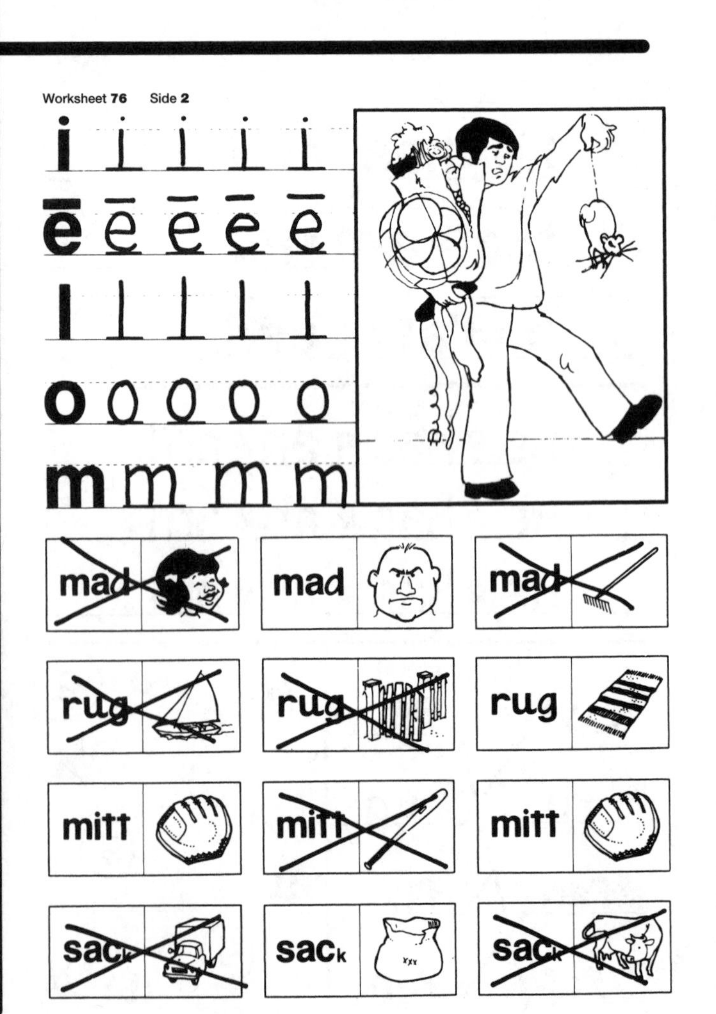
Worksheet 76 Side 2
i i i i i
ē ē ē ē ē
I I I I I
o o o o o
m m m m
mad
mad
mad
rug
rug
rug
mitt
mitt
mitt
sack
sack
sack

Name ______________________ Worksheet 77 Side 1

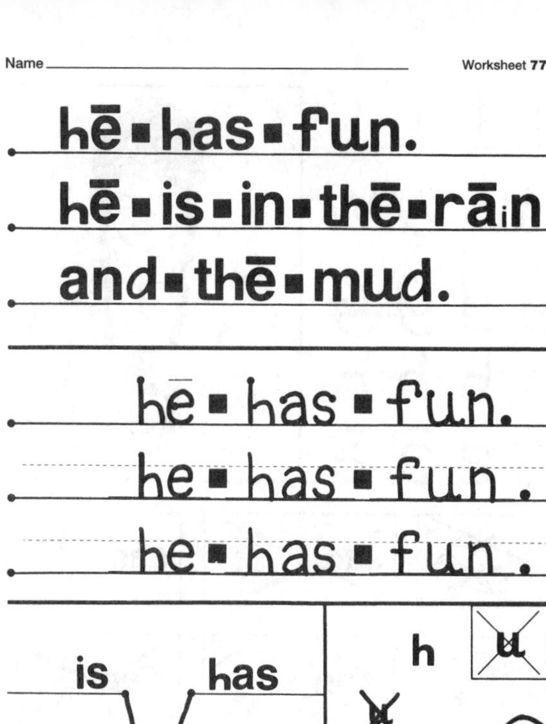

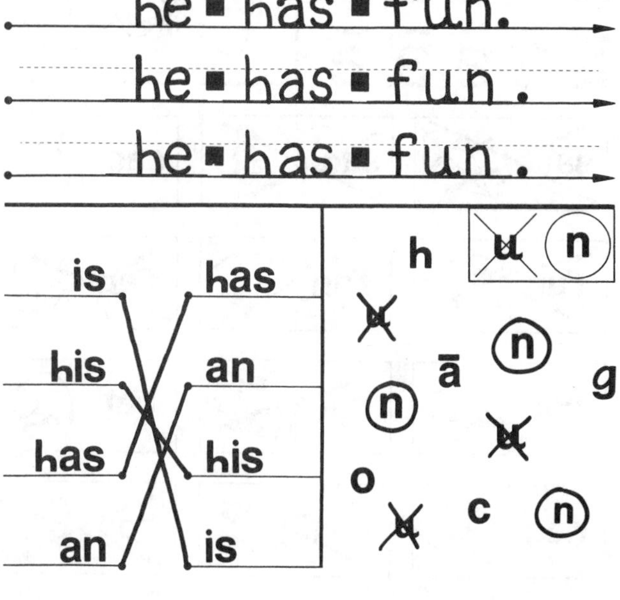

Worksheet 77 Side 2

Name ______________________ Worksheet 78 Side 1

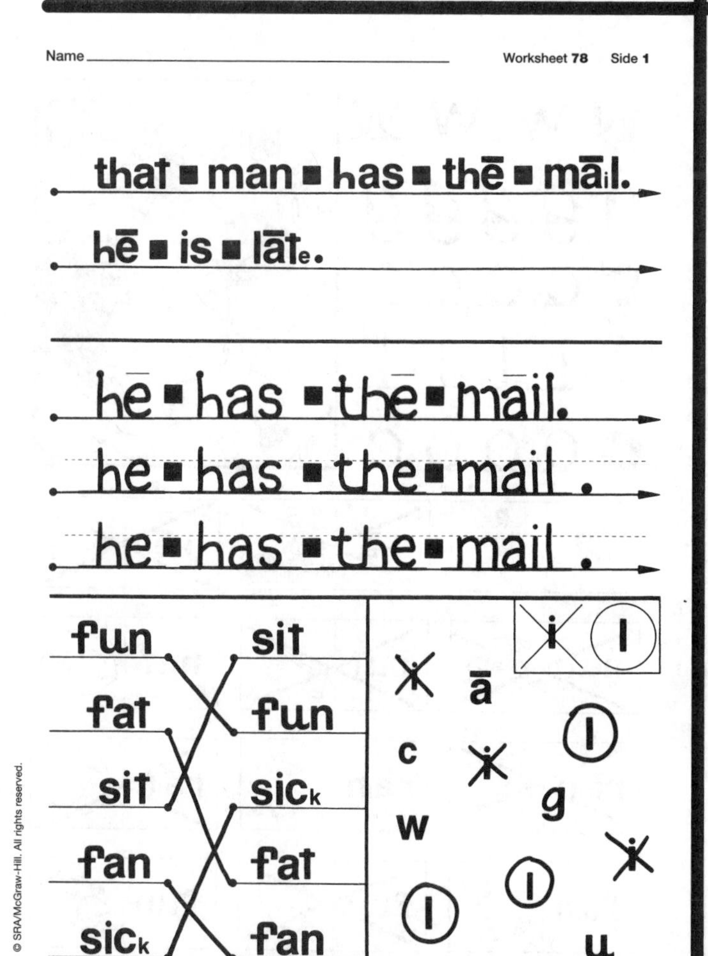

Worksheet 78 Side 2

Name ______________________ Worksheet 79 Side 1

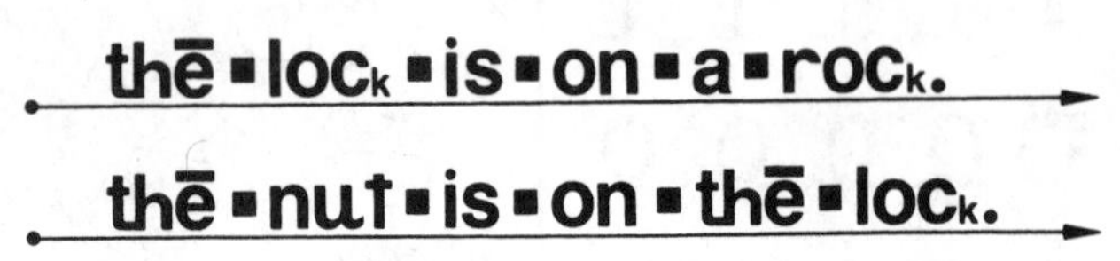

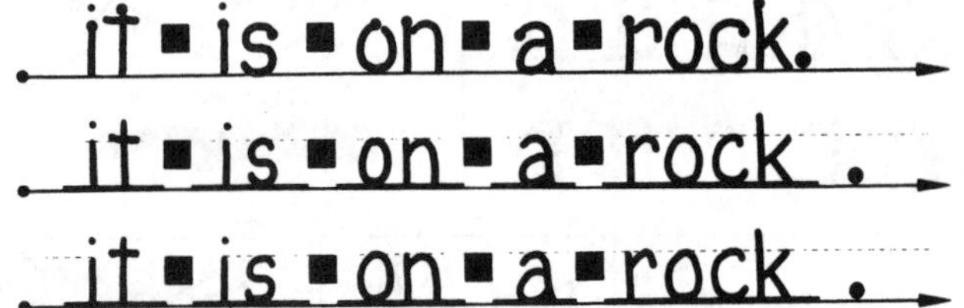

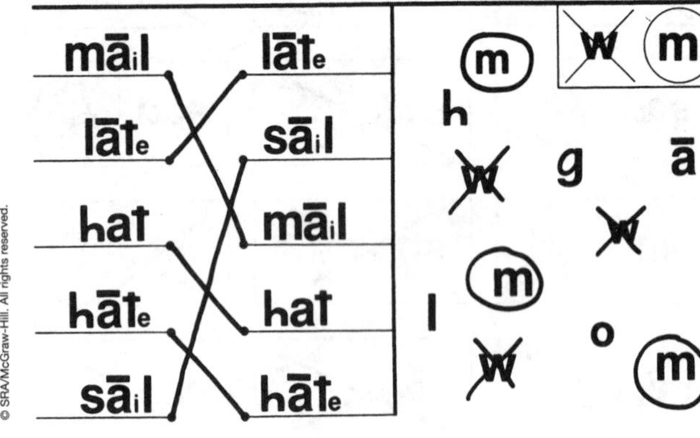

Worksheet 79 Side 2

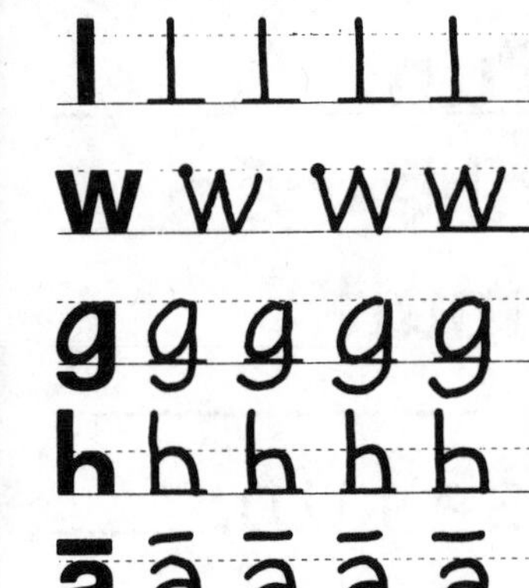

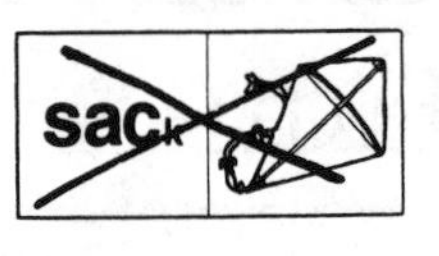

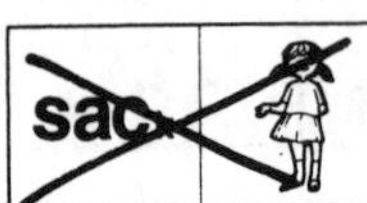

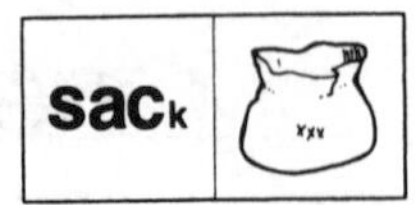

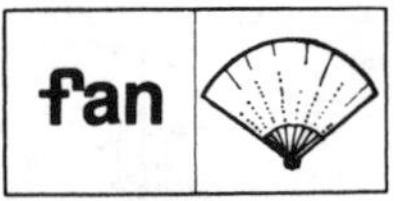

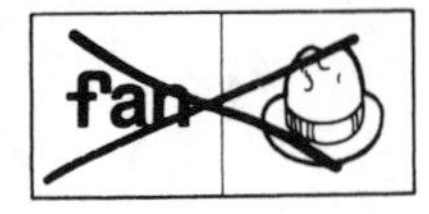

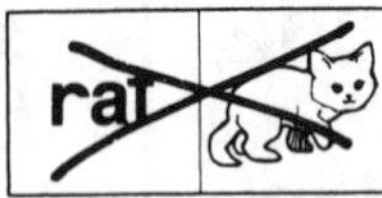

Name ______________________ Worksheet 80 Side 1

wē▪sēē▪a▪hut.▪wē▪will
run▪in▪thē▪hut.
wē▪will▪locₖ▪thē▪hut.

we▪see▪a▪hut.
we▪see▪a▪hut.
we▪see▪a▪hut.

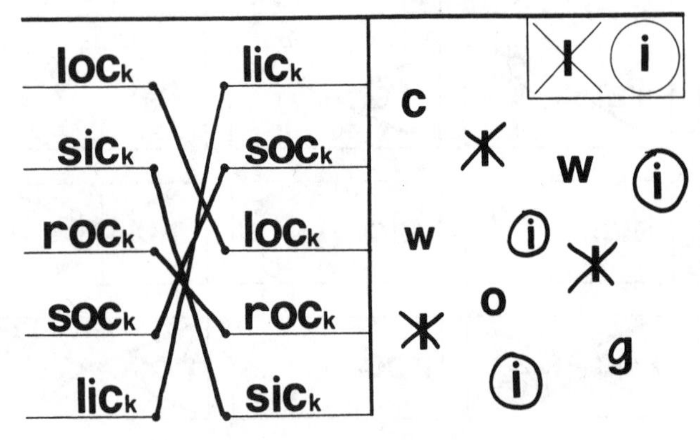

Worksheet 80 Side 2

w w w w
g g g g g
c c c c c
l l l l l
o o o o o

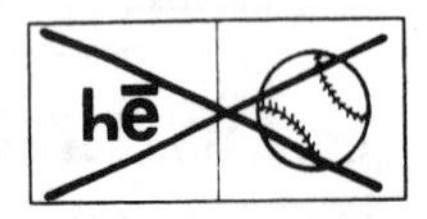

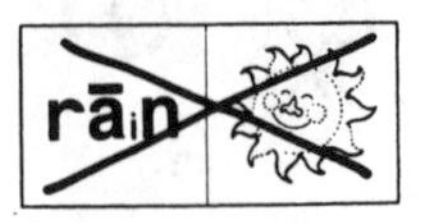

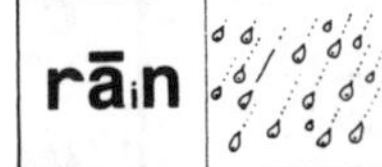

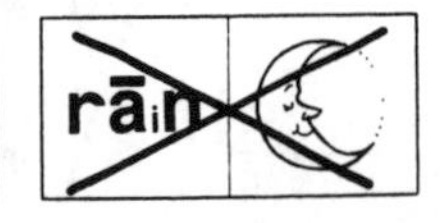

Name ____________________ Worksheet 81 Side 1

his ▪ nāmₑ ▪ is ▪ ron.

hē ▪ will ▪ run. ▪ and

hē ▪ will ▪ sēē ▪ mē.

his ▪ nāme ▪ is ▪ ron.

his ▪ name ▪ is ▪ ron.

his ▪ name ▪ is ▪ ron.

hut	hit
hat	hut
nut	not
hit	nut
not	hat

th sh

th h th sh ā w sh th l u sh

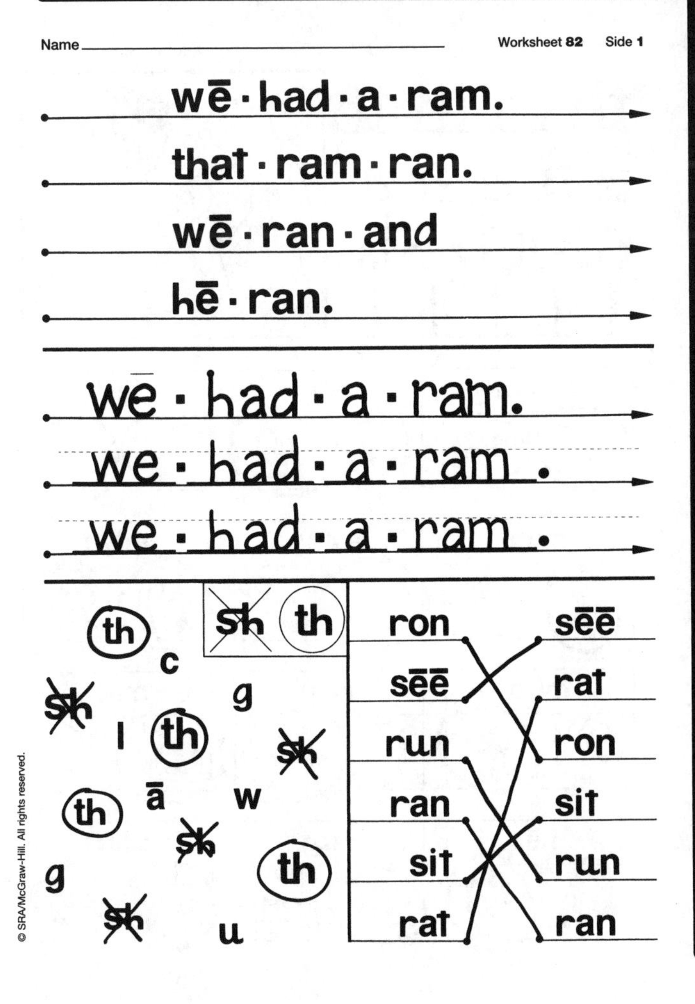

Worksheet 82 Side 2

sh sh sh

w w w w

g g g g g

u u u u u

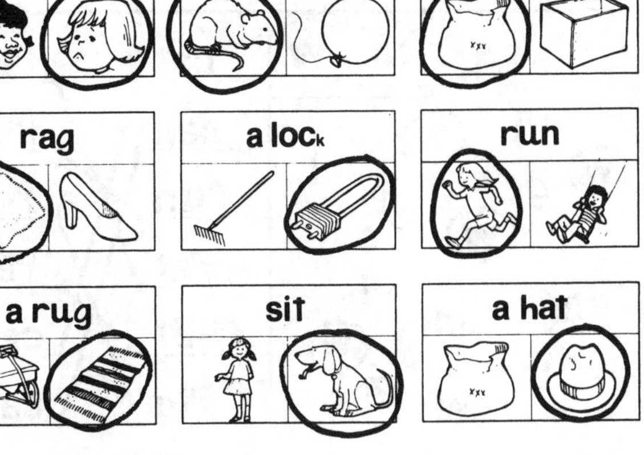

Name

Worksheet 83 Side 1

this·is·a·cat.
this·cat·has·fat
fēēt.·this·cat·can
run·in·thē·mud.

this·is·a·cat.
this·is·a·cat.
this·is·a·cat.

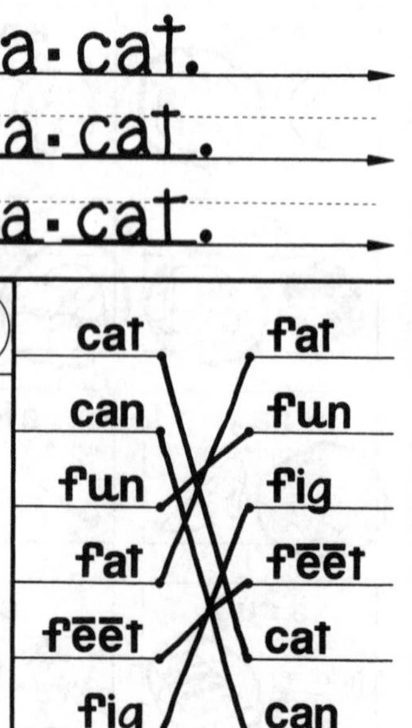

Worksheet 83 Side 2

th th th th
sh sh sh
w w w w
g g g g g

hut

a lock

a fan

hē

run

māil

mad

rāin

a rock

sick

fat

mitt
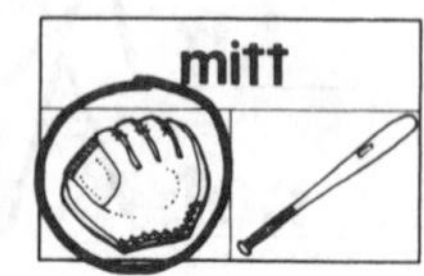

Name

Worksheet 84 Side 1

shē·has·a·cat.
that·cat·is
not·little.·that·cat
is·fat.

shē·has·a·cat.
she·has·a·cat.
she·has·a·cat.

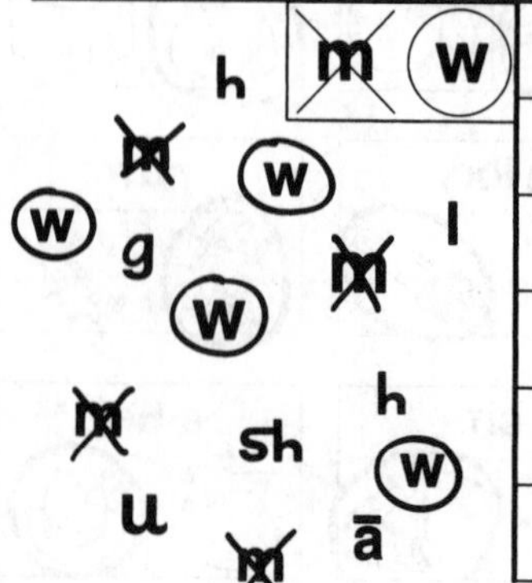

Worksheet 84 Side 2

th th th th
a a a a a
sh sh sh
l l l l l

a sack

sit
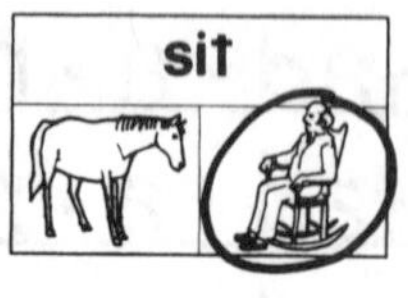
nut
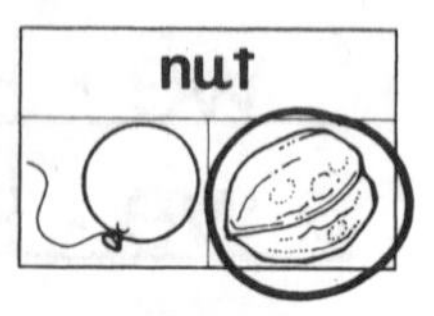

man

a rag

mēan

mud

rain

mail

hē

rug

a hut

Name ____________________ Worksheet **85** Side **1**

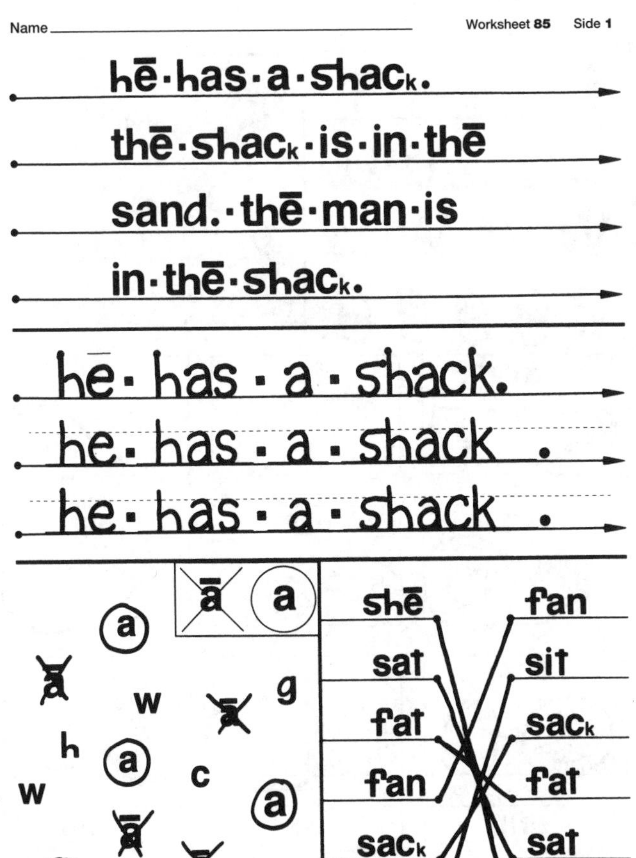
hē·has·a·shack.

thē·shack·is·in·thē

sand.·thē·man·is

in·thē·shack.

Worksheet **85** Side **2**

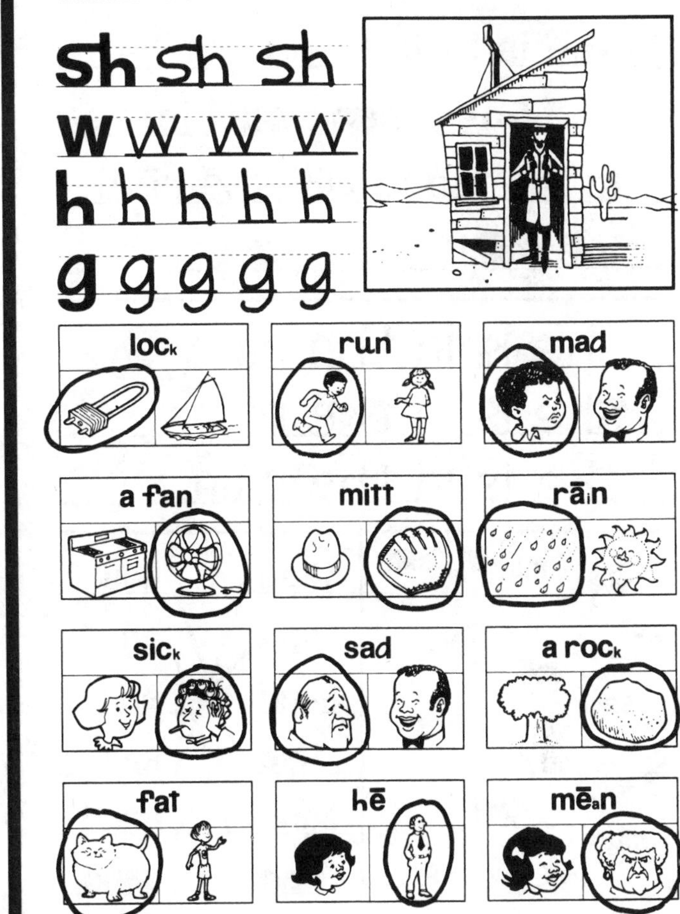

Name ____________________ Worksheet **86** Side **1**

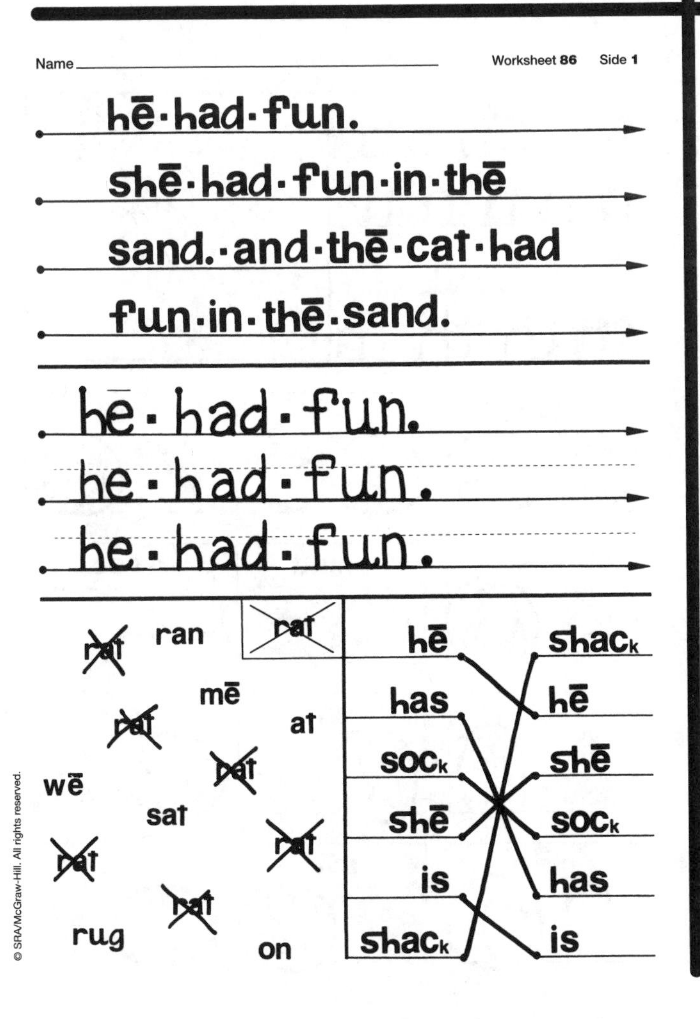
hē·had·fun.

shē·had·fun·in·thē

sand.·and·thē·cat·had

fun·in·thē·sand.

Worksheet **86** Side **2**

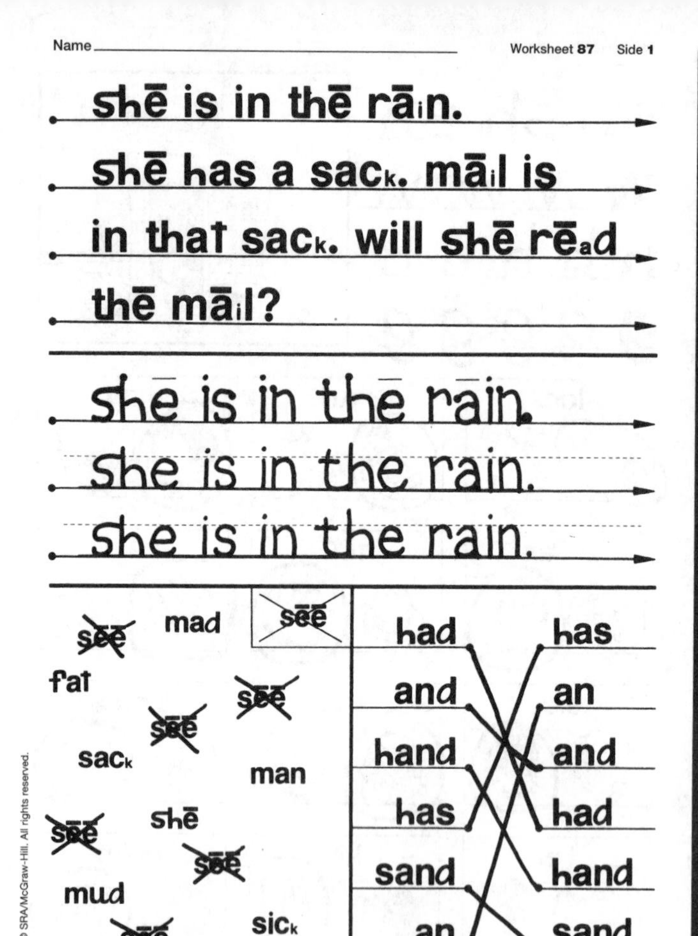

Name ____________________ Worksheet 87 Side 1

shē is in thē rāin.
shē has a sack. māil is
in that sack. will shē rēad
thē māil?

shē is in thē rāin.
she is in the rain.
she is in the rain.

see mad see
fat see
see
sack man
see shē
see
mud
see sick

had	has
and	an
hand	and
has	had
sand	hand
an	sand

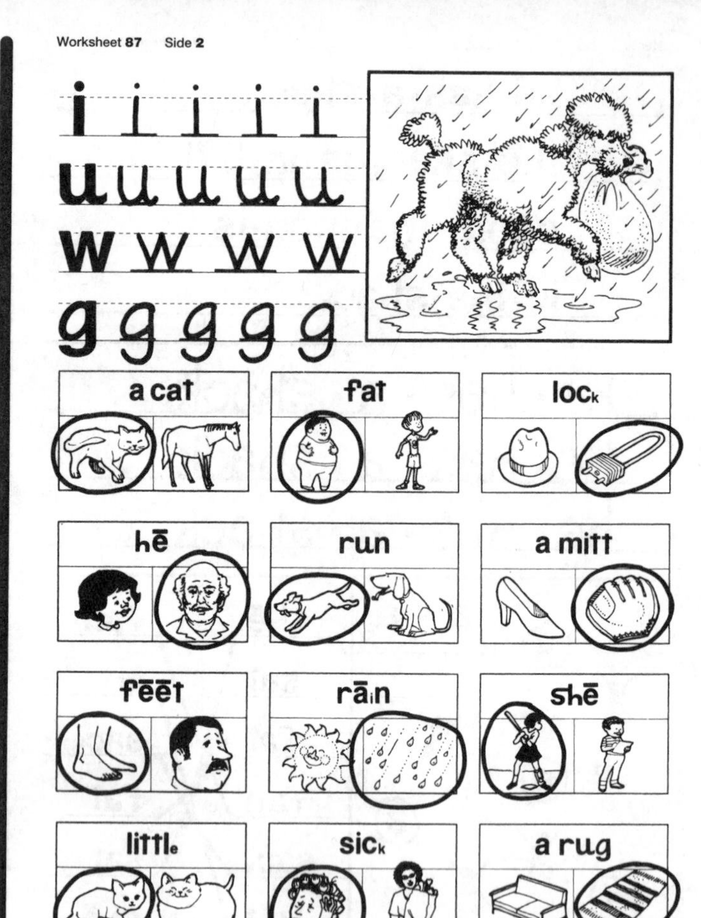

Worksheet 87 Side 2

i i i i i
u u u u u
w w w w
g g g g g

a cat	fat	lock
hē	run	a mitt
fēēt	rāin	shē
little	sick	a rug

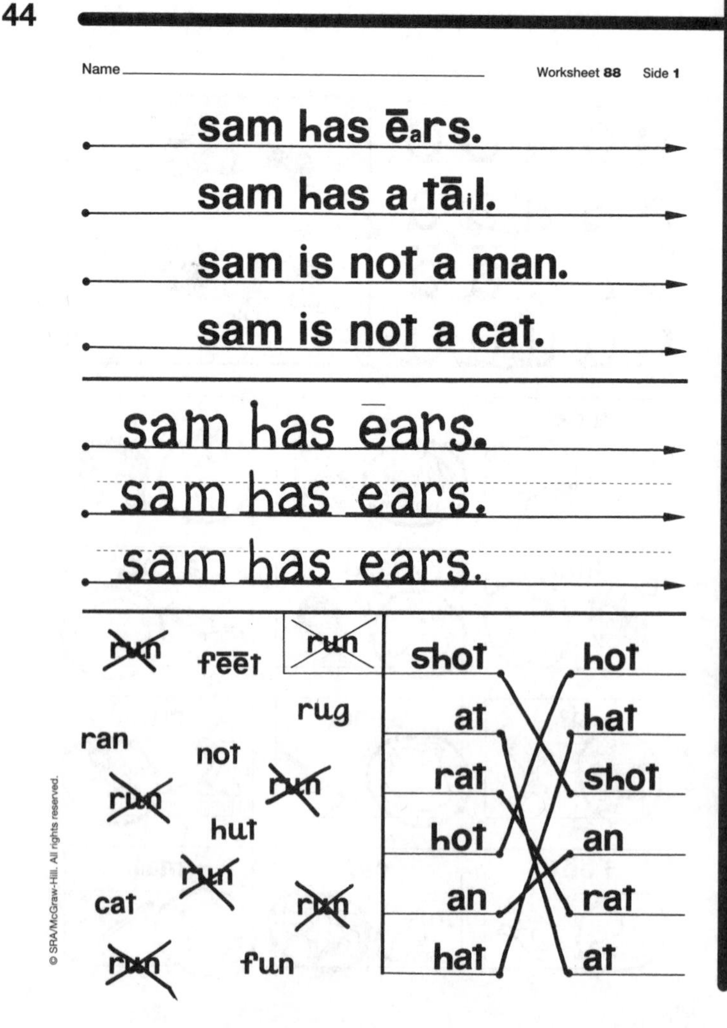

Name ____________________ Worksheet 88 Side 1

sam has ēars.
sam has a tāil.
sam is not a man.
sam is not a cat.

sam has ēars.
sam has ears.
sam has ears.

run fēēt run
rug
ran not
run run
hut
run
cat run
run fun

shot	hot
at	hat
rat	shot
hot	an
an	rat
hat	at

Worksheet 88 Side 2

sh sh sh
n n n n n
l l l l l
th th th th

shack	sand	sad
shē	mud	a rock
him	sit	cat
mēan	māil	a fan

Name ____________________ Worksheet 89 Side 1

thē sand is hot.
his fēēt got
hot. his hat is
not hot.

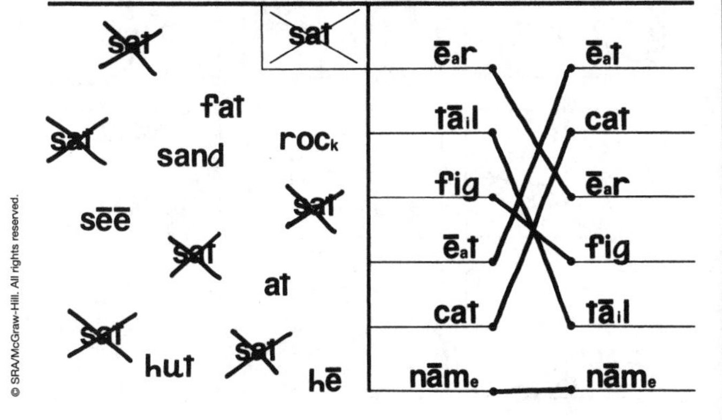

sat
fat
sat
sand
rocₖ
sēē
sat
sat
at
sat
hut
sat
hē

ēₐr	ēₐt
tāᵢl	cat
fig	ēₐr
ēₐt	fig
cat	tāᵢl
nāmₑ	nāmₑ

Worksheet 89 Side 2

h h h h h
n n n n n
w w w w
r r r r r

sacₖ
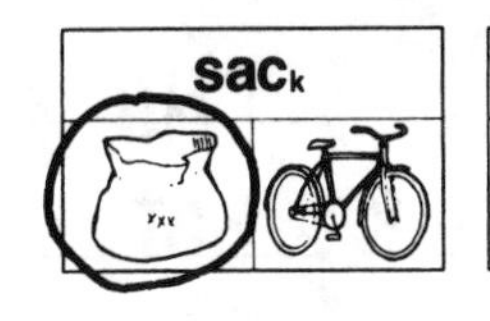
fēēt
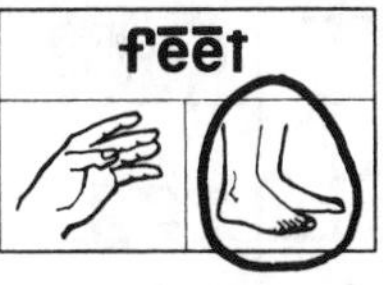
a locₖ
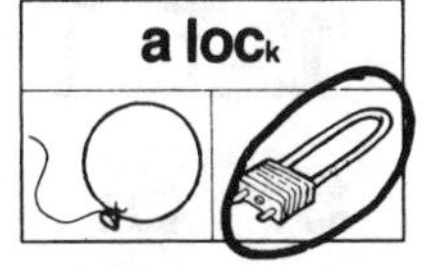
a rug

shē

fat

shacₖ

rāᵢn

hē

mad

littlₑ
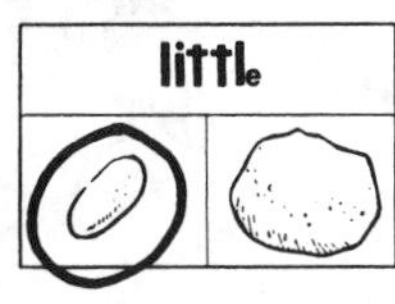
fan
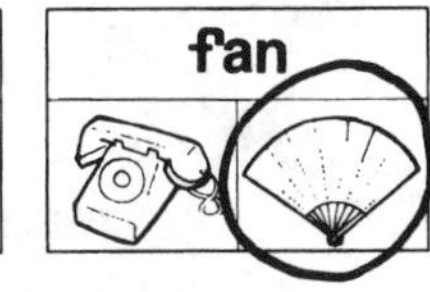

Name ____________________ Worksheet 90 Side 1

a fish mādₑ a wish.
"I wish I had fēēt. I wish
I had a tāᵢl. I wish I had
a hat. I wish I had a dish."

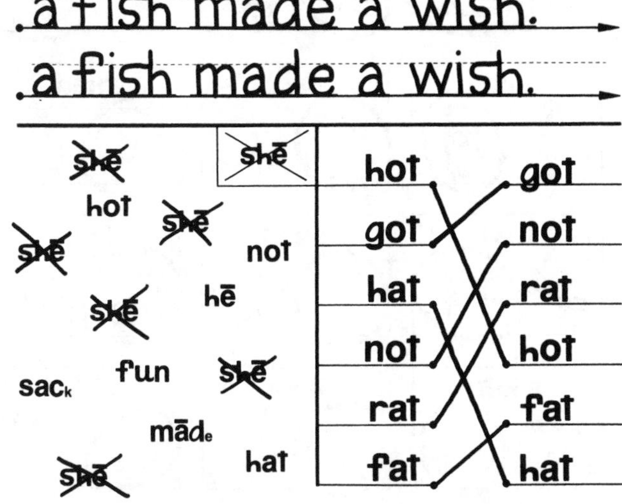

shē
hot
shē
shē
not
hē
shē
sacₖ
fun
shē
mādₑ
hat
shē

hot	got
got	not
hat	rat
not	hot
rat	fat
fat	hat

Worksheet 90 Side 2

f f f f f
a a a a a
I I I I
r r r r r

rag

sand

a hut

a rat

run

shē

māᵢl

a rug
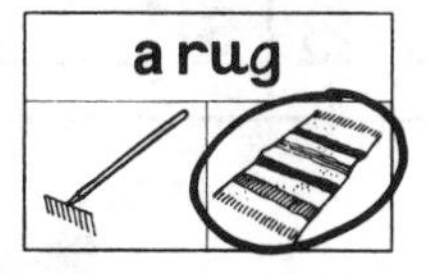
rocₖ

cat
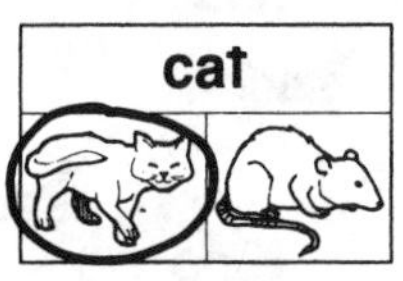
sicₖ

him

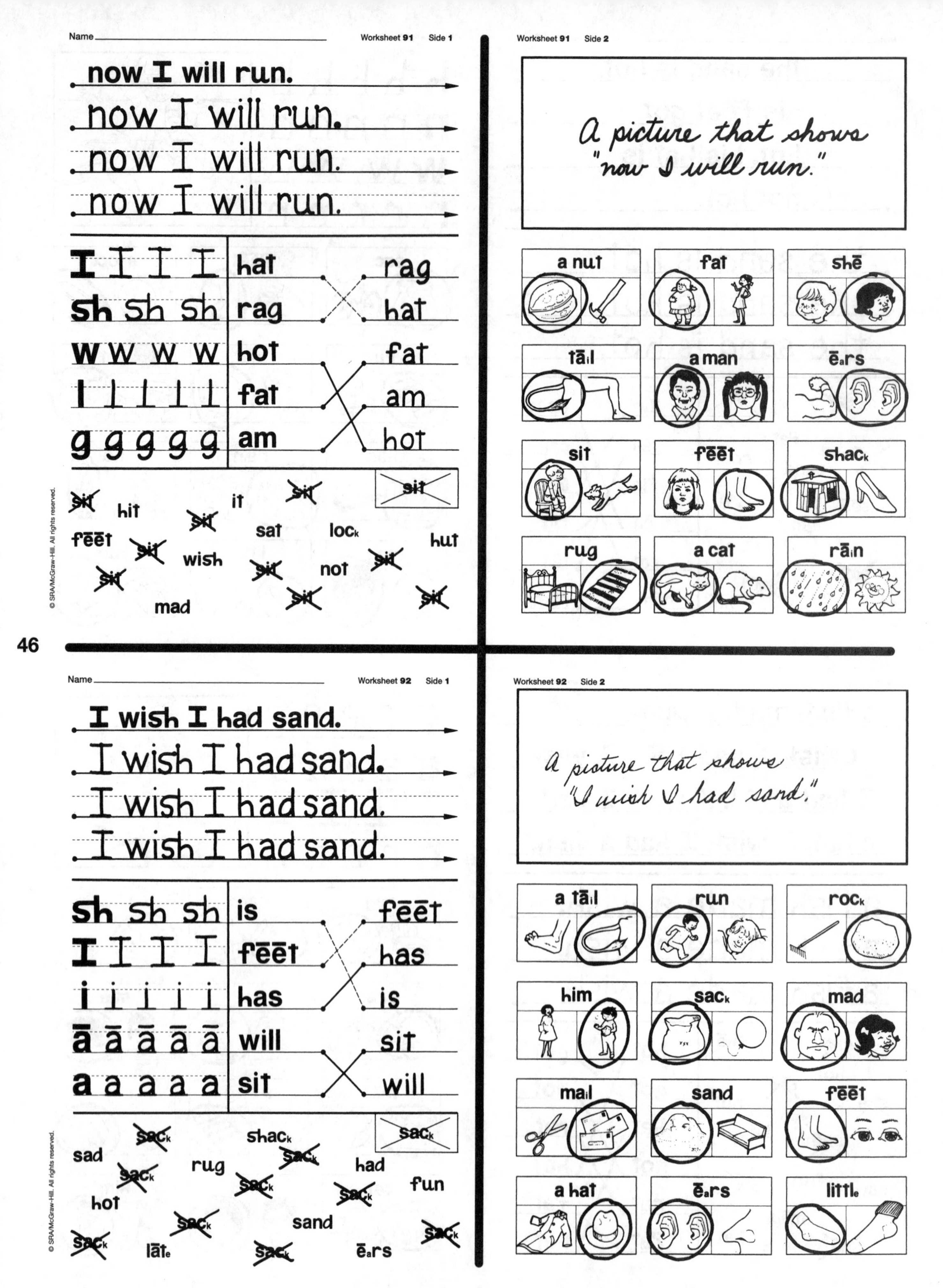

Name
Worksheet 91 Side 1
now I will run.
now I will run.
now I will run.
now I will run.
I I I I
sh sh sh
w w w w
I I I I I
g g g g g
hat
rag
hot
fat
am
rag
hat
fat
am
hot
sit
sit
hit
it
sit
feet
sit
sat
lock
hut
sit
wish
sit
not
sit
sit
sit
mad
sit
Worksheet 91 Side 2
A picture that shows "now I will run."
a nut
fat
she
tail
a man
ears
sit
feet
shack
rug
a cat
rain
Name
Worksheet 92 Side 1
I wish I had sand.
I wish I had sand.
I wish I had sand.
I wish I had sand.
sh sh sh
I I I I
i i i i i
ā ā ā ā ā
a a a a a
is
feet
has
will
sit
feet
has
is
sit
will
sack
sack
shack
sad
sack
sack
rug
had
sack
sack
fun
hot
sack
sand
sack
sack
late
sack
ears
Worksheet 92 Side 2
A picture that shows "I wish I had sand."
a tail
run
rock
him
sack
mad
mail
sand
feet
a hat
ears
little

Name ____________________ Worksheet 93 Side 1

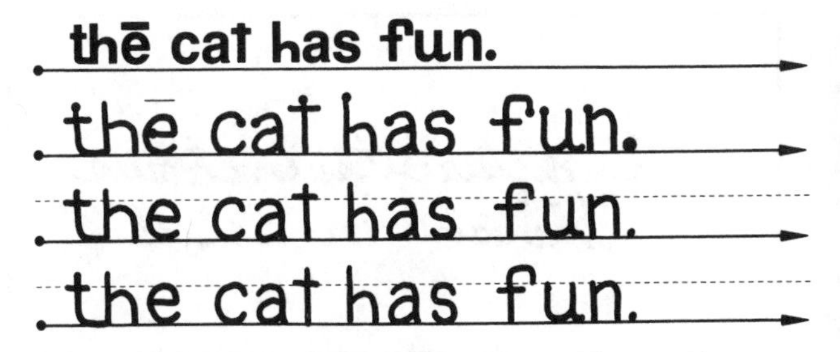

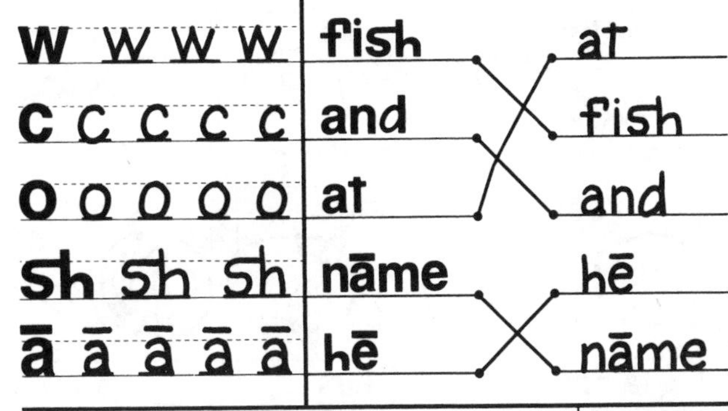

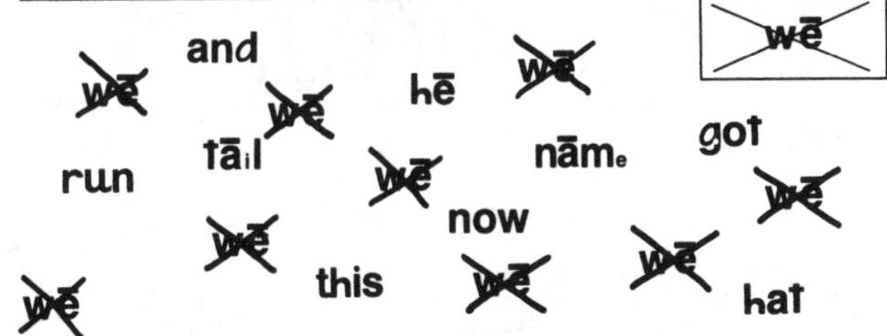

Worksheet 93 Side 2

A picture that shows "the cat has fun."

hat

a rat

shē

a fish

rāin

sad

a mitt

dish

ēars
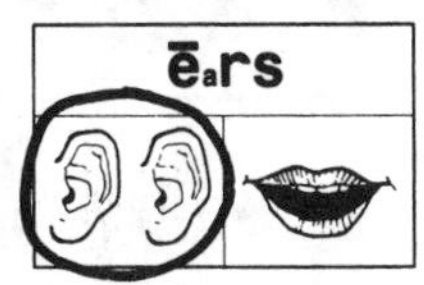

a cat

fan
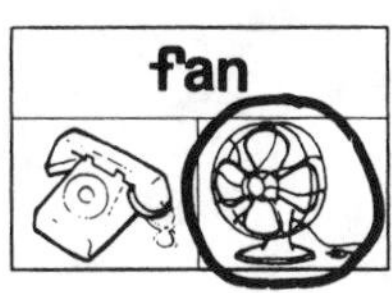

hē

Name ____________________ Worksheet 94 Side 1

thē fish had fun.

thē fish had fun.

the fish had fun.

the fish had fun.

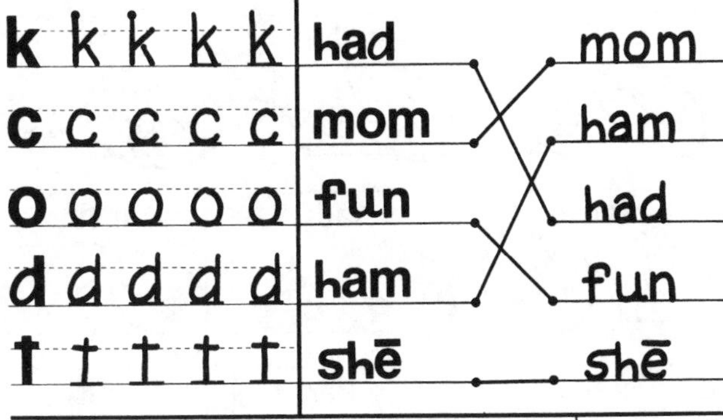

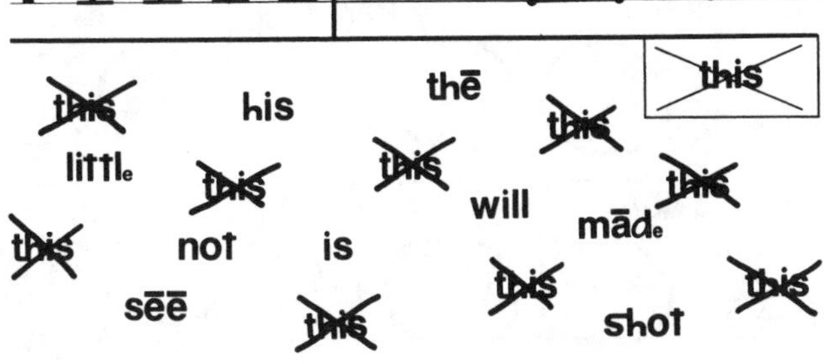

Worksheet 94 Side 2

A picture that shows "the fish had fun."

a fish

fat

sit
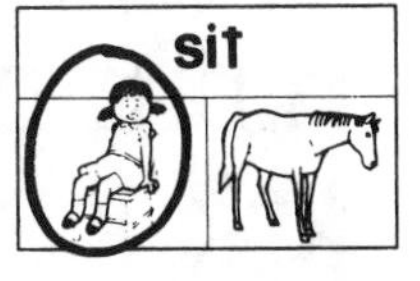

hill

fēēt
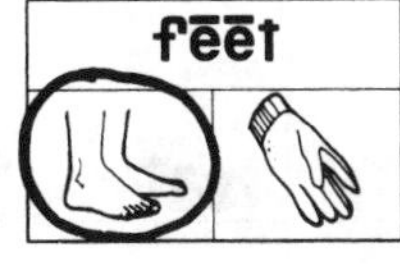

a rug

a man

sand
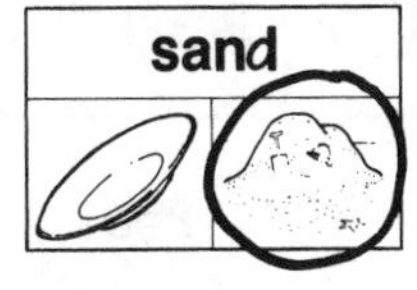

hut

hat

a dish

tāil
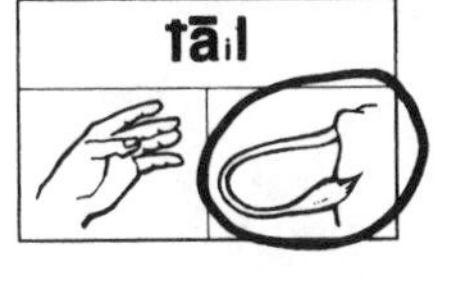

Name 

Worksheet **95** Side **1**

shē sat on a hill.

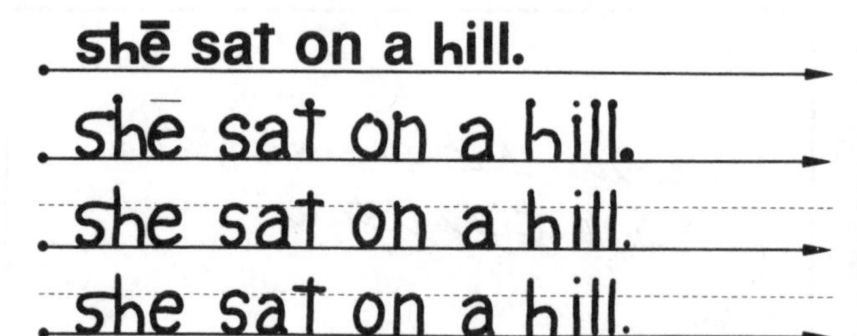

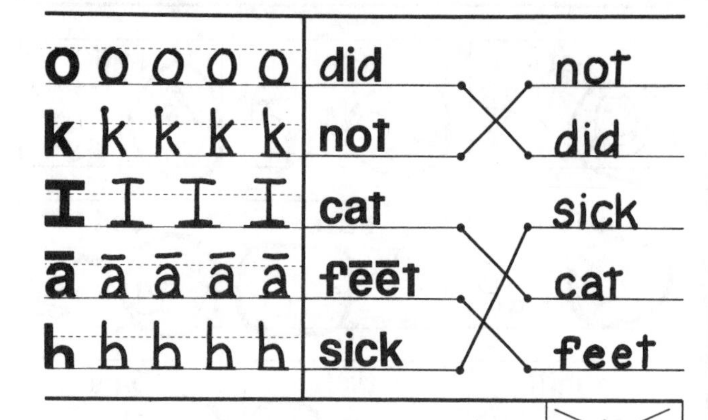

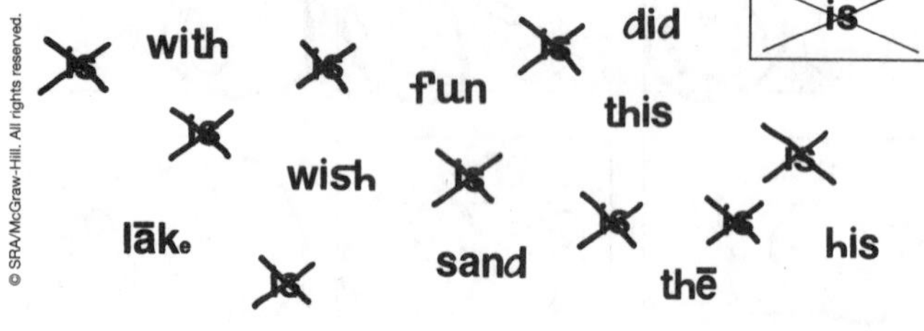

Worksheet **95** Side **2**

A picture that shows "she sat on a hill."

a dish	shē	rag

fēēt	**shack**	**a mitt**
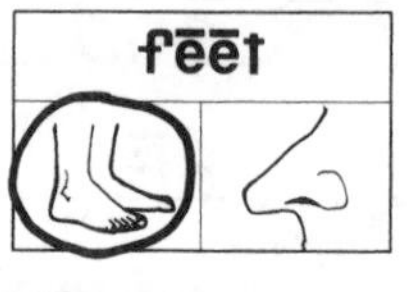		
a rāke	**him**	**fan**
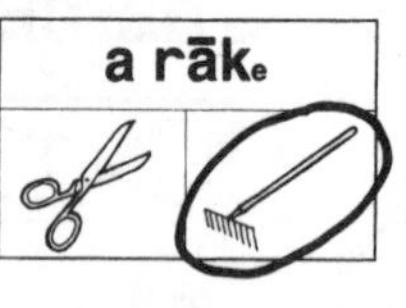		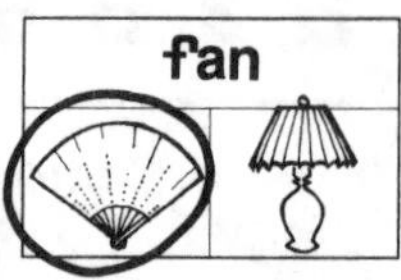
ēars	**lāke**	**sit**
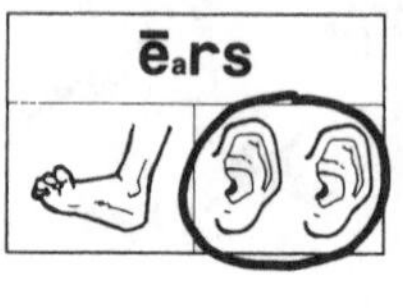		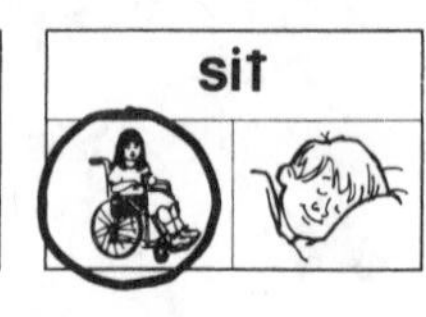

Name

Worksheet **96** Side **1**

shē said, "I āte."

she said, "I ate."
she said, "I ate."
she said, "I ate."

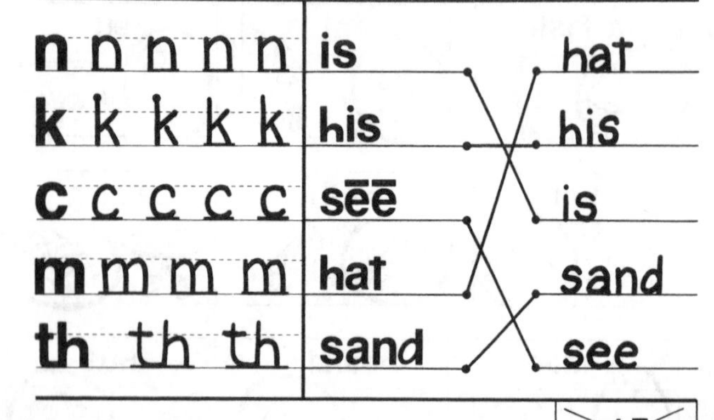

Worksheet **96** Side **2**

A picture that shows "she said 'I ate.'"

rāke	a dish	cat
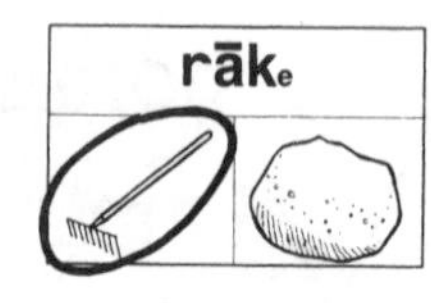		
mom	**tāil**	**little**
	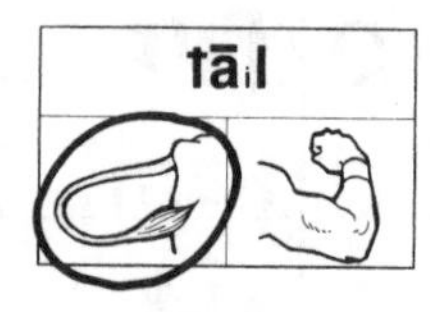	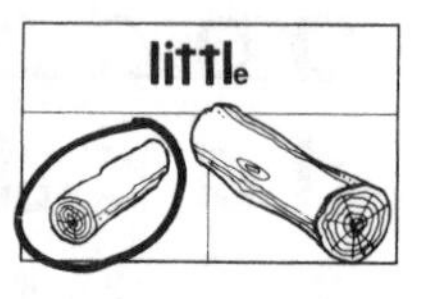
sand	**a rag**	**lāke**

a hill	**ēars**	**sack**
	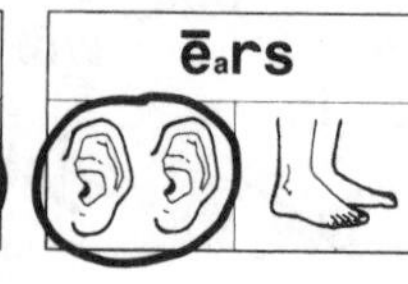	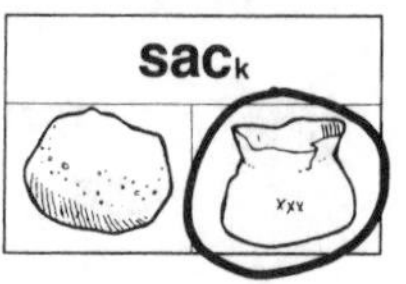

Name ______________________ Worksheet 97 Side 1

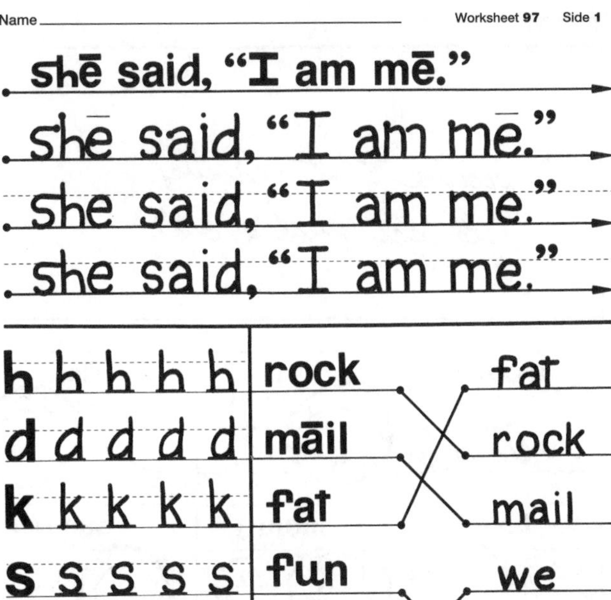

that

that fish that āte hot that at that that fat that now gun that mom this that that

Worksheet 97 Side 2

A picture that shows "she said 'I am me.'"

Name ______________________ Worksheet 98 Side 1

shē was not mad.

shē was not mad.

she was not mad.

she was not mad.

f f f f f	can	dish
k k k k k	dish	can
c c c c c	āte	man
r r r r r	man	got
m m m m	got	ate

nō

nō gāte nō am not hat nō nō sand nō nō tāil nō cow wish nō hit nō

Worksheet 98 Side 2

A picture that shows "she was not mad."

Name ____________________ Worksheet **99** Side **1**

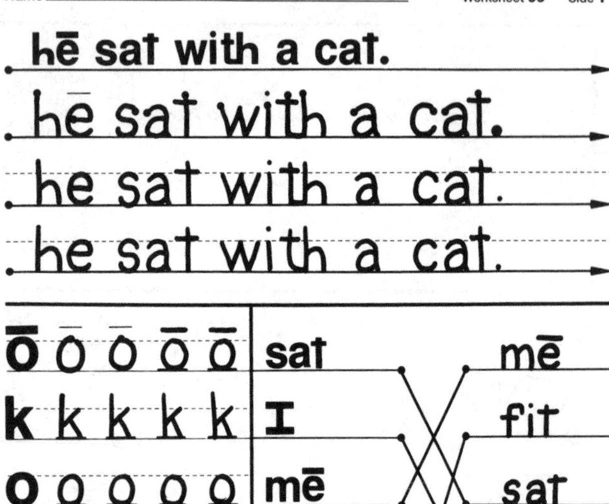

hē sat with a cat.

hē sat with a cat.

he sat with a cat.

he sat with a cat.

ō ō ō ō ō ō
k k k k k k
o o o o o o
ā ā ā ā ā ā
u u u u u u

sat	mē
I	fit
mē	sat
his	I
fit	his

~~thē~~

thē shē cat thē hē thē āte thē fish hug thē thē little thē nō thē thē thē lick

Worksheet **99** Side **2**

A picture that shows "he sat with a cat."

a cow 	fan 	fish 
lāke 	mom 	sand 
ēars 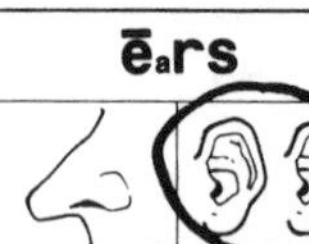	a mitt 	fēēt 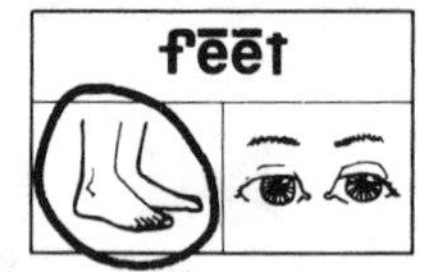
a rag 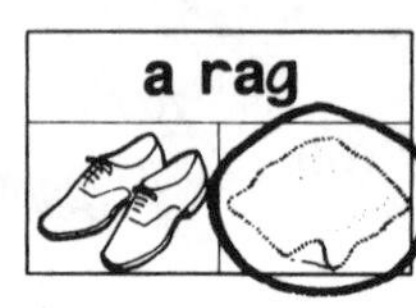	lock 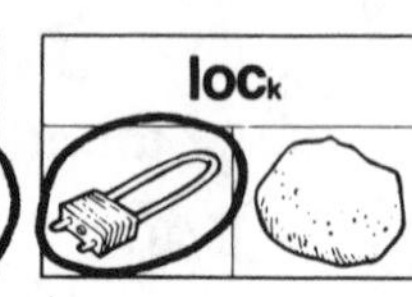	him 

Name ____________________ Worksheet **100** Side **1**

hē has nō tēēth.

hē has nō tēēth.

he has no teeth.

he has no teeth.

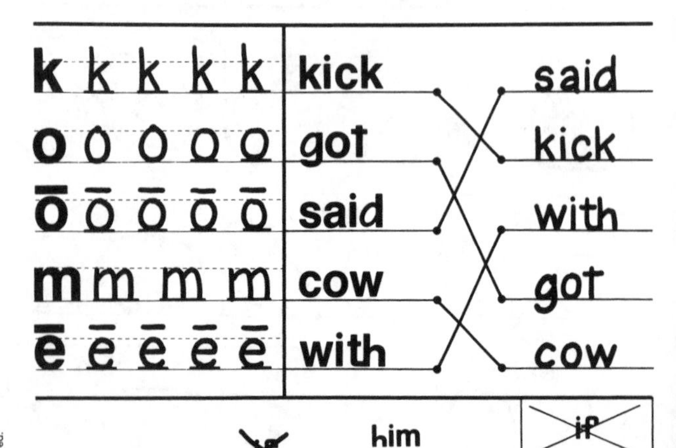

k k k k k
o o o o o o
ō ō ō ō ō ō
m m m m m
ē ē ē ē ē ē

kick	said
got	kick
said	with
cow	got
with	cow

~~if~~

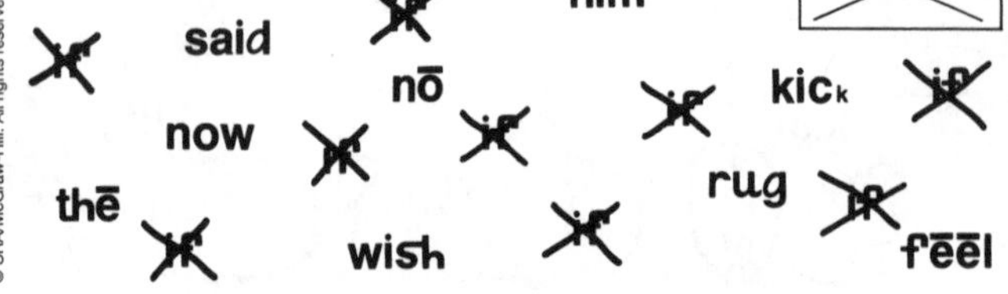

if said if him nō if now if if kick if thē rug if if wish fēēl

Worksheet **100** Side **2**

A picture that shows "he has no teeth."

lāke 	cow 	tāil 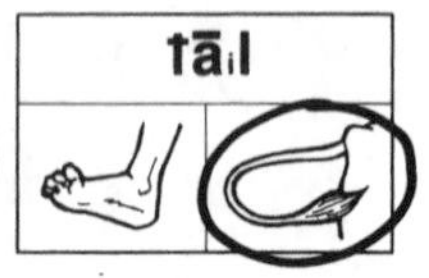
shē 	dish 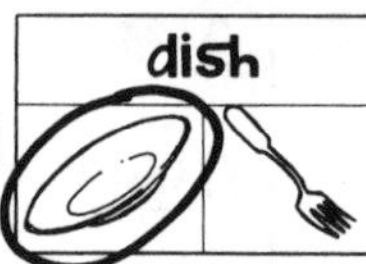	a rāke 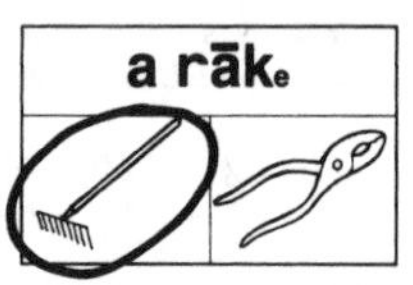
hill 	a shack 	sick 
a cat 	sack 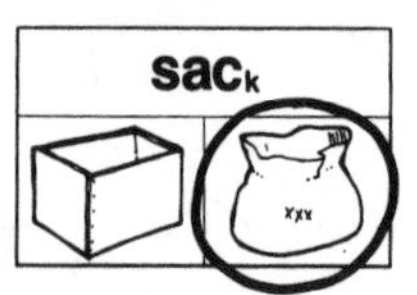	fat 

Name ____________________

Worksheet **101** Side **1**

I can kiss a cat.

I can kiss a cat.

I can kiss a cat.

I can kiss a cat.

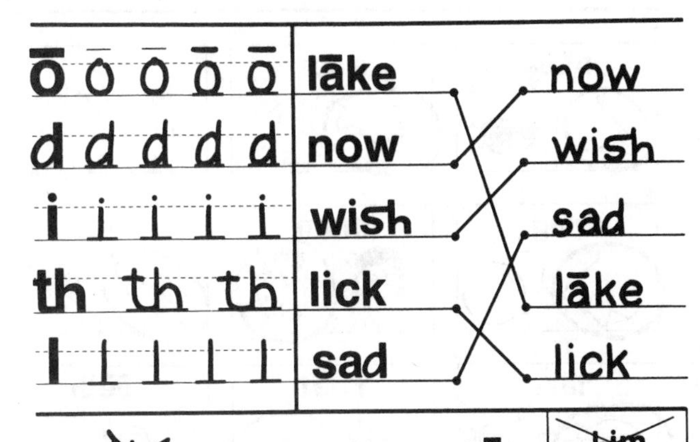

ō ō ō ō ō	lāke	now
d d d d d	now	wish
i i i i i	wish	sad
th th th	lick	lāke
l l l l l	sad	lick

~~him~~ | hit | ~~him~~ | hat | cāke | ~~him~~ | ~~him~~ | hug | ~~him~~ | ~~him~~ | nō | ~~him~~ | ēat | kiss | if | ~~him~~ | ~~him~~ | will | ~~him~~

Worksheet **101** Side **2**

A picture that shows "I can kiss a cat."

a rug

fēēt
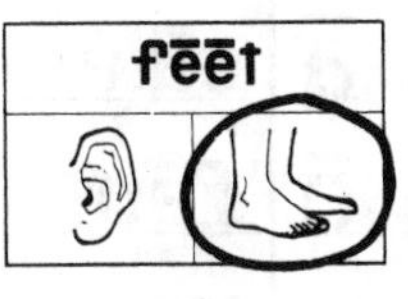

him

hut

māil

ēars
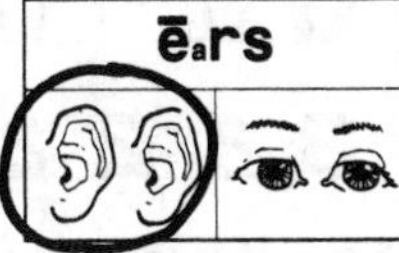

kiss

mom

a lāke

a rock
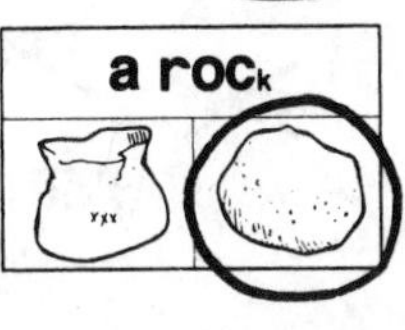

hat

lick

Name ____________________

Worksheet **102** Side **1**

a cat is on thē cow.

a cat is on thē cow.

a cat is on the cow.

a cat is on the cow.

ō ō ō ō ō	sō	mad
k k k k k	run	sō
I I I I	mad	sick
sh sh sh	nō	run
u u u u u	sick	nō

~~and~~ | thē | ~~and~~ | sat | ~~and~~ | ~~and~~ | rat | lick | ~~and~~ | āte | nō | ~~and~~ | ~~and~~ | ~~and~~ | man | sand | him | ~~and~~ | ~~and~~

Worksheet **102** Side **2**

A picture that shows "a cat is on the cow."

a cat
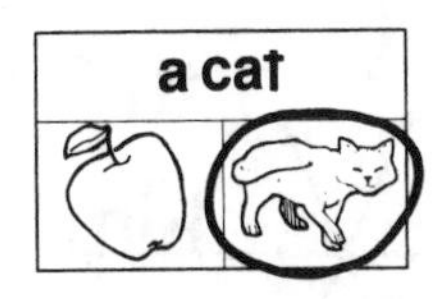

sand
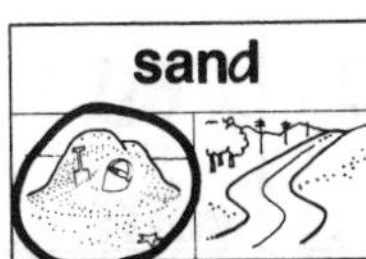

shē

sad

a fish

shack

a rāke

sit

a cow

lock
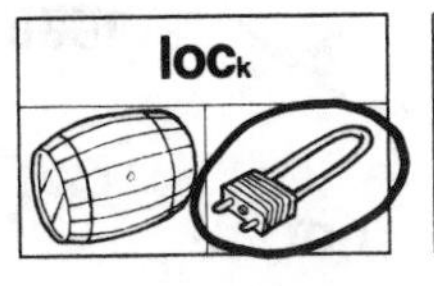

hē

mitt
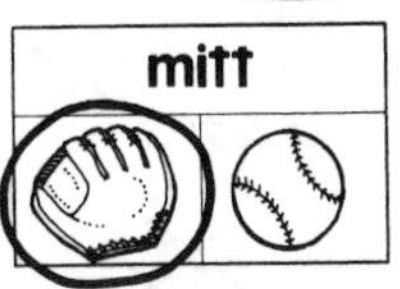

Name ______________________ Worksheet 103 Side 1

I can hōld thē hats.

I can hōld thē hats.

I can hold the hats.

I can hold the hats.

ā ā ā ā ā	cāke	fan
ō ō ō ō ō	fan	cāke
o o o o o	it	was
a a a a a	was	man
v v v v v	man	it

cow

cow kiss cow have cow cat cow wish if cow cow cow cow now how lāt fēēt cow

Worksheet 103 Side 2

A picture that shows "I can hold the hats."

nōse

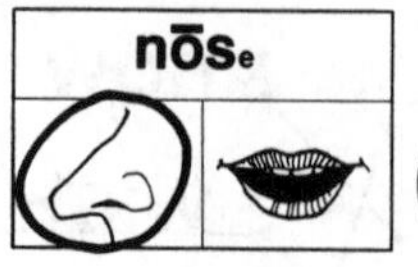

a cat

fat

rag

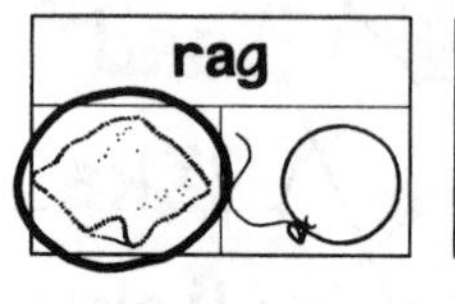

mom

a dish

lāke

fēēt

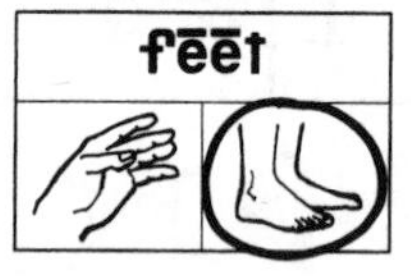

tēēth

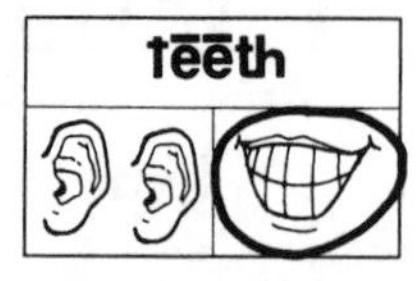

kiss

a cow

lick

Name ______________________ Worksheet 104 Side 1

wē have sacks.

wē have sacks.

we have sacks.

we have sacks.

th th th	rag	thē
sh sh sh	him	him
h h h h h	thē	rag
l l l l l	rug	sēē
g g g g g	sēē	rug

can

can fish can nō can can cat tēēth sand can and can cow can can can is not

Worksheet 104 Side 2

A picture that shows "we have sacks."

kitten

hit

ēars

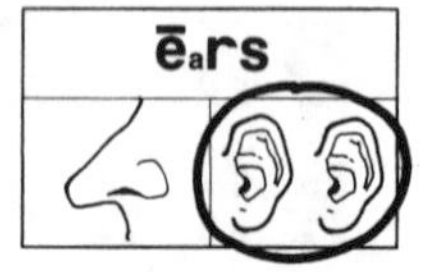

shē

a sack

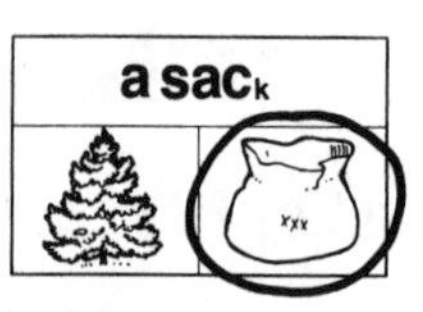

sand

rāke

a rock

lock

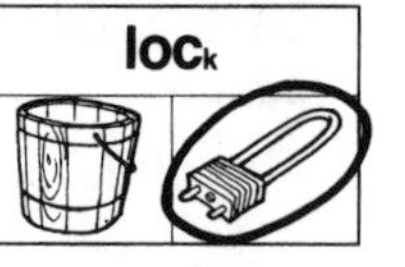

a rug

tēēth

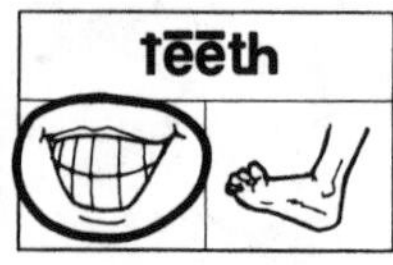

fan

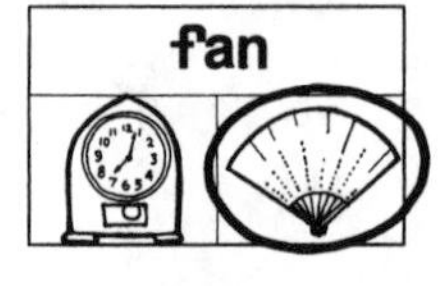

Name ____________________ Worksheet **105** Side **1**

thē ōld man shāvₑs.

the old man shaves.

the old man shaves.

the old man shaves.

v v v v v	in	can
w w w w	can	in
n n n n n	gāte	a
u u u u u	this	gāte
h h h h h	a	this

now

now lick not now mē now āte now if now kittₑn cow can now has now

Worksheet **105** Side **2**

a picture that shows "the old man shaves."

a cow	lākₑ	hill

mom	**kiss**	**a rocₖ**

tēēth	**mitt**	**a dish**
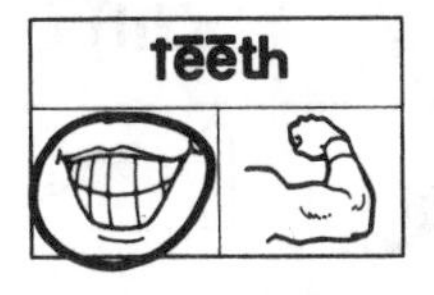		
a fish	**nōsₑ**	**shacₖ**
	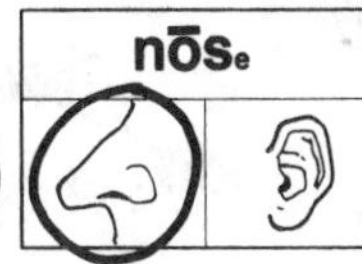	

Name ____________________ Worksheet **106** Side **1**

givₑ mē a socₖ.

give me a sock.

give me a sock.

give me a sock.

ō ō ō ō ō	lāte	hōld
I I I I	that	lāte
v v v v v	hōld	that
k k k k k	rock	mē
u u u u u	mē	rock

hats

hats sit hats at hats rocₖ littlₑ hats hats ōld hats hats now havₑ can wē hats hats hats

Worksheet **106** Side **2**

a picture that shows "give me a sock."

thē hats	ōld	a sacₖ

mad	**ēₐrs**	**mom**
	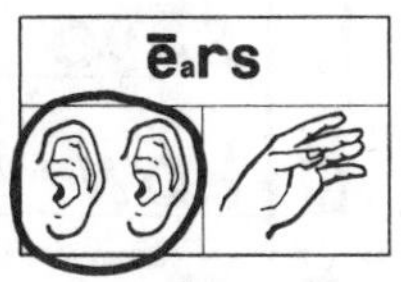	
a dish	**nōsₑ**	**locₖ**
	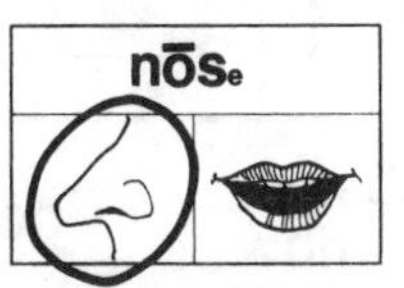	
fēēt	**sad**	**kittₑn**
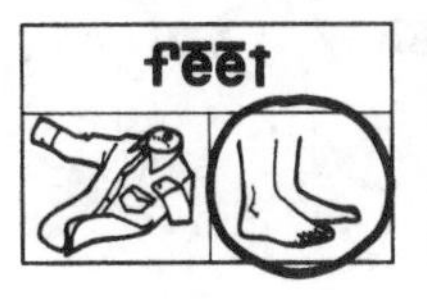		

Name ____________________ Worksheet **107** Side **1**

thē man was cōld.

the man was cold.

the man was cold.

the man was cold.

w w w w w	shē	ran
k k k k k	mitt	hats
v v v v v	ran	said
f f f f f	hats	shē
ā ā ā ā ā	said	mitt

~~nēēd~~

will ~~nēēd~~ did ~~nēēd~~ ~~nēēd~~ can fēēt sand nō ~~nēēd~~ ~~nēēd~~ ~~nēēd~~ ~~nēēd~~ tēēth ~~nēēd~~ hōld ~~nēēd~~ ~~nēēd~~ ēat

Worksheet **107** Side **2**

a picture that shows "the man was cold."

a sack 	tēēth 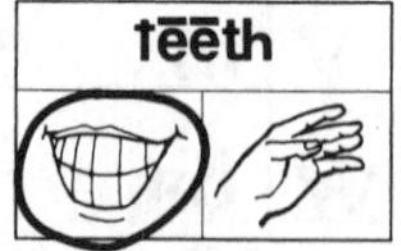	thē rocks 
kiss 	shē 	shack 
fan 	a man 	sand 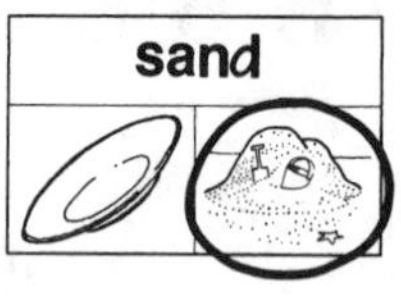
a tāil 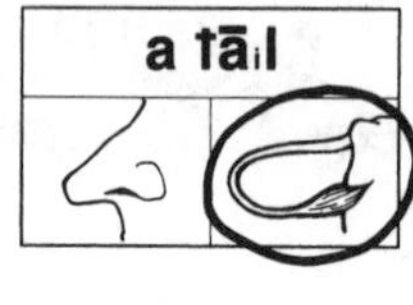	dish 	sit 

Name ____________________ Worksheet **108** Side **1**

thē gōat āte thē cōat.

the goat ate the coat.

the goat ate the coat.

the goat ate the coat.

g g g g g	hit	ōld
c c c c c	ōld	how
k k k k k	sāve	I
d d d d d	how	hit
t t t t t	I	sāve

~~nŏt~~

~~nŏt~~ nōse ~~nŏt~~ now ~~nŏt~~ sack fish ~~nŏt~~ hē ~~nŏt~~ ~~nŏt~~ hāte that ~~nŏt~~ ~~nŏt~~ got ~~nŏt~~ is

Worksheet **108** Side **2**

A picture that shows "the goat ate his coat."

thē sacks 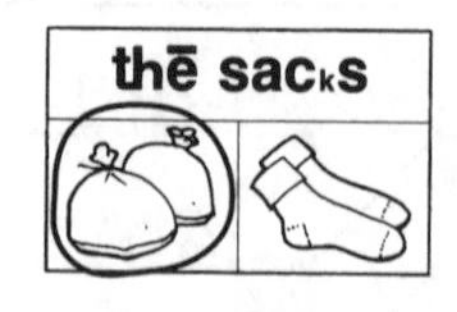	a rug 	tāil 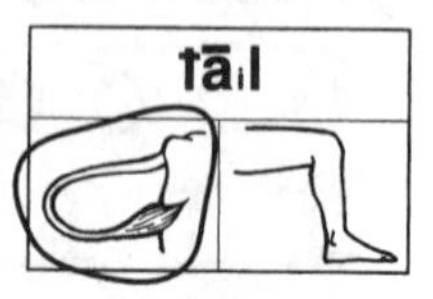
lick 	shack 	hē 
a rāke 	nōse 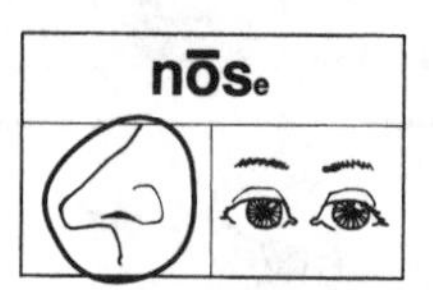	shē 
fēēt 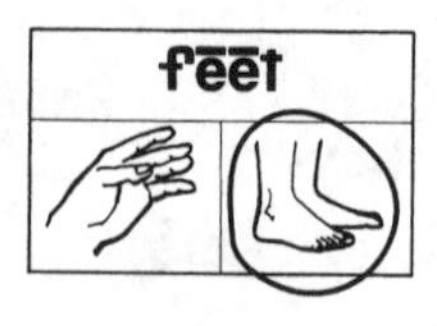	hut 	māil 

Name ____________________ Worksheet **109** Side **1**

a cow got on a rock.

a cow got on a rock.

a cow got on a rock.

a cow got on a rock.

p p p p p	sat	mud
v v v v v	hē	sat
d d d d d	now	hē
g g g g g	mud	nāme
s s s s s	nāme	now

on ~~man~~ ~~man~~ said ~~man~~
~~man~~ not
~~man~~ sand ~~man~~ ~~man~~
~~man~~ shāve
mad sō ~~man~~
rock ~~man~~ nēēd

Worksheet **109** Side **2**

a picture that shows "a cow got on a rock."

shack	ēars	hut
	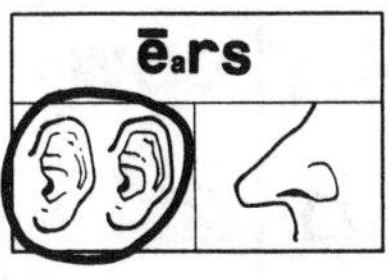	
a fish	him	ōld

lāke	a mitt	a sack

mom	fēēt	a cow
	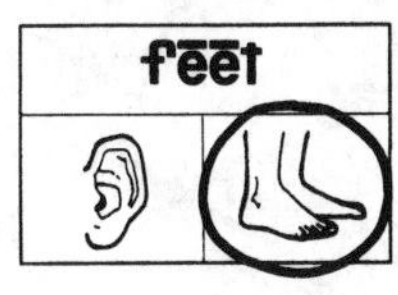	

Name ____________________ Worksheet **110** Side **1**

hē had sand on him.

hē had sand on him.

he had sand on him.

he had sand on him.

p p p p p	sock	ham
g g g g g	of	to
v v v v v	run	sock
t t t t t	ham	of
I I I I	to	run

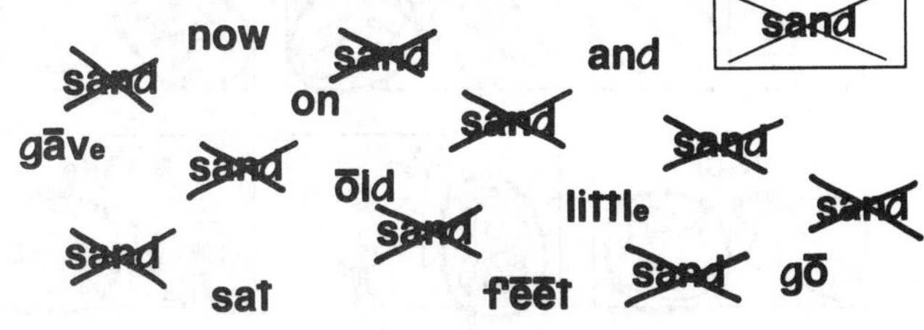

Worksheet **110** Side **2**

a picture that shows "he had sand on him."

a cōat	hill	lock

a tāil	tēēth	a dish
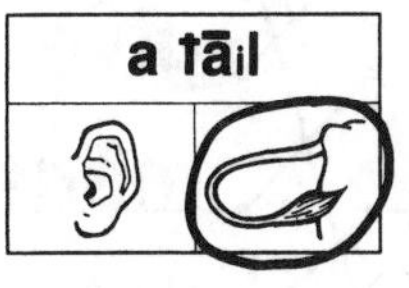	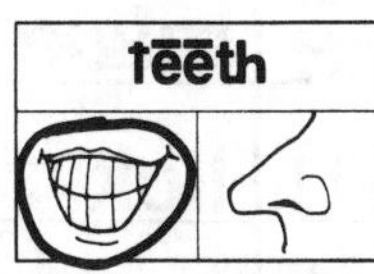	
nōse	hut	gōat
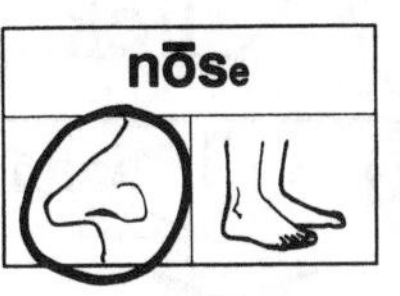		
shē	a rāke	cōld

Name ____________________

Worksheet **111** Side **1**

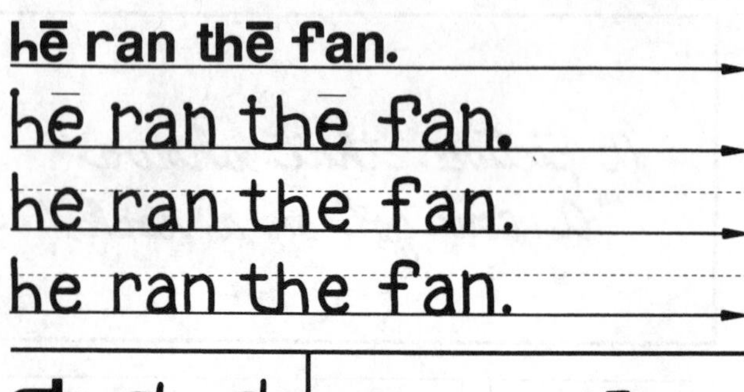

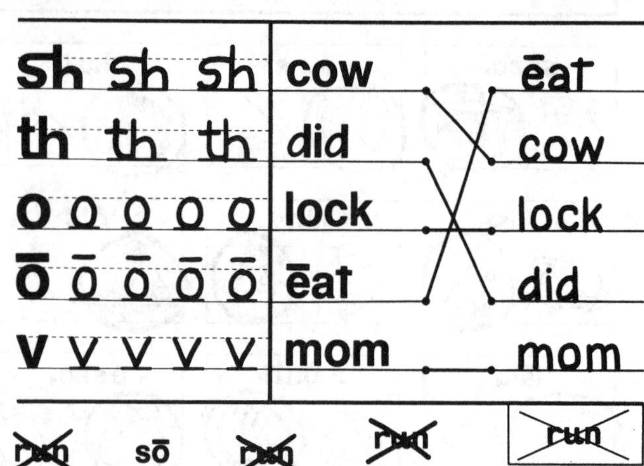

run

run sō run run

run

lāte is fun run

rag run

run run run

sand did got rug

Worksheet **111** Side **2**

a picture that shows "he ran the fan."

gōat

man

māil

fish

cōld

kitten

a rāke

kiss

fēēt

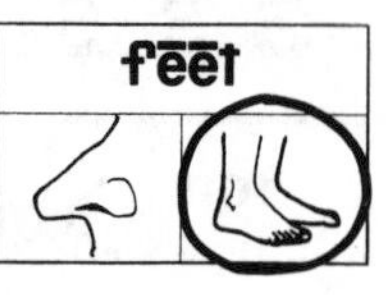

a shack

a fan

ēars

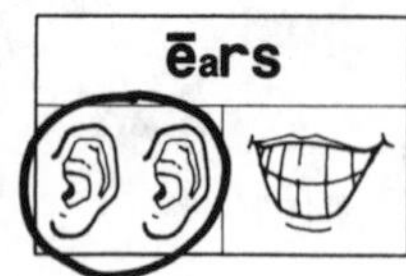

Name ____________________

Worksheet **112** Side **1**

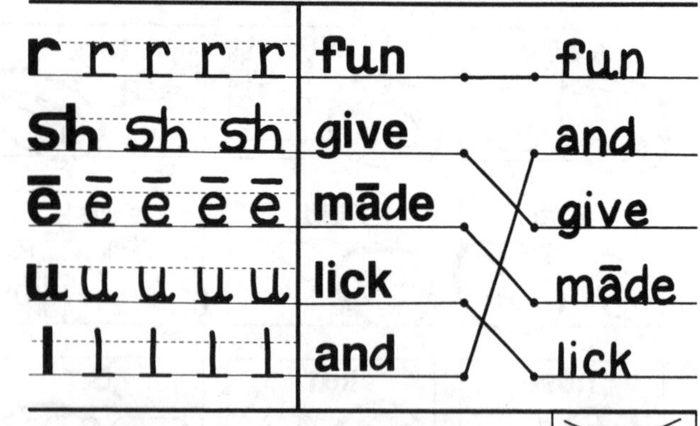

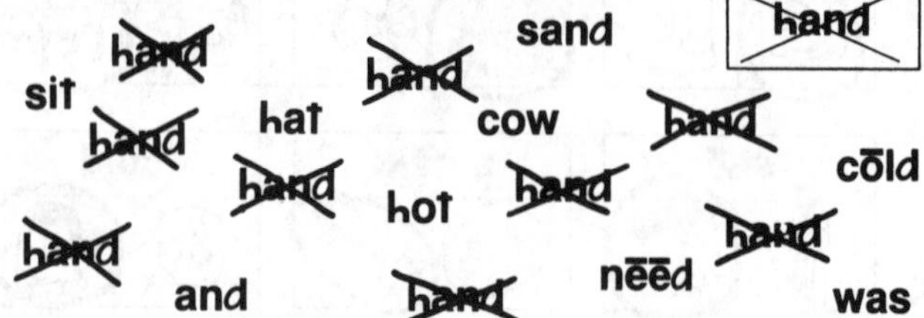

Worksheet **112** Side **2**

A picture that shows "the dog ate the car."

thē cōats

cow

cōld

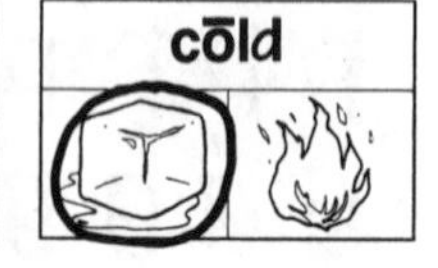

mitt

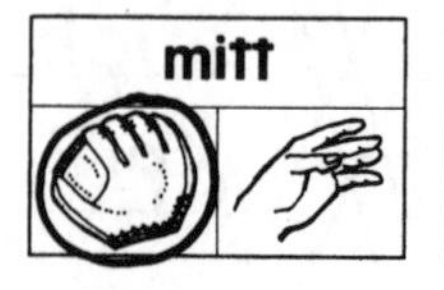

a nōse

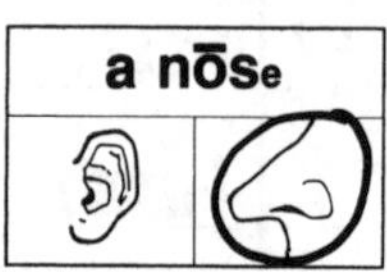

gāte

a rāke

socks

a rug

sack

hē

a lāke

Name ______________________ Worksheet **113** Side **1**

the gōat sat on a log.

the gōat sat on a log.

the goat sat on a log.

the goat sat on a log.

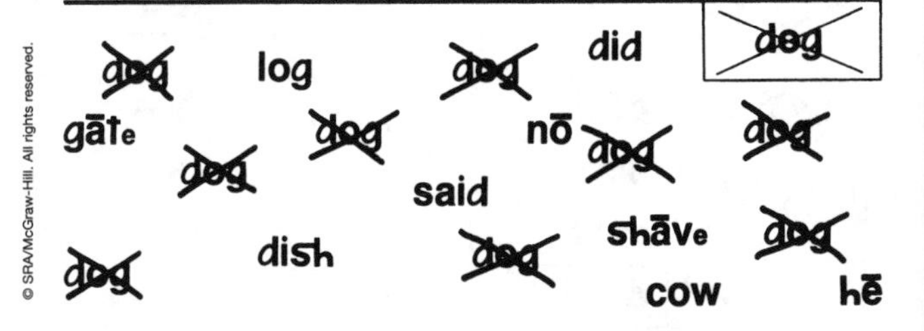

dog

dog log dog did gāte dog dog nō dog dog said dog dish dog shāve dog cow hē

Worksheet **113** Side **2**

A picture that shows "the goat sat on a log."

rock	sand	a cow
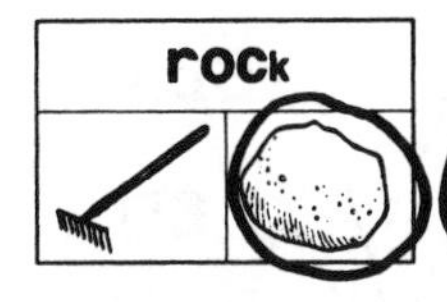		

tēēth	sun	mom
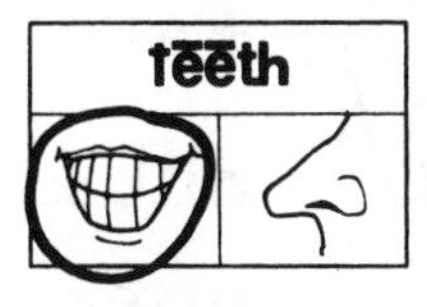		

socks	a cōat	ēars
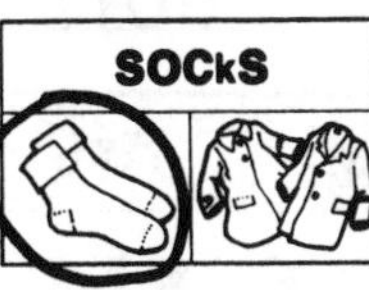		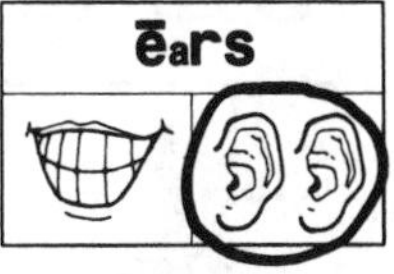

tāil	hill	a gōat
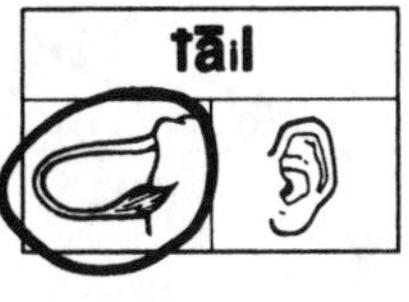	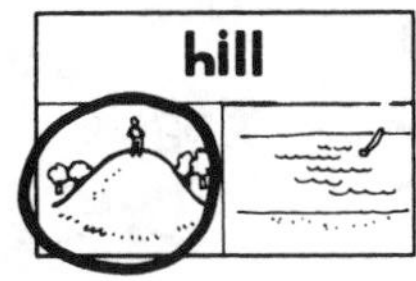	

Name ______________________ Worksheet **114** Side **1**

a man sat on a gōat.

a man sat on a gōat.

a man sat on a goat.

a man sat on a goat.

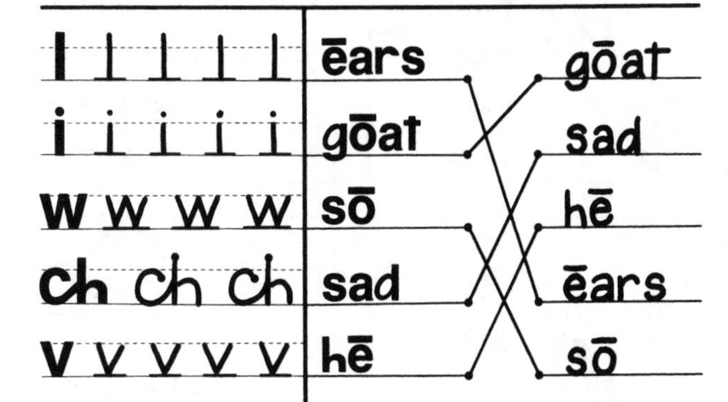

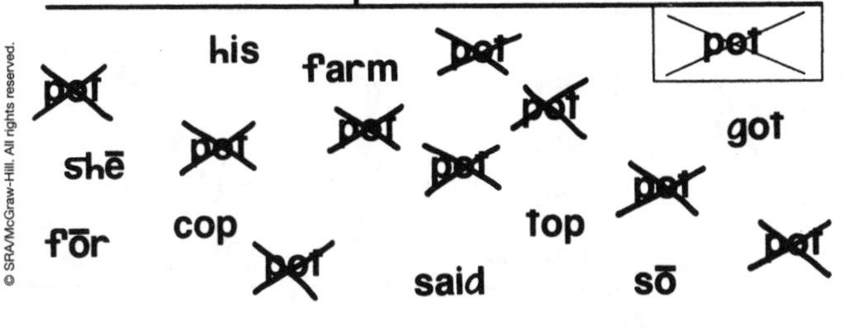

Worksheet **114** Side **2**

A picture that shows "a man sat on a goat."

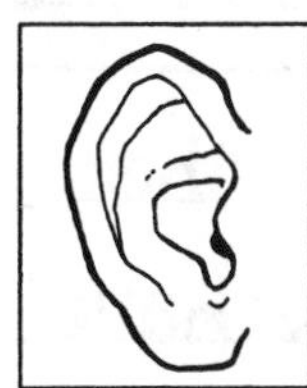

~~nōse~~
~~tēēth~~
ēar
~~car~~

~~eat~~
cow
~~nut~~
~~look~~

~~sock~~
~~fan~~
~~lāke~~
rock

~~rat~~
~~fish~~
rāke
~~hut~~

gōat
~~cōat~~
~~cat~~
~~got~~

~~nō~~
nōse
~~on~~
~~not~~

Name ____________________ Worksheet **115** Side **1**

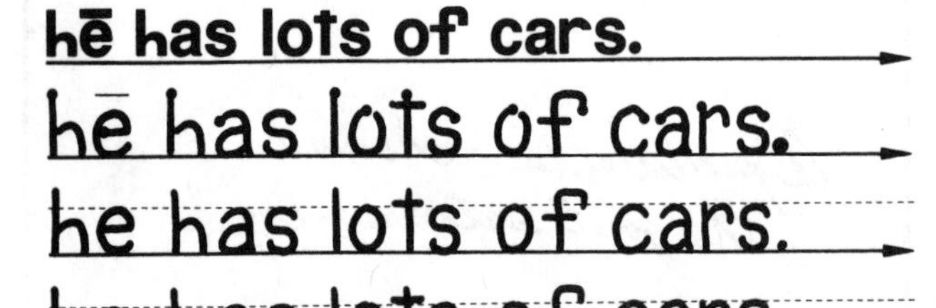

hē has lots of cars.

hē has lots of cars.

he has lots of cars.

he has lots of cars.

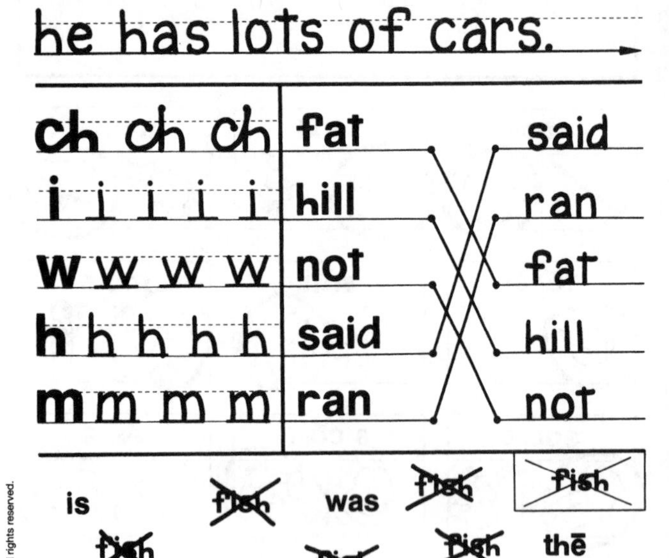

ch ch ch	fat	said
i i i i i	hill	ran
w w w w	not	fat
h h h h h	said	hill
m m m m	ran	not

~~fish~~

is ~~fish~~ was ~~fish~~ ~~fish~~ ~~fish~~ ~~fish~~ thē fat wish am ~~fish~~ ~~fish~~ fog ~~fish~~ ~~fish~~ now ~~fish~~ lāte

Worksheet **115** Side **2**

A picture that shows "he has lots of cars."

~~man~~
~~eat~~
~~tāil~~
car

~~rug~~
rat
~~gāte~~
~~rāke~~

dog
~~rag~~
~~rock~~
~~cow~~

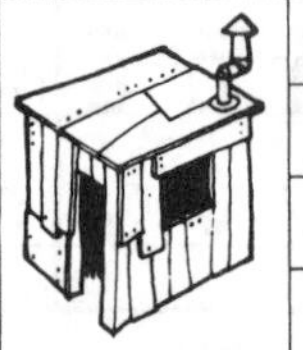

~~log~~
~~dish~~
shack
~~gōat~~

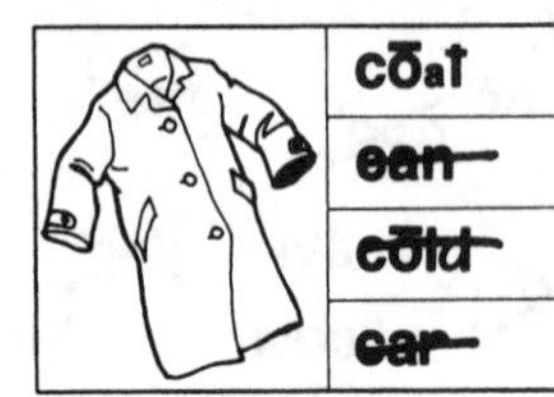

cōat
~~ean~~
~~cold~~
~~car~~

~~tāil~~
~~āte~~
māil
~~shāve~~

Name ____________________ Worksheet **116** Side **1**

thē dog said, "nō."

thē dog said, "nō."

the dog said, "no."

the dog said, "no."

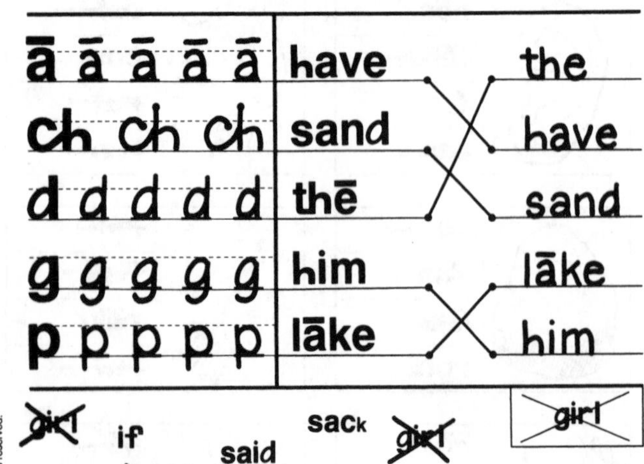

ā ā ā ā ā	have	the
ch ch ch	sand	have
d d d d d	thē	sand
g g g g g	him	lāke
p p p p p	lāke	him

~~girl~~

~~girl~~ if said sack ~~girl~~ ~~girl~~ log not ~~girl~~ sō ~~girl~~ ~~girl~~ ~~girl~~ ~~girl~~ gōat fēet ~~girl~~ sand

Worksheet **116** Side **2**

A picture that shows "the dog said, 'no.'"

~~nōse~~
~~fan~~
log
~~cow~~

fish
~~dog~~
~~dish~~
~~nut~~

~~not~~
gōat
~~gāte~~
~~gun~~

~~tāil~~
~~rock~~
lāke
~~sack~~

~~sad~~
sand
~~and~~
~~fan~~

sēat
~~fēet~~
~~shē~~
~~said~~

Name ______________________ Worksheet **117** Side **1**

a girl was in a cāve.

a girl was in a cāve.

a girl was in a cave.

a girl was in a cave.

s s s s s	rock		it
ch ch ch	mē		rock
f f f f f	dog		mē
v v v v v	it		dog
p p p p p	cow		cow

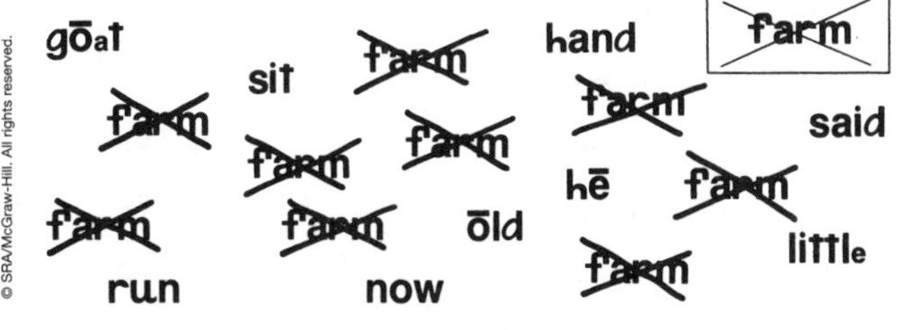

gōat sit ~~farm~~ hand ~~farm~~ ~~farm~~ ~~farm~~ ~~farm~~ ~~farm~~ said hē ~~farm~~ ~~farm~~ ~~farm~~ ōld little ~~farm~~ run now

Worksheet **117** Side **2**

A picture that shows "a girl was in a cave."

~~hē~~
~~fish~~
~~man~~
shē

~~mad~~
fat
~~sad~~
~~mēan~~

lock
~~cōat~~
~~sack~~
~~hut~~

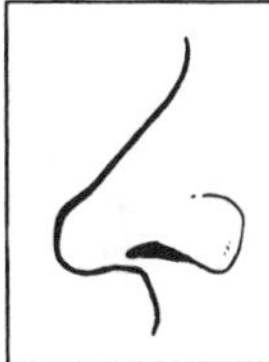

~~log~~
~~mom~~
nōse
~~feet~~

~~ran~~
rōad
~~dog~~
~~car~~

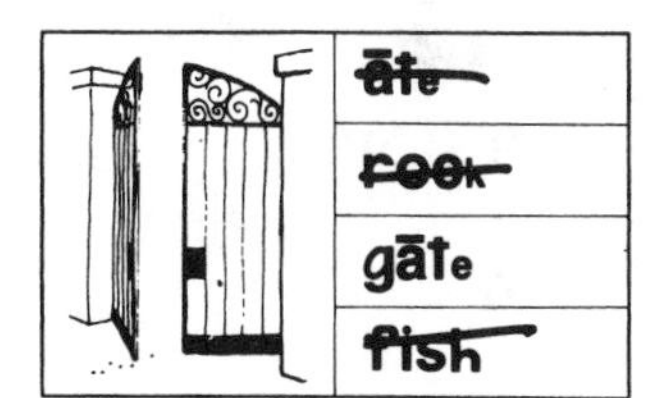

~~āte~~
~~rock~~
gāte
~~fish~~

Name ______________________ Worksheet **118** Side **1**

hē has lots of pots.

hē has lots of pots.

he has lots of pots.

he has lots of pots.

o o o o o	pot		nāme
v v v v v	nāme		tar
sh sh sh	kiss		kiss
w w w w	tar		pot
a a a a a	hut		hut

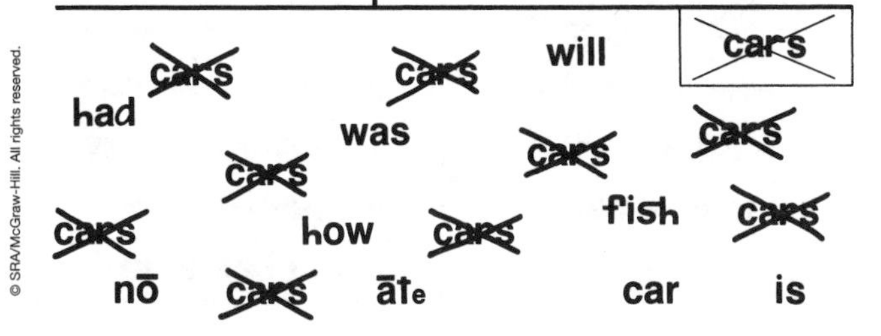

~~cars~~ ~~cars~~ will had was ~~cars~~ ~~cars~~ ~~cars~~ fish ~~cars~~ how ~~cars~~ ~~cars~~ nō ~~cars~~ āte car is

Worksheet **118** Side **2**

A picture that shows "he has lots of pots."

~~hat~~
cōat
~~rug~~
~~dog~~

cat
~~fish~~
~~cow~~
~~gōat~~

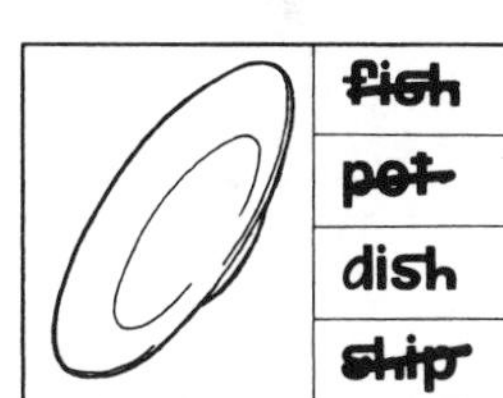

~~fish~~
~~pot~~
dish
~~ship~~

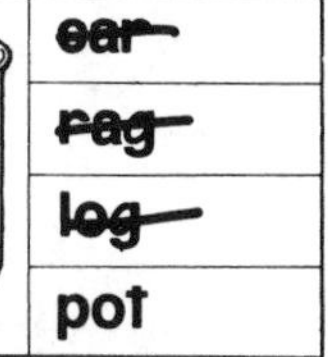

~~ear~~
~~rag~~
~~log~~
pot

~~fat~~
~~cow~~
~~car~~
farm

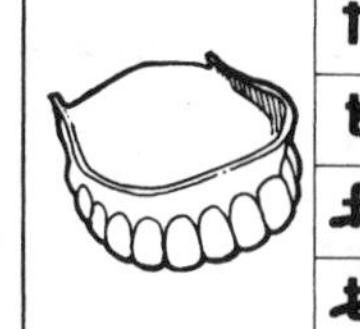

tēēth
~~this~~
~~fēēt~~
~~the~~

Name ______________________ Worksheet **119** Side **1**

Worksheet **119** Side **2**

a picture that shows "she sat in the lake."

	~~eat~~ girl ~~man~~ ~~pot~~
	rōad ~~gāte~~ ~~lāke~~ ~~dish~~
	~~nōse~~ ~~fēēt~~ tāil ~~ēars~~
	~~cop~~ ~~sand~~ ~~ear~~ sack
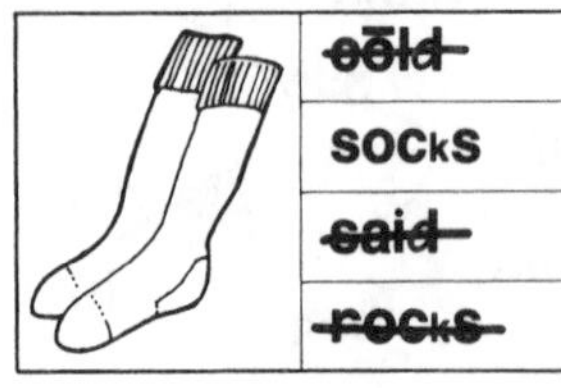	~~cōld~~ socks ~~said~~ ~~rocks~~
	rāke ~~cāke~~ ~~cat~~ ~~hōld~~

Name ______________________ Worksheet **120** Side **1**

A picture that shows this sentence

the girl got wet.
the girl got wet.
the girl got wet.

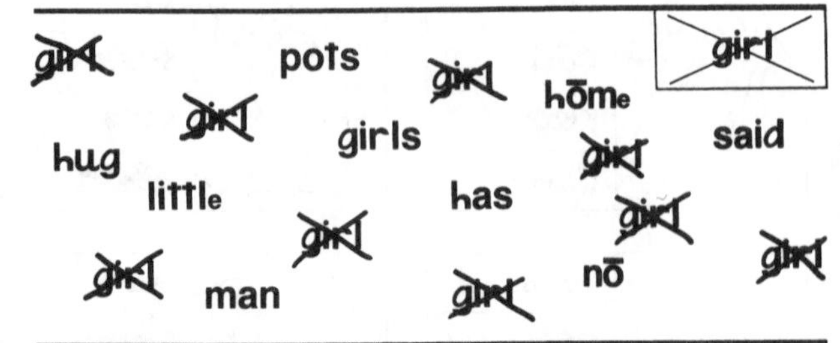

ron was in the rāin.
hē got wet.

1. ron was in the...
   • rat • rāin • sand
2. hē got...
   • fat • sick • wet

Worksheet **120** Side **2**

e e e e e e | p p p p p p
d d d d d d | w w w w w
g g g g g g | I I I I I

~~the man has a sack.~~	hē is in the sun.
hē has a mitt.	~~it is in the mud.~~
~~sam is mad.~~	~~the man is not fat.~~
~~hē māde a fuss.~~	~~hē āte a nut.~~

~~I am on the log.~~	~~a rat is on a rug.~~
~~wē will ēat fish.~~	~~hē sat on a rock.~~
hē is in a car.	~~wē have sand.~~
~~hē has a fan.~~	a girl has a gōat.

Name ____________________ Worksheet 121 Side 1

A picture that shows this sentence

the girl got a cat.
the girl got a cat.
the girl got a cat.

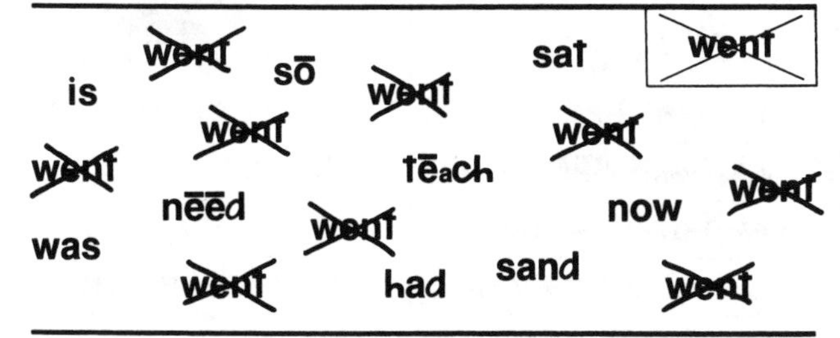

the girl went to a shop.
shē got a cat.

1. the girl went to a...
   - ship
   - car
   - shop

2. shē got a...
   - cat
   - dog
   - car

Worksheet 121 Side 2

d d d d d d | n n n n n n
e e e e e e | s s s s s s
p p p p p p | r r r r r r

~~that man is mōan.~~
a girl has a sack.
~~a man will ēat ham.~~
~~hē āte a fig.~~

the man has a cow.
~~hē is in the mud.~~
~~a girl has a fan.~~
~~a nut is on a log.~~

~~the girl can run.~~
~~hē has the māil.~~
shē has a pot.
~~wē will sit in sand.~~

sleeping cat picture

~~shē ran and ran.~~
this cat is fat.
~~wē lock the nut.~~
~~a man is in a shack.~~

Name ____________________ Worksheet 122 Side 1

A picture that shows this sentence

the cow sat in a car.
the cow sat in a car.
the cow sat in a car.

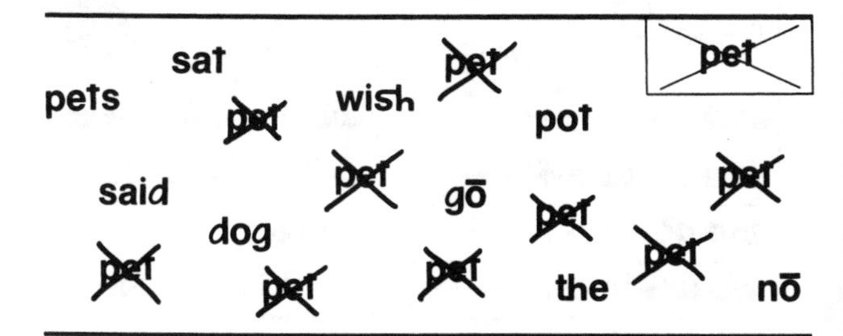

the cow was on the rōad.
the men got mad.

1. the cow was on the...
   - car
   - rōad
   - farm

2. the men got...
   - sad
   - māde
   - mad

Worksheet 122 Side 2

t t t t t t | u u u u u u
d d d d d d | I I I I I
p p p p p p | ch ch ch ch

~~a cat has fat fēēt.~~
~~hē will ēat fish.~~
shē is in the mud.
~~a gōat is on a car.~~

~~hē has a pot.~~
~~a gōat āte a sock.~~
~~wē are not sad.~~
the dog is on a log.

~~his cat is fat.~~
shē has the māil.
~~hē has a shack.~~
~~sam āte corn.~~

this man is ōld.
~~his fēēt are wet.~~
~~shē is in a car.~~
~~that dog is mad.~~

Name ______________________ Worksheet 123 Side 1

A picture that shows this sentence

it is fun to pet pigs.
it is fun to pet pigs.
it is fun to pet pigs.

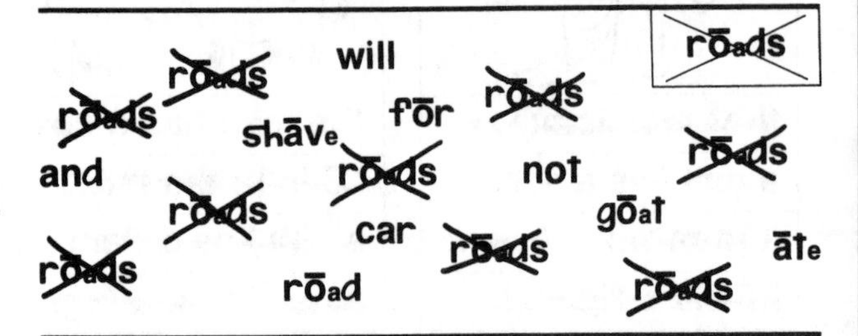

roads

the gōat went to the park.
the girl went to the farm.

1. the gōat went...
- in a car
- in the rāin
- to the park

2. the girl went to the...
- car
- farm
- park

Worksheet 123 Side 2

d d d d d d | m m m m m
w w w w w w | h h h h h h
f f f f f f | l l l l l l

- the pet has nō top.
- shē will fēēd a pig.
- shē sat in a lāke.
- the fish has a hat.

- wē are on a ship.
- shē will ēat cōrn.
- now I am cōld.
- the man has socks.

- the girl can run.
- a gōat is in mud.
- mom has a sock.
- that is his dog.

- his fēēt got hot.
- shē is on a hill.
- I will run.
- hē sat on a gāte.

Name ______________________ Worksheet 124 Side 1

A picture that shows this sentence

he had a red nose.
he had a red nose.
he had a red nose.

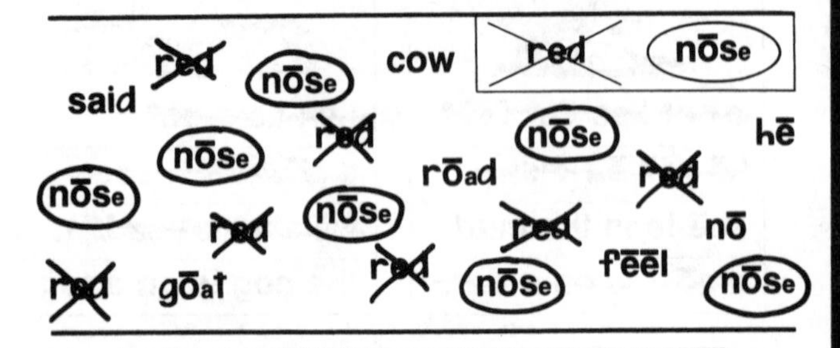

red nōse

the little dog had a red nōse.
hē was mad.

1. the little dog had a...
- big nōse
- hot nōse
- red nōse

2. hē was...
- sad
- mad
- big

Worksheet 124 Side 2

b b b b b b | t t t t t t
ā ā ā ā ā ā | c c c c c c
g g g g g g | i i i i i i

- shē can kick.
- I am not a fish.
- the gōat āte a hat.
- wē are in the rāin.

- wē can gō in a car.
- shē will kiss him.
- hē has a big fish.
- I fēēd the cat.

- his ēars are little.
- shē sat with a cat.
- mom has a rāke.
- hē will ēat cāke.

- hē sat on a log.
- the man has a cow.
- shē has nō tēēth.
- this rat is fat.

Name

Worksheet **125** Side **1**

A picture that shows this sentence

she got a red hat.

she got a red hat.

she got a red hat.

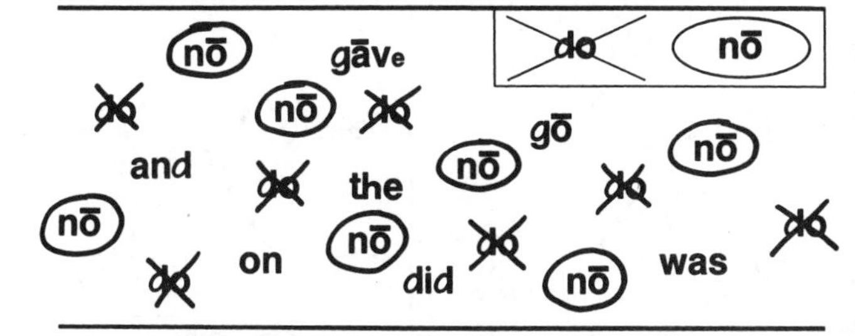

the fish got a hat.
the cow got a car.

1. the fish got...
   - (a hat) • a gōat • a fish
2. the cow got a...
   - • cat (• car) • cow

Worksheet **125** Side **2**

d d d d d d | c c c c c c

b b b b b b | ē ē ē ē ē ē

g g g g g g | r r r r r r

- ~~a cow can lick mē.~~
- the girl got wet.
- ~~hē has a hat.~~
- ~~I have cōrn.~~

- ~~wē will ēat cōrn.~~
- ~~I am not fat.~~
- ~~a man is on a rōad.~~
- shē has socks.

- hē has a gōat.
- ~~the girl is cōld.~~
- ~~shē ran in the sand.~~
- ~~that dog is mad.~~

- ~~a dog is in a car.~~
- shē sat on a log.
- ~~that is a cop.~~
- ~~I can run.~~

Name

Worksheet **126** Side **1**

A picture that shows this sentence

the bug bit the log.

the bug bit the log.

the bug bit the log.

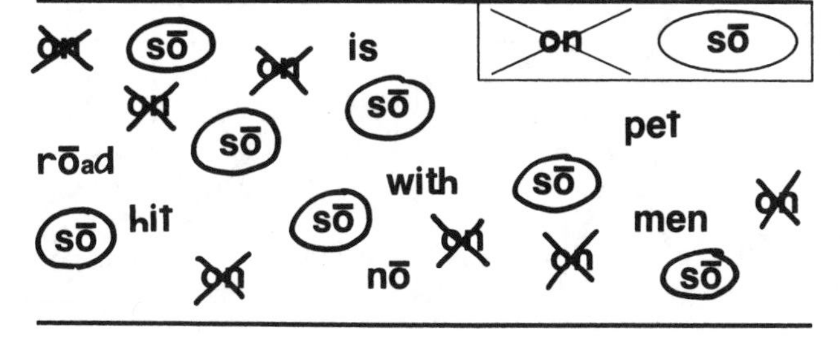

the bug got mad.
sō shē bit a log.

1. the bug...
   - • got big (• got mad) • got sad
2. sō shē bit a...
   - • dog • lock (• log)

Worksheet **126** Side **2**

sh sh sh sh | ā ā ā ā ā ā

o o o o o o | v v v v v v

b b b b b b | p p p p p p

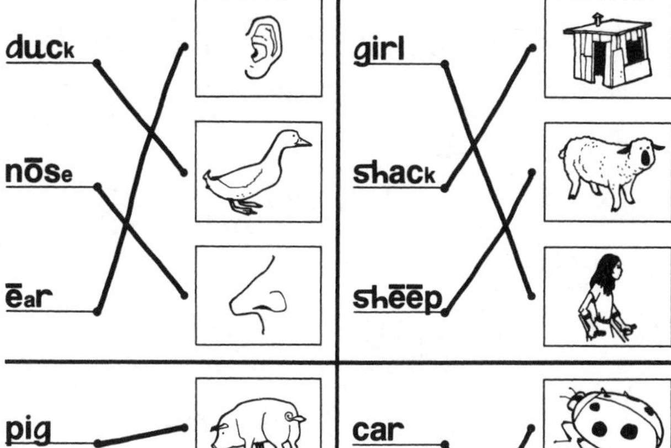

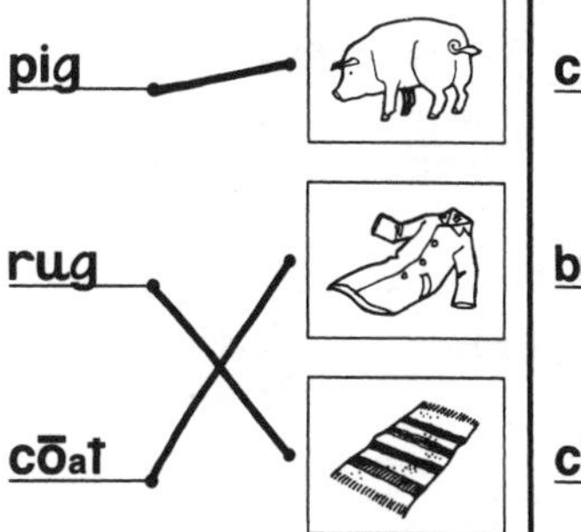

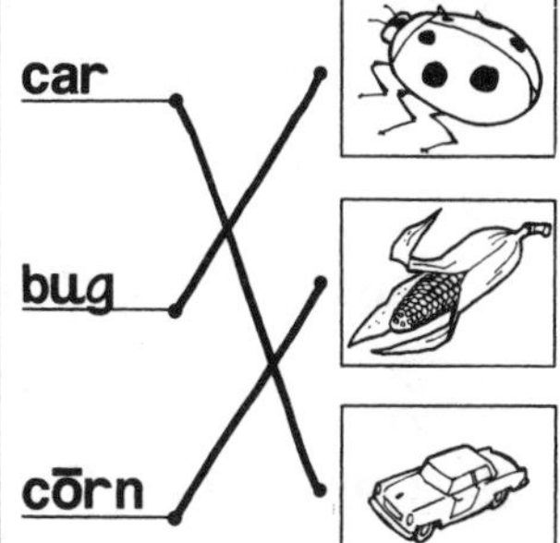

Worksheet 127 Side 1

A picture that shows this sentence

she ate the log.

she ate the log.

she ate the log.

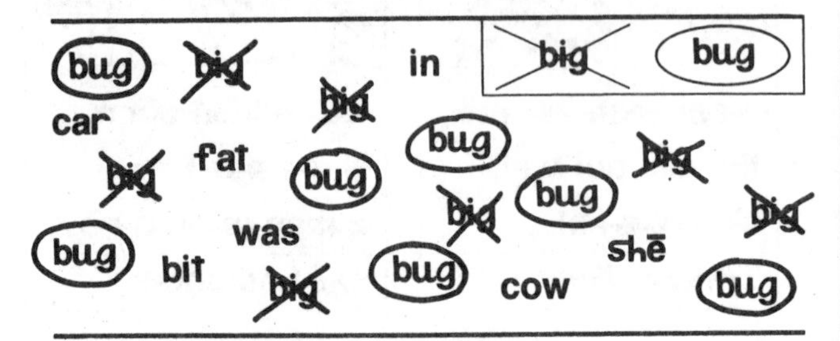

a big bug met a little bug.
hē said, "let's gō ēat."

1. a big bug met a little...
•big •dog •bug

2. hē said, "let's gō..."
•hōme •ēat •slēēp

Worksheet 127 Side 2

I I I I I ō ō ō ō ō ō
b b b b b b ch ch ch ch
k k k k k k h h h h h h

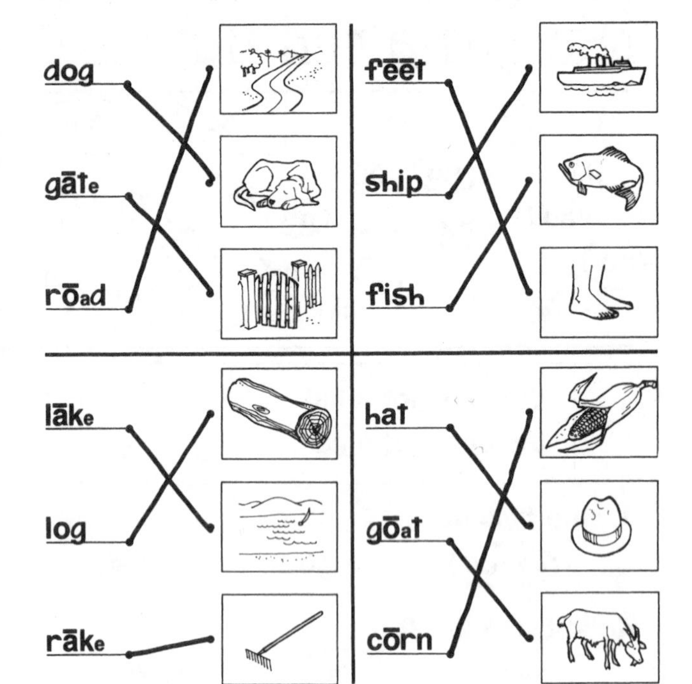

64

Worksheet 128 Side 1

Name

A picture that shows this sentence

the bug was on a dog.

the bug was on a dog.

the bug was on a dog.

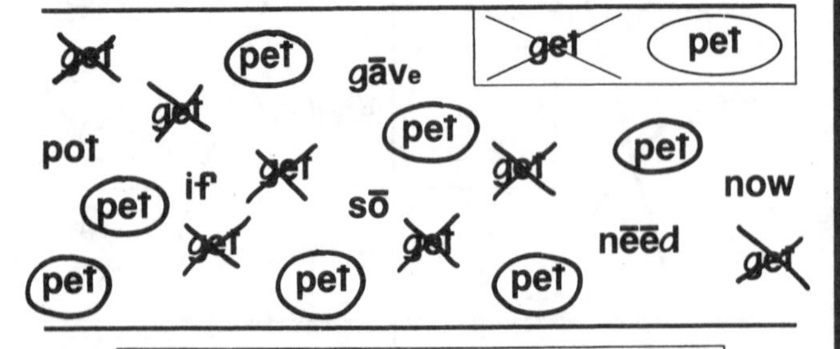

the dog said, "I am a dog.
I am not a bus."

1. the dog said, "I am a...
•log •frog •dog

2. I am not a..."
•bug •bus •bēē

Worksheet 128 Side 2

b b b b b b ē ē ē ē ē ē
e e e e e e I I I I I I
ch ch ch ch th th th th

Name ______________________ Worksheet 129 Side 1

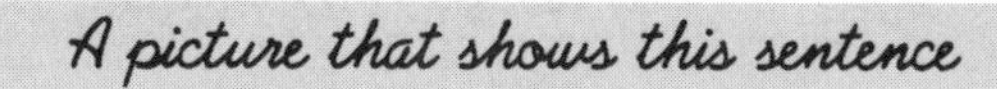

A picture that shows this sentence

a man had a tub.
a man had a tub.
a man had a tub.

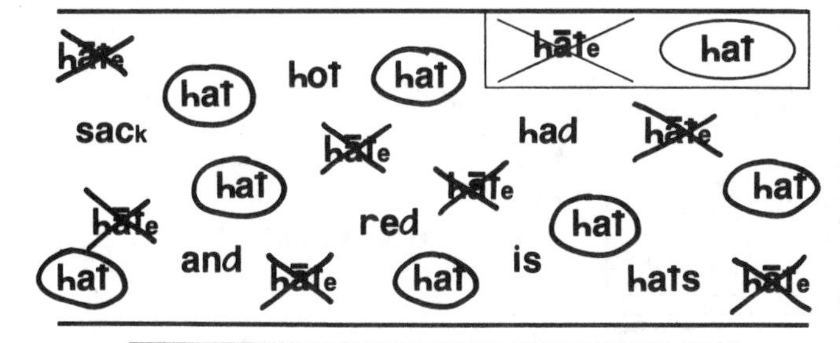

hāte hat hot hat sack hāte had hāte hat hāte hat hāte red hat hat and hāte hat is hats hāte

the man had a tub.
hē said, "I lIke to rub, rub."

1. the man had a...
   • tub • top • bug

2. hē said, "I lIke to..."
   • run, run • rēad, rēad • rub, rub

Worksheet 129 Side 2

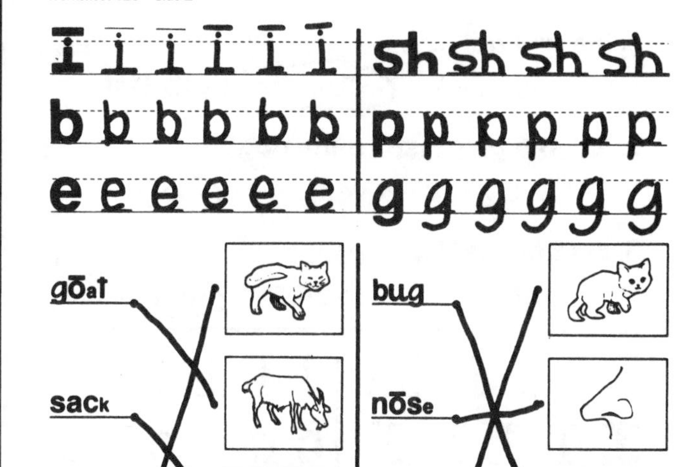

I I I I I I | sh sh sh sh
b b b b b b | p p p p p p
e e e e e e | g g g g g g

gōat, sack, cat | bug, nōse, kitten

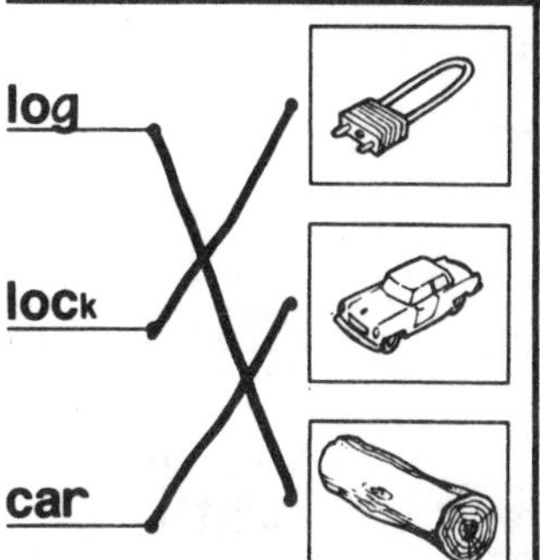

log, lock, car

hat, fish, duck

Name ______________________ Worksheet 130 Side 1

A picture that shows this sentence

she met a fat cat.
she met a fat cat.
she met a fat cat.

talk girl tāke girl talk girl talk sō talk ship talk it girl girl girl got girl talk girl with talk talk walk

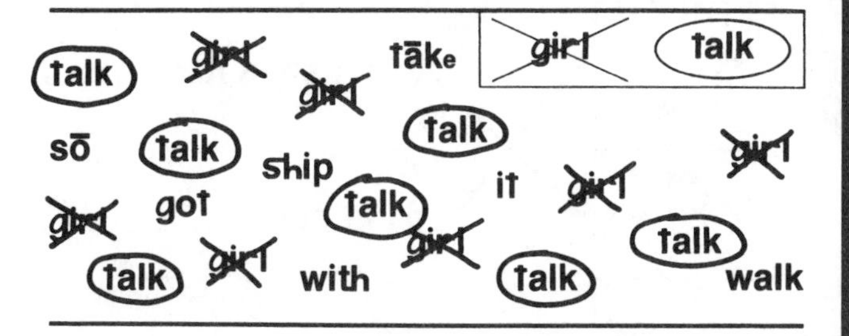

"can cats talk?" the girl said.
the cat said, "I can talk."

1. "can cats talk?" the...
   • man said • girl said • gōat said

2. the cat said, "I can..."
   • talk • run • wish

Worksheet 130 Side 2

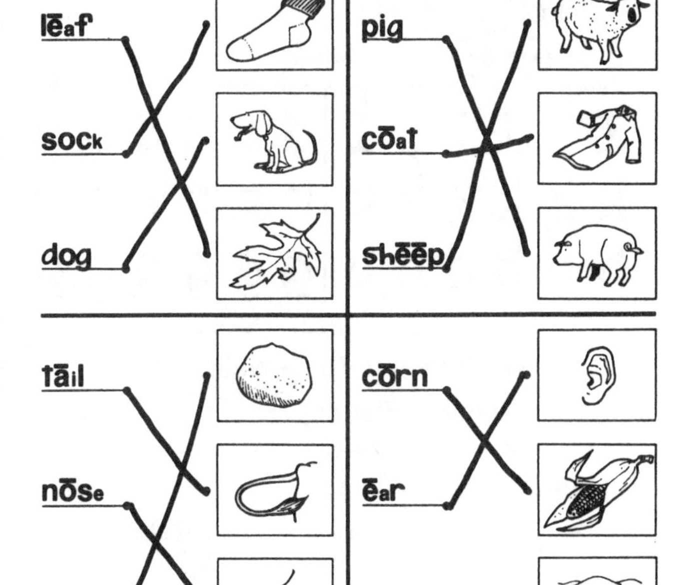

b b b b b b | r r r r r r
ch ch ch ch | I I I I I I
f f f f f f | l l l l l l

lēaf, sock, dog | pig, cōat, shēēp

tāil, nōse, rock | cōrn, ēar, lāke

Name ______________________ Worksheet 131 Side 1

1. the girl got...

- ten fish
- (fīve fish) — circled
- nō fish

2. did shē give fish to the dog?

- yes
- (nō) — circled

3. the dog went...

- hōme
- to slēēp
- (in the lāke) — circled

I I I I I I | l l l l l l
I I I I I | c c c c c c
sh sh sh sh | ā ā ā ā ā ā

a man had a car.
the car was red.

1. a man had a...

- card
- cat
- (car) — circled

2. the car was...

- big
- (red) — circled
- little

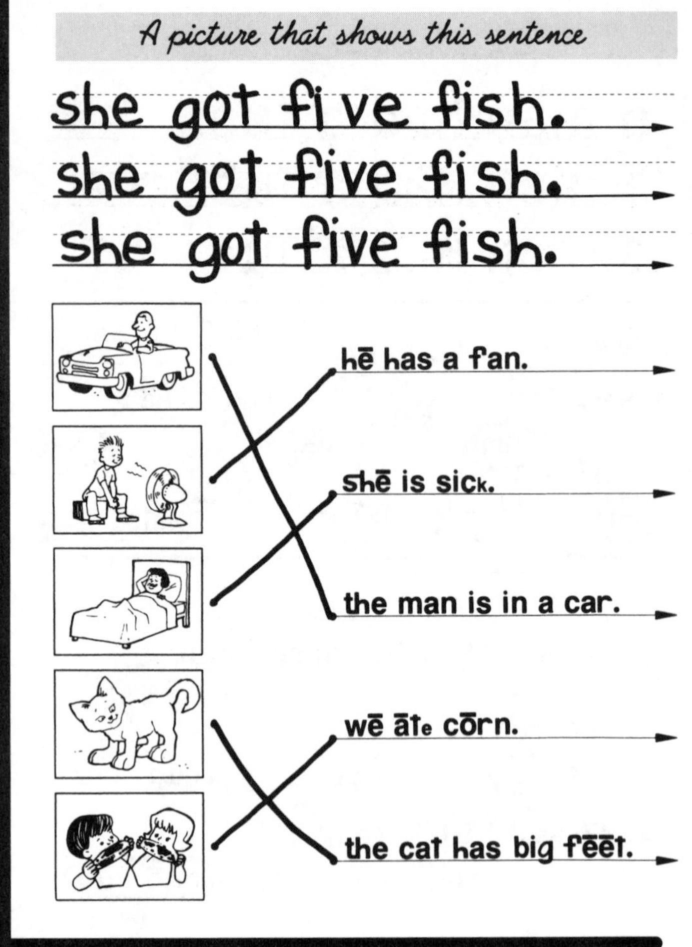

Worksheet 131 Side 2

A picture that shows this sentence

she got fi ve fish.
she got five fish.
she got five fish.

hē has a fan.

shē is sick.

the man is in a car.

wē āte cōrn.

the cat has big fēēt.

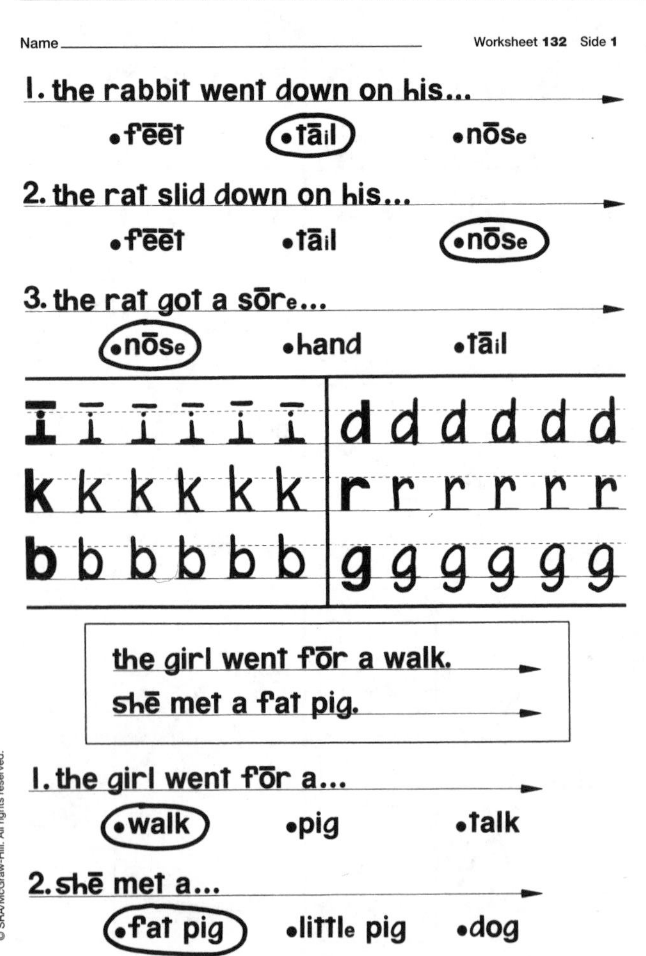

Name ______________________ Worksheet 132 Side 1

1. the rabbit went down on his...

- fēēt
- (tāil) — circled
- nōse

2. the rat slid down on his...

- fēēt
- tāil
- (nōse) — circled

3. the rat got a sōre...

- (nōse) — circled
- hand
- tāil

I I I I I I | d d d d d d
k k k k k k | r r r r r r
b b b b b b | g g g g g g

the girl went fōr a walk.
shē met a fat pig.

1. the girl went fōr a...

- (walk) — circled
- pig
- talk

2. shē met a...

- (fat pig) — circled
- little pig
- dog

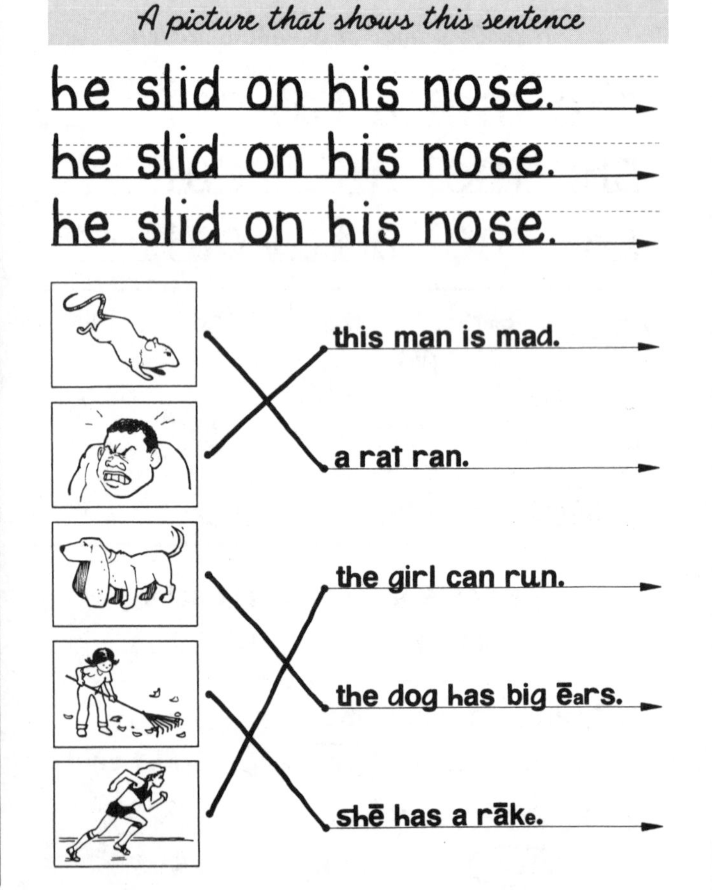

Worksheet 132 Side 2

A picture that shows this sentence

he slid on his nose.
he slid on his nose.
he slid on his nose.

this man is mad.

a rat ran.

the girl can run.

the dog has big ēars.

shē has a rāke.

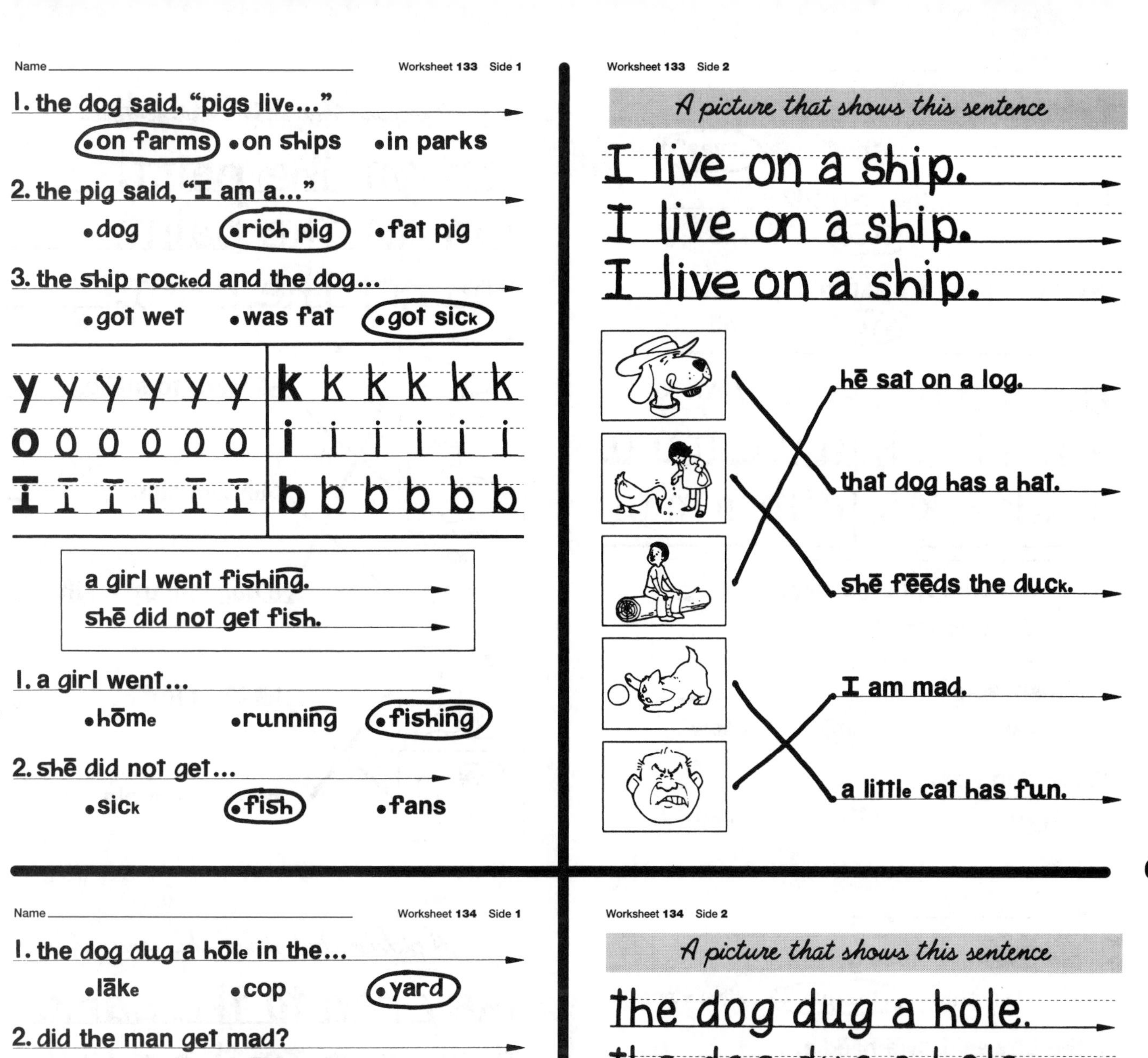

Name ____________________ Worksheet **133** Side **1**

1. the dog said, "pigs live..."
   - •on farms (circled)
   - •on ships
   - •in parks

2. the pig said, "I am a..."
   - •dog
   - •rich pig (circled)
   - •fat pig

3. the ship rocked and the dog...
   - •got wet
   - •was fat
   - •got sick (circled)

y y y y y y	k k k k k k
o o o o o o	i i i i i i
I I I I I I	b b b b b b

a girl went fishing.
shē did not get fish.

1. a girl went...
   - •hōme
   - •running
   - •fishing (circled)

2. shē did not get...
   - •sick
   - •fish (circled)
   - •fans

Worksheet **133** Side **2**

A picture that shows this sentence

I live on a ship.
I live on a ship.
I live on a ship.

hē sat on a log.

that dog has a hat.

shē fēēds the duck.

I am mad.

a little cat has fun.

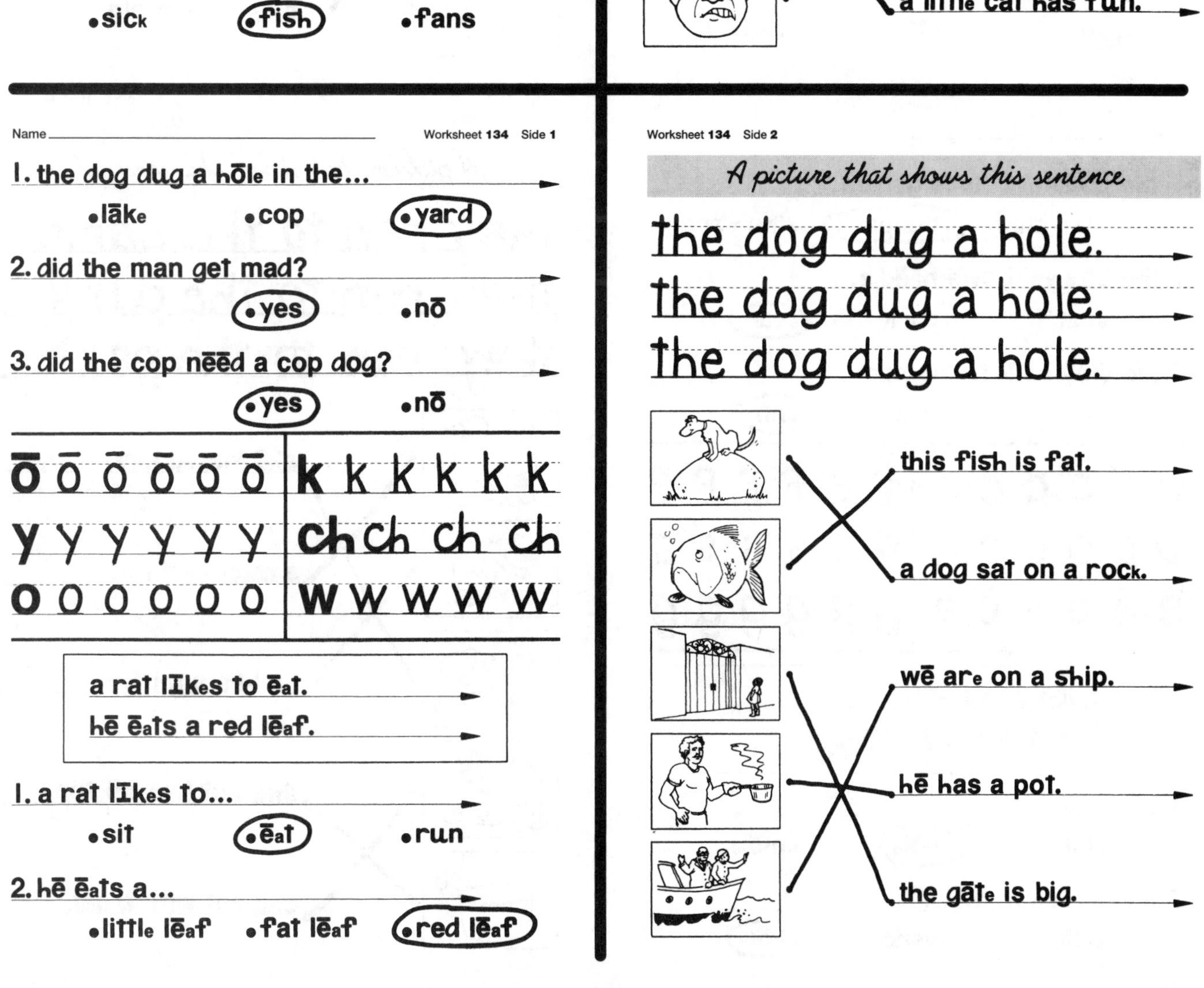

Name ____________________ Worksheet **134** Side **1**

1. the dog dug a hōle in the...
   - •lāke
   - •cop
   - •yard (circled)

2. did the man get mad?
   - •yes (circled)
   - •nō

3. did the cop nēēd a cop dog?
   - •yes (circled)
   - •nō

ō ō ō ō ō ō	k k k k k k
y y y y y y	ch ch ch ch
o o o o o o	w w w w w

a rat līkes to ēat.
hē ēats a red lēaf.

1. a rat līkes to...
   - •sit
   - •ēat (circled)
   - •run

2. hē ēats a...
   - •little lēaf
   - •fat lēaf
   - •red lēaf (circled)

Worksheet **134** Side **2**

A picture that shows this sentence

the dog dug a hole.
the dog dug a hole.
the dog dug a hole.

this fish is fat.

a dog sat on a rock.

wē are on a ship.

hē has a pot.

the gāte is big.

Name ______________________ Worksheet 135 Side 1

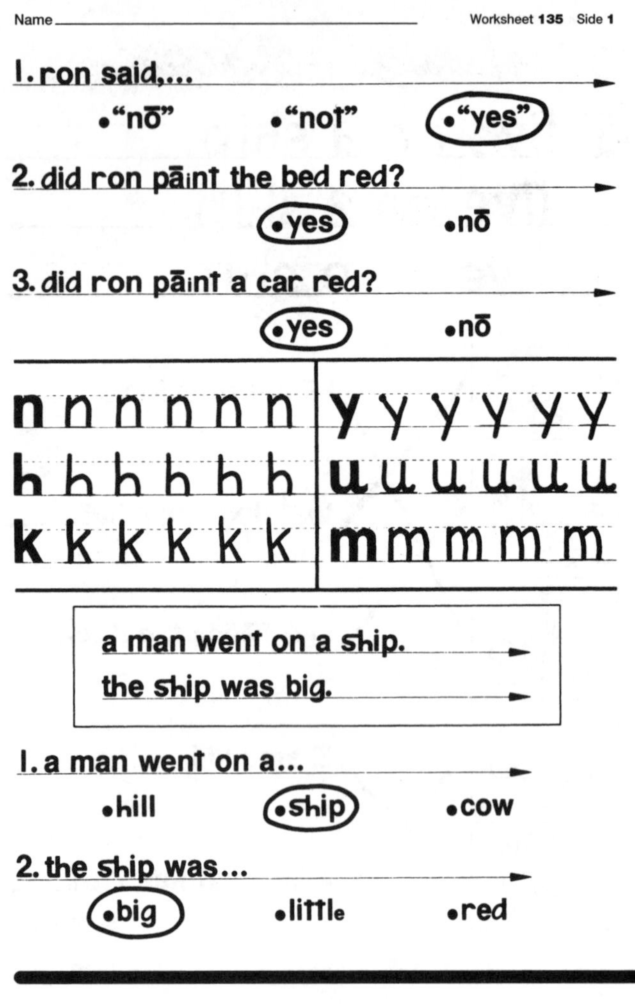

1. ron said,...

•"nō" •"not" •"yes"

2. did ron paint the bed red?

•yes •nō

3. did ron paint a car red?

•yes •nō

n n n n n n	y y y y y y
h h h h h h	u u u u u u
k k k k k k	m m m m m

a man went on a ship.
the ship was big.

1. a man went on a...

•hill •ship •cow

2. the ship was...

•big •little •red

Worksheet 135 Side 2

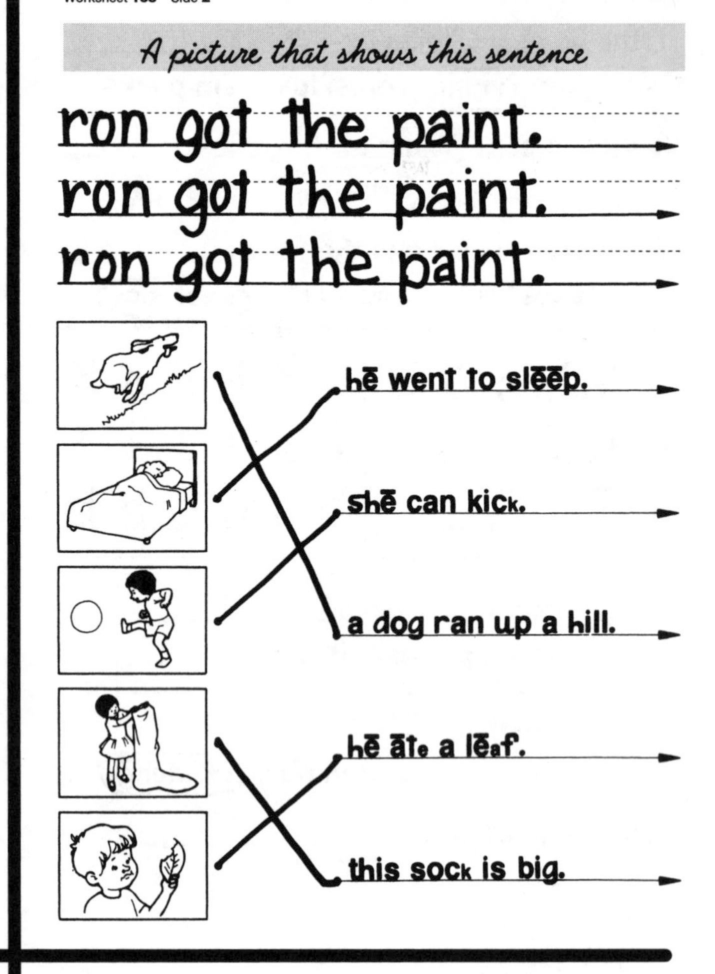

A picture that shows this sentence

ron got the paint.
ron got the paint.
ron got the paint.

hē went to slēēp.

shē can kick.

a dog ran up a hill.

hē āte a lēaf.

this sock is big.

Name ______________________ Worksheet 136 Side 1

1. the boy said, "let's gō to..."

•the ship •the park •the farm

2. the boy said, "wē nēēd a..."

•cat •park •car

3. did they ride to the park?

•yes •nō

c c c c c c	f f f f f f
o o o o o o	s s s s s s
ē ē ē ē ē ē	g g g g g g

a dog dug a hōle.
a man fell in the hōle.

1. a dog dug a...

•hill •hōle •mōle

2. a man fell in the...

•lāke •yard •hōle

Worksheet 136 Side 2

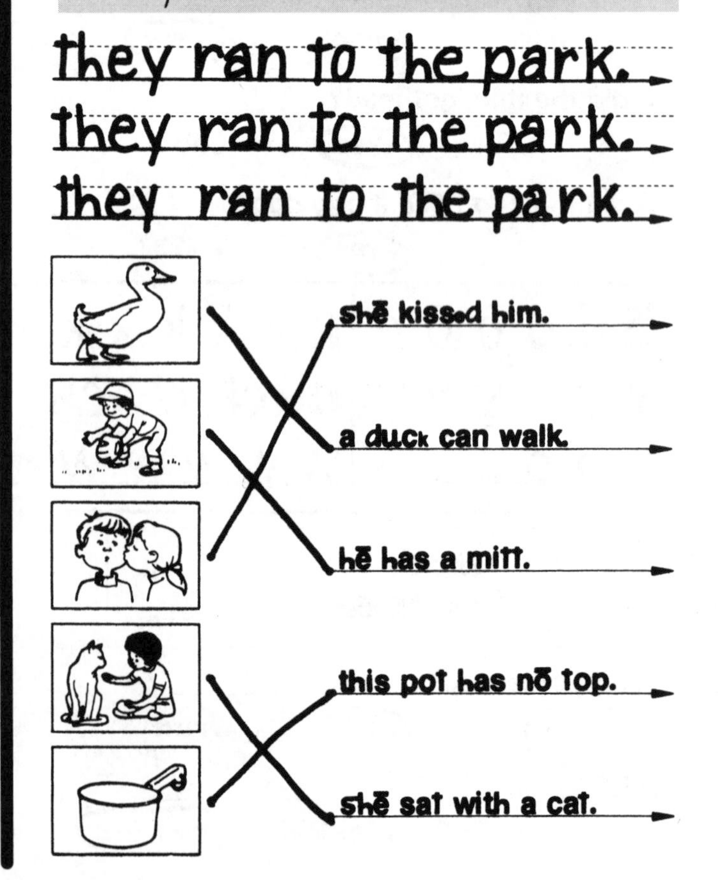

A picture that shows this sentence

they ran to the park.
they ran to the park.
they ran to the park.

shē kissed him.

a duck can walk.

hē has a mitt.

this pot has nō top.

shē sat with a cat.

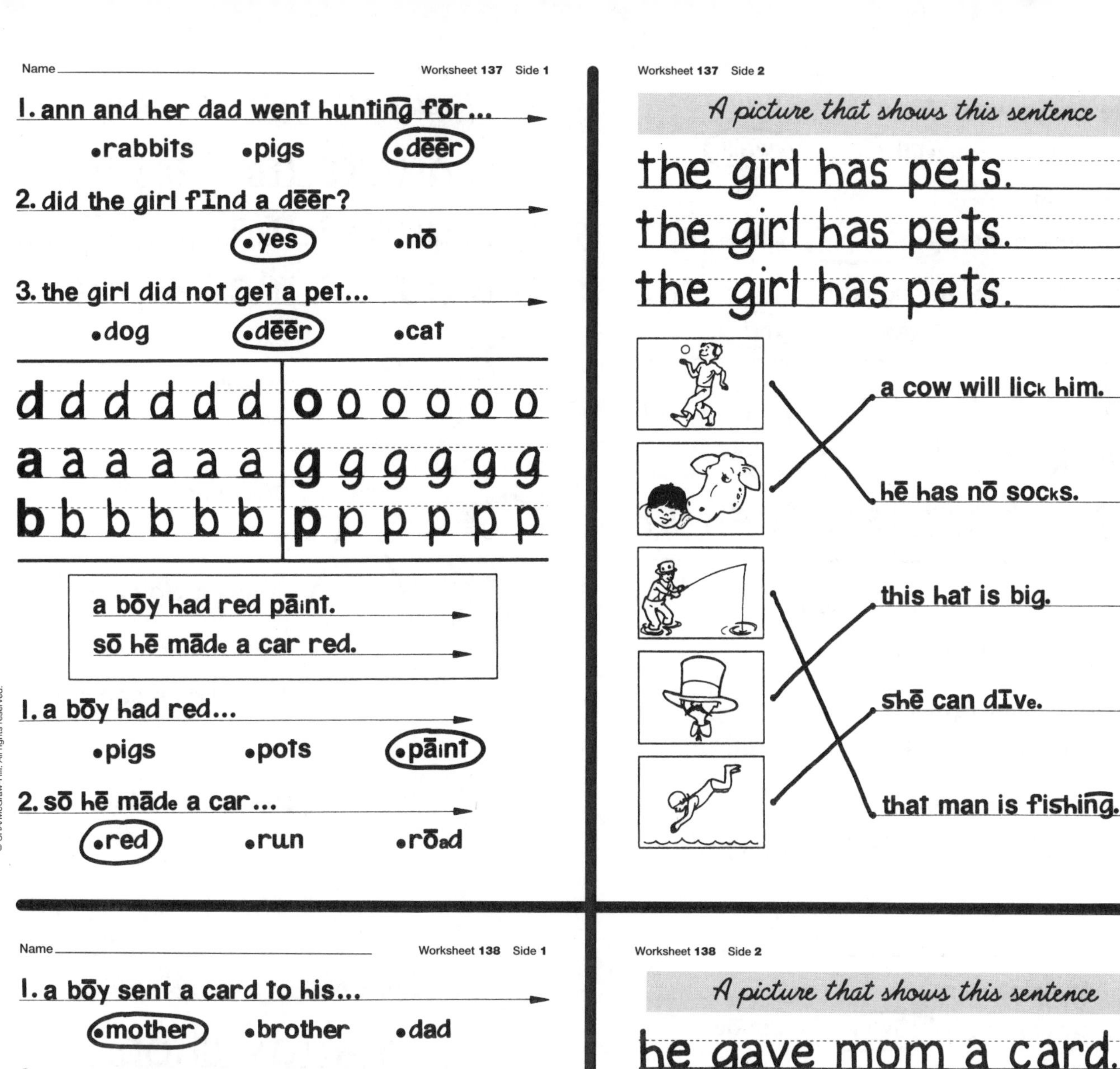

Name ____________________ Worksheet 137 Side 1

1. ann and her dad went hunting for...
- rabbits
- pigs
- (dēēr) — circled

2. did the girl fInd a dēēr?
- (yes) — circled
- nō

3. the girl did not get a pet...
- dog
- (dēēr) — circled
- cat

d d d d d d	o o o o o o
a a a a a a	g g g g g g
b b b b b b	p p p p p p

a bōy had red pāint.
sō hē māde a car red.

1. a bōy had red...
- pigs
- pots
- (pāint) — circled

2. sō hē māde a car...
- (red) — circled
- run
- rōad

Worksheet 137 Side 2

A picture that shows this sentence

the girl has pets.
the girl has pets.
the girl has pets.

a cow will lick him.
hē has nō socks.
this hat is big.
shē can dIve.
that man is fishing.

Name ____________________ Worksheet 138 Side 1

1. a bōy sent a card to his...
- (mother) — circled
- brother
- dad

2. the cop gāve the card to her...
- mother
- (brother) — circled
- dad

3. a bōy said, "give mē that..."
- man
- (card) — circled
- fish

p p p p p p	w w w w w
e e e e e e	ā ā ā ā ā ā
h h h h h h	ē ē ē ē ē ē

a girl met a bōy.
shē said, "let's dig a hōle."

1. a girl met a...
- dog
- (bōy) — circled
- pig

2. shē said, "let's..."
- sit
- run
- (dig a hōle) — circled

Worksheet 138 Side 2

A picture that shows this sentence

he gave mom a card.
he gave mom a card.
he gave mom a card.

this bug is little.
shē fēēds the pig.
the gōat āte a can.
that cop was mad.
hē has a duck.

Printed in the United States of America

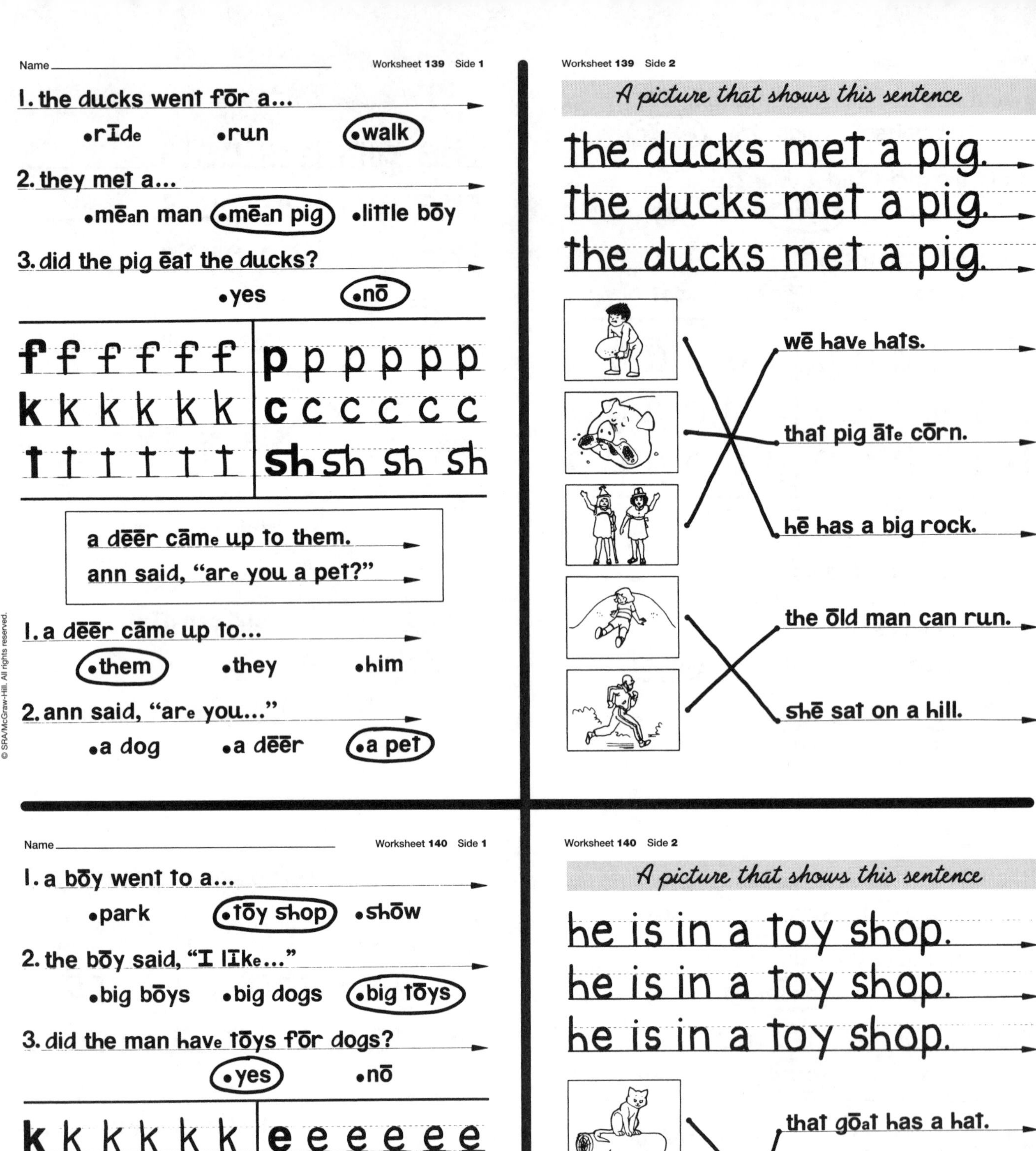

Name ________________ Worksheet **139** Side **1**

1. the ducks went fōr a...
   - rīde
   - run
   - **walk** (circled)
2. they met a...
   - mēan man
   - **mēan pig** (circled)
   - little bōy
3. did the pig ēat the ducks?
   - yes
   - **nō** (circled)

f f f f f f | p p p p p p
k k k k k k | c c c c c c
t t t t t t | sh sh sh sh

a dēēr cāme up to them.
ann said, "are you a pet?"

1. a dēēr cāme up to...
   - **them** (circled)
   - they
   - him
2. ann said, "are you..."
   - a dog
   - a dēēr
   - **a pet** (circled)

Worksheet **139** Side **2**

A picture that shows this sentence

the ducks met a pig.
the ducks met a pig.
the ducks met a pig.

wē have hats.
that pig āte cōrn.
hē has a big rock.
the ōld man can run.
shē sat on a hill.

Name ________________ Worksheet **140** Side **1**

1. a bōy went to a...
   - park
   - **tōy shop** (circled)
   - shōw
2. the bōy said, "I līke..."
   - big bōys
   - big dogs
   - **big tōys** (circled)
3. did the man have tōys fōr dogs?
   - **yes** (circled)
   - nō

k k k k k k | e e e e e e
b b b b b b | u u u u u u
p p p p p p | l l l l l l

his mother got a card.
it said, "I love you."

1. his mother got a...
   - car
   - farm
   - **card** (circled)
2. it said, "I..."
   - hēar you
   - **love you** (circled)
   - sēē you

Worksheet **140** Side **2**

A picture that shows this sentence

he is in a toy shop.
he is in a toy shop.
he is in a toy shop.

that gōat has a hat.
a cat was on a log.
her mom has socks.
this pig is fat.
shē fēēds the shēēp.

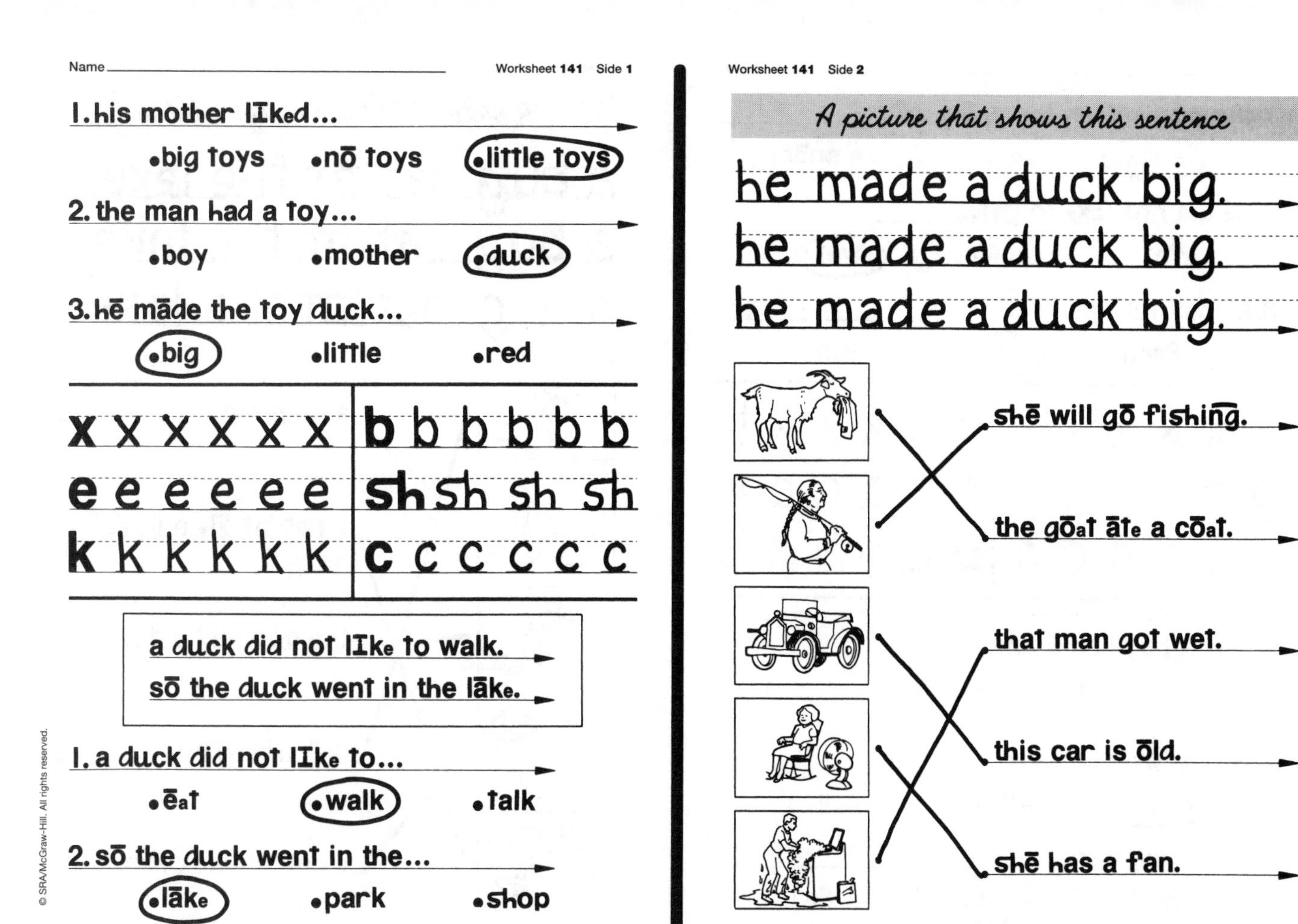
Name
Worksheet 141 Side 1
1. his mother lIked...
•big toys •nō toys •little toys
2. the man had a toy...
•boy •mother •duck
3. hē māde the toy duck...
•big •little •red
x x x x x x b b b b b b
e e e e e e sh sh sh sh
k k k k k k c c c c c c
a duck did not lIke to walk.
sō the duck went in the lāke.
1. a duck did not lIke to...
•ēat •walk •talk
2. sō the duck went in the...
•lāke •park •shop
Worksheet 141 Side 2
A picture that shows this sentence
he made a duck big.
he made a duck big.
he made a duck big.
shē will gō fishing.
the gōat āte a cōat.
that man got wet.
this car is ōld.
shē has a fan.

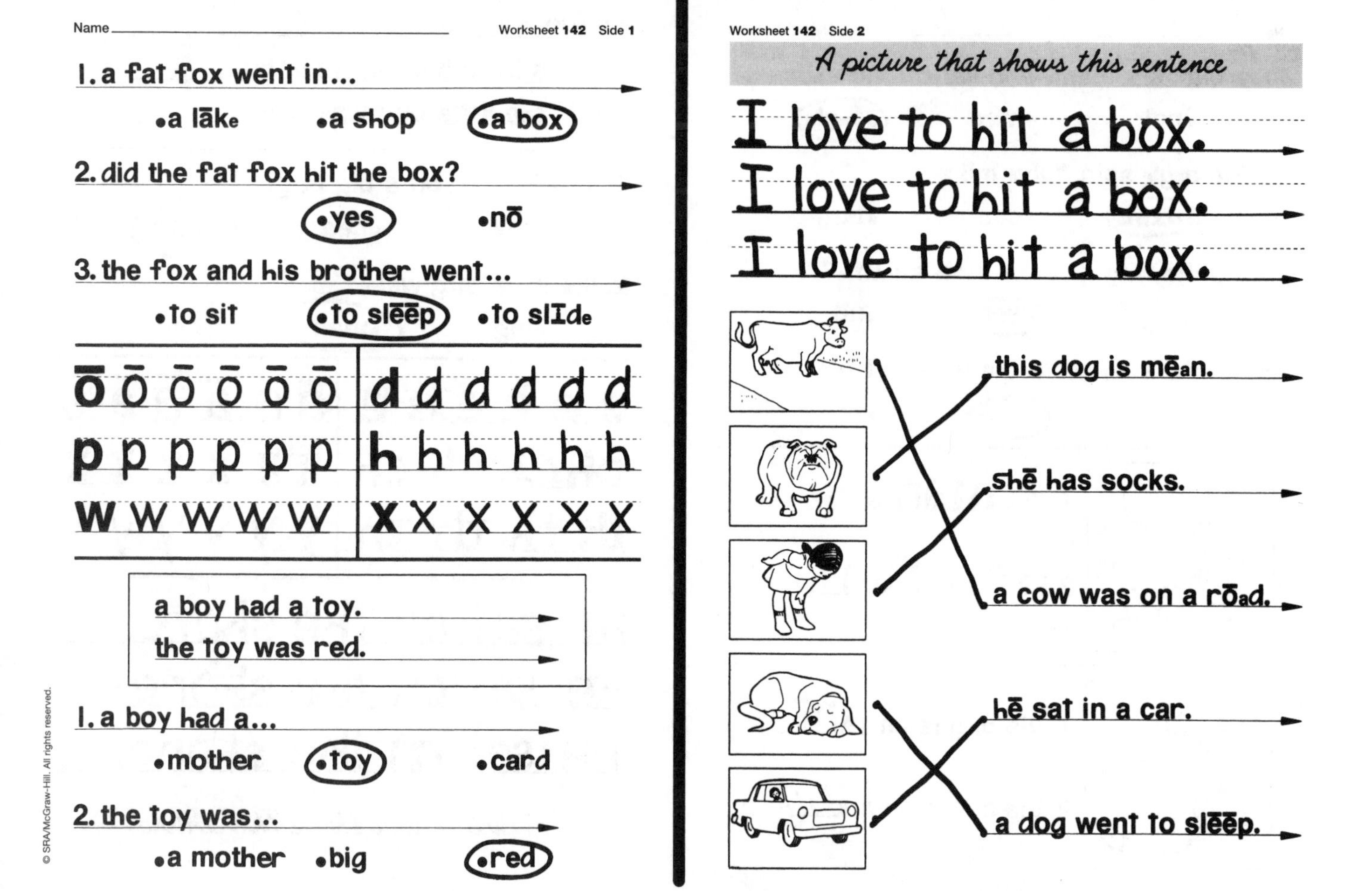
Name
Worksheet 142 Side 1
1. a fat fox went in...
•a lāke •a shop •a box
2. did the fat fox hit the box?
•yes •nō
3. the fox and his brother went...
•to sit •to slēēp •to slIde
ō ō ō ō ō ō d d d d d d
p p p p p p h h h h h h
w w w w w w x x x x x x
a boy had a toy.
the toy was red.
1. a boy had a...
•mother •toy •card
2. the toy was...
•a mother •big •red
Worksheet 142 Side 2
A picture that shows this sentence
I love to hit a box.
I love to hit a box.
I love to hit a box.
this dog is mēan.
shē has socks.
a cow was on a rōad.
hē sat in a car.
a dog went to slēēp.

Name ____________________ Worksheet **143** Side **1**

1. the bug sat on the shōre of...

(•a lāke) •a cāke •a snāke

2. hē did not līke to get...

•fat •shōre (•wet)

3. hē did not have a...

•farm (•car) •hōme

x x x x x x	k k k k k k
p p p p p p	c c c c c c
o o o o o o	b b b b b b

a boy had a box.
a fox went in the box.

1. a boy had a...

(•box) •fox •car

2. a fox went in...

•a hōle (•the box) •a fox

Worksheet **143** Side **2**

A picture that shows this sentence

a bug sat at the lake.
a bug sat at the lake.
a bug sat at the lake.

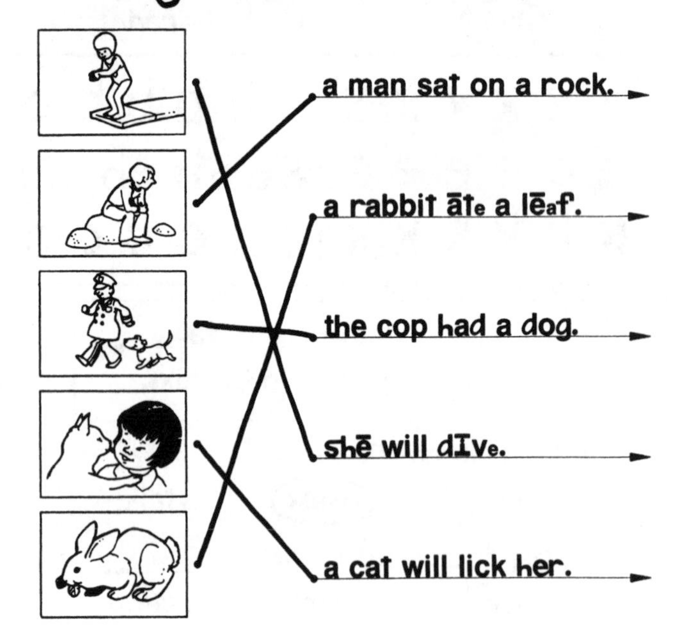

Name ____________________ Worksheet **144** Side **1**

1. a big ____ cāme and sat on the shōre.

•rat •man (•ēagle)

2. the eagle said, "give mē a ____."

(•dīme) •can •bug

3. did the bug give the eagle a dīme?

(•yes) •nō

4. did the bug gō to the other sīde?

(•yes) •nō

1. the man is fat.
2. hē has a fan.

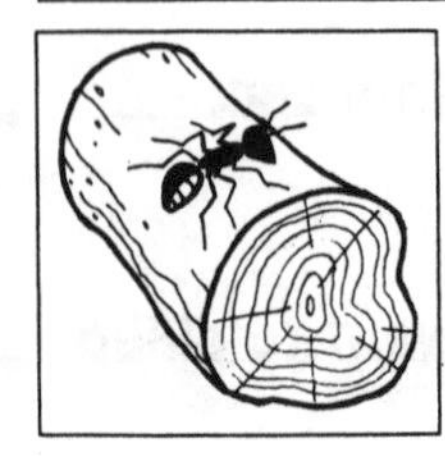

1. the bug is an ant.
2. the ant is on a log.

Worksheet **144** Side **2**

a little bug bit a big bug.
the little bug was mad.

1. a little ____ bit a big bug.

•man •bag (•bug)

2. the little bug was ____.

•big (•mad) •red

e e e e e e	ā ā ā ā ā ā
ch ch ch ch ch	x x x x x x
th th th th th	y y y y y y

hē sat on the shōre.
he sat on the shore.
he sat on the shore.

A picture that shows this sentence

Name ______________________ Worksheet **145** Side **1**

1. a bug and a ___ met on a rōad.
   - **(pig)** • man • gōat
2. the bug bit a ___.
   - • dog **(log)** • bug
3. the pig bit ___.
   - **(his leg)** • the bug • a man
4. did the pig bīte better?
   - **(yes)** • nō

1. she has a cat.
2. they are on a rug.

1. the man is at the lāke.
2. hē has a fish.

Worksheet **145** Side **2**

hē līked to ēat.
sō hē āte bēans and cāke.

1. hē ___ to ēat.
   - • hātes **(līked)** • did not līke
2. sō hē āte bēans and ___.
   - • cōrn • fish **(cāke)**

t t t t t t | o o o o o o
i i i i i i | I I I I I I
e e e e e e | n n n n n n

"I bīte," a bug said.
"I bite," a bug said.
"I bite," a bug said.

A picture that shows this sentence

Name ______________________ Worksheet **146** Side **1**

1. a girl went to the shop with her ___.
   - • car **(cat)** • dog
2. then they went to the ___.
   - • lāke **(park)** • car
3. shē said, "you can not ___ to mē."
   - **(talk)** • walk • sit
4. did the cat talk?
   - **(yes)** • nō

1. the cat is sitting.
2. hē is on the bed.

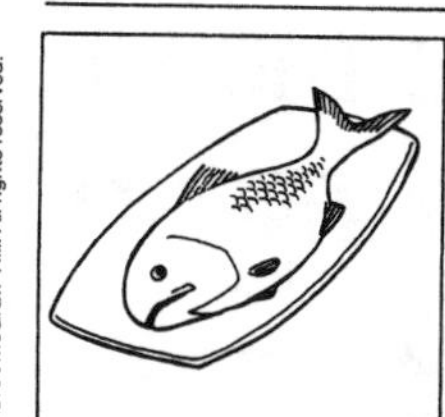

1. the fish is not wet.
2. it is in the dish.

Worksheet **146** Side **2**

shē had a dog.
the dog did not talk.

1. shē had a ___.
   - • log • bug **(dog)**
2. the ___ did not talk.
   - • fox **(dog)** • bug

J J J J J J | d d d d d d
e e e e e e | y y y y y y
t t t t t t | x x x x x x

I can talk to you.
I can talk to you.
I can talk to you.

A picture that shows this sentence

Name ____________________ Worksheet 147 Side 1

1. the girl said, "cats can not ____."

(•talk) •walk •slēēp

2. ann said, "can I have that ____?"

•can (•cat) •bug

3. the ____ said, "I will not gō with you."

•girl •ann (•cat)

4. ann said, "I will lēave this ____."

(•park) •dark •stōre

1. the man is a cop.

2. hē has a cat.

1. she has a dog.

2. they are on a log.

Worksheet 147 Side 2

the man lIked to swim.
sō hē jumped into the lāke.

1. the ____ lIked to swim.

•boy (•man) •cow

2. sō hē ____ into the lāke.

•ran (•jumped) •fell

e e e e e e | n n n n n n
r r r r r r | t t t t t t
j j j j j j | f f f f f f

cats do not talk.
cats do not talk.
cats do not talk.

A picture that shows this sentence

Name ____________________ Worksheet 148 Side 1

1. some girls went to the ____.

•shōre (•moon) •shop

2. a girl said, "I will fInd some ____."

(•fun) •sun •nuts

3. the moon cow said, "come with ____."

•you •him (•mē)

4. the ____ jumped into the pool.

•man •boy (•cow)

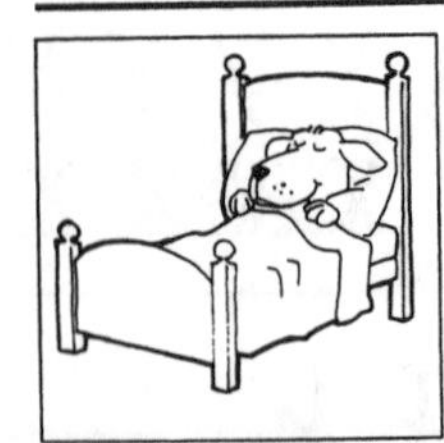

1. that dog is slēēping.

2. hē is in bed.

1. a toy is in her hand.

2. it is a toy ship.

Worksheet 148 Side 2

the man had a pet cow.
hē talked to the cow.

1. the man had a pet ____.

•cat •car (•cow)

2. hē ____ to the cow.

•ran (•talked) •walked

d d d d d d | b b b b b b
p p p p p p | j j j j j j
y y y y y y | a a a a a a

she went to the moon.
she went to the moon.
she went to the moon.

A picture that shows this sentence

Name ____________________ Worksheet **149** Side **1**

1. the ōld car did not ____ .
   - start (circled) • stop • shop
2. do rats have cars?
   - yes 
3. did the big man start the car?
   - yes (circled) • nō
4. the big man will kēēp sitting in ____ .
   - the bus • the cāve 

1. a cat is on a pig.
2. they are on a bus.

1. a man is on the moon.
2. hē has a moon ship.

Worksheet **149** Side **2**

a girl went rīding in a car.
shē went to a farm.

1. a girl went ____ in a car.
   - rīding (circled) • talking • walking
2. shē went to a ____ .
   - farm (circled) • park • shop

e e e e e e | p p p p p p
m m m m m | u u u u u u
g g g g g g | h h h h h h

the car did not start.
the car did not start.
the car did not start.

A picture that shows this sentence

Name ____________________ Worksheet **150** Side **1**

1. an ōld ____ was in the barn.
   - dog • car 
2. a ____ said, "have you sēēn a hōrse?"
   - man (circled) • car • cat
3. did the ōld man fīnd a hōrse?
   - yes (circled) • nō
4. did the ōld hōrse līke to gō fōr a rīde?
   - yes (circled) • nō

1. the man is fat.
2. his car is ōld.

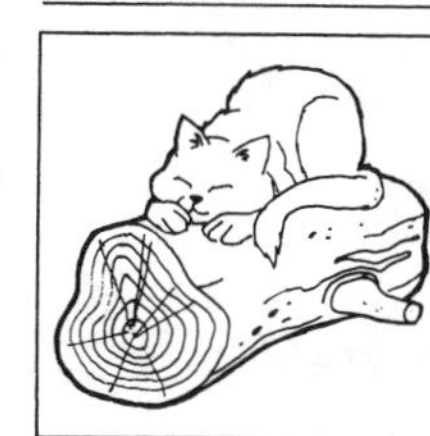

1. a cat is slēēping.
2. shē is on a log.

Worksheet **150** Side **2**

a girl had a hōrse.
shē went rīding on a hōrse.

1. a ____ had a hōrse.
   - man • gōat 
2. shē went rīding on a ____ .
   - hat • hōrse (circled) • gōat

u u u u u u | p p p p p p
J J J J J J | o o o o o o
y y y y y y | e e e e e e

they went riding.
they went riding.
they went riding.

A picture that shows this sentence

Name ______________________________ Worksheet **151** Side **1**

1. bill lIked to gō ____.

•rIding (•fishing) •hunting

2. bill did not get ____.

(•fish) •fat •mad

3. bill had a ____ on his lIne.

•bug •rug (•tug)

4. bill had an ōld ____.

•boy •fish (•box)

1. this dog is mad.

2. a bug bit his leg.

1. shē is hot.

2. shē has a fan.

Worksheet **151** Side **2**

a girl went fishing.
shē got fIve fish.

1. a girl went ____.

•walking (•fishing) •running

2. shē got ____ fish.

(•fIve) •nIne •nō

ȳ ȳ ȳ ȳ ȳ ȳ | s s s s s s
p p p p p p | b b b b b b
r r r r r r | c c c c c c

bill did not get fish.
bill did not get fish.
bill did not get fish.

A picture that shows this sentence

Name ______________________________ Worksheet **152** Side **1**

1. did bill get fish?

•yes (•nō)

2. the boys said, "you have an ōld ____."

•car (•box) •fox

3. bill said, "that box is filled with ____."

•fish •boys (•gōld)

4. bill was ____.

(•not sad) •a bug •gōld

1. the cop is on a hōrse.

2. the hōrse has a hat.

1. shē got a fish.

2. hē got a can.

Worksheet **152** Side **2**

a man went in a sāil bōat.
hē had a lot of fun.

1. a man went in a ____.

(•sāil bōat) •little bōat •sāil gōat

2. hē had a lot ____.

•of bōats (•of fun) •of cows

Ī Ī Ī Ī Ī Ī | a a a a a a
o o o o o o | u u u u u u
i i i i i i | e e e e e e

"it is gold," he said.
"it is gold," he said.
"it is gold," he said.

A picture that shows this sentence

Name

Worksheet 153 Side 1

1. the ēagle said, "I līke to ____."
run •fly •fish

2. the hōrse said, "can you ____ mē to fly?"
•love •wish •tēach

3. did the hōrse fly to the top of a barn?
•yes •nō

4. hē ran into the ____ of the barn.
•sīde •top •back

1. the man has a bug.

2. the bug is on his hat.

1. that cat is slēēping.

2. shē is on a rug.

Worksheet 153 Side 2

an ēagle līked to fly.
hē did not sit in a trēē.

1. an ēagle līked ____.
•to ēat •to sit •to fly

2. hē did not sit in ____.
•a trēē •a park •a bed

b b b b b b | v v v v v v
k k k k k k | f f f f f f
j j j j j j | i i i i i i

an ēagle līkes to fly.
an eagle likes to fly.
an eagle likes to fly.

A picture that shows this sentence

Name

Worksheet 154 Side 1

1. did the hōrse fly to the top of a car?
•yes •nō

2. the hōrse ran into the ____ of the car.
•top •sīde •back

3. the hōrse ran with the ēagle on his ____.
•top •sīde •back

4. did they have fun?
•yes •nō

1. this dog is in a car.

2. a cat is on the car.

1. this pig has fun.

2. hē is in the mud.

Worksheet 154 Side 2

an ōld car did not run.
the girl got mad at the car.

1. an ōld ____ did not run.
•cat •car •cow

2. the girl got ____ at the car.
•bad •sad •mad

p p p p p p | h h h h h h
x x x x x x | k k k k k k
ȳ y y ȳ ȳ ȳ | j j j j j j

the hōrse ran.
the horse ran.
the horse ran.

A picture that shows this sentence

Name ________________ Worksheet 155 Side 1

1. shē brushed her tēēth ____ tīmes a dāy.
•nīne •six •nō

2. shē had a ____ tooth brush.
•toy •red •gōld

3. did her tēēth shīne līke the moon?
•yes •nō

4. did her mother have the tooth brush?
•yes •nō

1. the gōat is on a log.

2. hē has a hat.

1. this man is a cop.

2. hē is fat.

Worksheet 155 Side 2

bill had a brush.
it was not a tooth brush.

1. bill had a ____.
•brush •car •bat

2. was it a tooth brush?
•yes •nō

qu qu qu d d d d d d
c c c c c c f f f f f f
b b b b b b g g g g g g

I need a tooth brush.
I need a tooth brush.
I need a tooth brush.

A picture that shows this sentence

Name ________________ Worksheet 156 Side 1

1. the girl slipped on her ____.
•rug •fēēt •dog

2. the dog was brushing his ____.
•tēēth •nōse •fēēt

3. the dog had the red ____ brush.
•hand •tooth •nāil

4. did the dog's tēēth shīne now?
•yes •nō

1. that bug is an ant.

2. it is on a can.

1. shē has a dog.

2. they are on the rug.

Worksheet 156 Side 2

bill went to the park.
hē went in the big pool.

1. bill went to the ____.
•pond •farm •park

2. hē went in the ____ pool.
•bad •big •little

qu qu qu ō ō ō ō ō ō
x x x x x x ā ā ā ā ā ā
k k k k k k ȳ ȳ ȳ ȳ ȳ ȳ

the girl smīled.
the girl smīled.
the girl smīled.

A picture that shows this sentence

Name ____________

Worksheet 157 Side 1

1. an ēagle āte cāke and ham and ____.

- nuts
- (corn) ← circled
- bēans

2. hē got ____.

- (fatter) ← circled
- better
- sadder

3. a little eagle sat ____ a trēē.

- on
- (under) ← circled
- at

4. then a ____ cāme hunting fōr ēagles.

- man
- boy
- (tīger) ← circled

1. this cat is slēēping.
2. shē is in bed.

1. the man is sitting.
2. hē is on a fish.

Worksheet 157 Side 2

a girl līked to talk.
shē talked to the māil man.

1. a girl līked ____.

- to walk
- to sit
- (to talk) ← circled

2. shē talked to the ____.

- (māil man) ← circled
- sad man
- moon man

j j j j j j | y y y y y y
z z z z z z | e e e e e e
k k k k k k | r r r r r r

a fat ēagle sat.
a fat eagle sat.
a fat eagle sat.

A picture that shows this sentence

Name ____________

Worksheet 158 Side 1

1. the fat ēagle cāme down on the ____.

- ēagle
- (tīger) ← circled
- hōrse

2. the ____ ran far away.

- ēagle
- (tīger) ← circled
- boy

3. do the ēagles māke fun of the fat ēagle?

- yes
- (nō) ← circled

4. they give him ____ and ham and cōrn.

- cans
- nuts
- (cāke) ← circled

1. this dog runs.
2. shē has a hat.

1. the man is a cop.
2. his car is ōld.

Worksheet 158 Side 2

a tīger sat under a trēē.
hē was looking fōr rabbits.

1. a tīger sat ____ a trēē.

- in
- nēar
- (under) ← circled

2. hē was looking fōr ____.

- girls
- (rabbits) ← circled
- pigs

z z z z z z | n n n n n n
f f f f f f | e e e e e e
u u u u u u | r r r r r r

they gāve him cake.
they gave him cake.
they gave him cake.

A picture that shows this sentence

Name

Worksheet 159 Side 1

1. a man lIked to ___ .

•slēēp •fish •gō fast

2. did hē talk fast?

•yes •nō

3. the egg slipped and fell on his ___ .

•head •fēēt •nōse

4. the mēat pIe hit his ___ .

•mother •wIfe •fēēt

1. that pig is wet.

2. hē is in the mud.

1. this man is hot.

2. hē has a fan.

Worksheet 159 Side 2

a girl walked down the rōad.
shē met a big fox.

1. a girl ___ down the rōad.

•looked •walked •ran

2. shē met a big ___ .

•log •fox •dog

z z z z z z m m m m m

ū ū ū ū ū ū n n n n n n

b b b b b b r r r r r r

hē āte a mēat pIe.

he ate a meat pie.

he ate a meat pie.

A picture that shows this sentence

Name

Worksheet 160 Side 1

1. the ___ said, "I will slōw down."

•mother •wIfe •man

2. sō hē did not gō ___ in his car.

•rIding •fast •slōw

3. did hē walk fast?

•yes •nō

4. did hē ēat fast?

•yes •nō

1. the man is at the lāke.

2. hē is on a log.

1. that dog is sitting.

2. shē is on a bed.

Worksheet 160 Side 2

hē fell in the mud.
his nōse had mud on it.

1. hē ___ in the mud.

•walked •sat •fell

2. his ___ had mud on it.

•nōse •hat •fēēt

o o o o o o k k k k k k

ū ū ū ū ū ū t t t t t t

f f f f f f g g g g g g

"I ēat fast," hē said.

"I eat fast," he said.

"I eat fast," he said.

A picture that shows this sentence